THE MICHIGAN ROADSIDE NATURALIST

T0355721

THE MICHIGAN ROADSIDE NATURALIST

J. Alan Holman and Margaret B. Holman

THE UNIVERSITY OF MICHIGAN PRESS | Ann Arbor

Copyright © by the University of Michigan 2003
All rights reserved
Published in the United States of America by
The University of Michigan Press
Printed and bound by CPI Group (UK) Ltd, Croydon, CR0 4YY

2006   2005   2004   2003   4   3   2   1

A CIP catalog record for this book is available from the British Library.

Library of Congress Cataloging-in-Publication Data

Holman, J. Alan, 1931–
   The Michigan roadside naturalist / J. Alan Holman and Margaret B.
Holman.
      p.   cm.
   Includes bibliographical references and index.
   ISBN 0-472-09675-3 — ISBN 0-472-06675-7 (pbk.)
      1. Natural history—Michigan—Guidebooks.   2. Historic
sites—Michigan—Guidebooks.   3. Michigan—Guidebooks.   I. Holman,
Margaret B.   II. Title.
QH105.M5 H66   2003
508.774—dc21   2003012934

   ISBN13 978-0-472-09675-6 (cloth)
   ISBN13 978-0-472-06675-9 (paper)
   ISBN13 978-0-472-02459-9 (electronic)

Two pleasant peninsulas surrounded by blue freshwater seas.
Rolling glacial hills. The smell of cedar and pines.
An encounter with a bear and her cubs.
Smoked-fish houses on a long pier.
The whimsical Upper Peninsula of writer John Travers.
Indian "arrowheads" in a field.
Big dunes by the lake. Boulders in a stream.
A doe and her fawn at meadow's edge. Lumberjack lore.
Young Ernest Hemingway fishing for trout.
Beautiful bays. Waterfalls. Quaking bogs.
Ski slopes in winter. Ice Age mastodont bones.
Morel mushrooms. A blueberry patch.
A dead porcupine on the road.
A green frog jumping in the water.
An old man hunched over a hole in the ice.
Loon calls. Storms on the Great Lakes.
A rowboat on a still pond.
A lone fly fisherman standing in a stream at dawn.
Petoskey stones on a beach.
The Straits of Mackinac. An old fort.
A soaring eagle.
Wave-cut cliffs of Lake Superior.

These are visions of some of Michigan's rich geological, biological, and archaeological heritage. This book is a roadside guide to such sights.

—JAH, MBH

PREFACE

Michigan's highways traverse a wonderful mix of geological, biological, and archaeological features that are often missed by busy travelers whose main purpose is getting from one place to another. Some of these sights may be easily recognized from the car window, while others may be enjoyed by making short diversions. This book is meant to be a guide for the discovery of such features, either for persons merely passing through, or for those who wish to more thoroughly enjoy the natural treasures of the state.

The first part of the book suggests how to prepare for your trip through the "Great Lakes State," including what to read before you leave and what to take along. Next we describe the state's four regional landscape ecosystems, two in the Lower Peninsula and two in the Upper Peninsula. Then comes an introduction to the geology, biology, and archaeology of Michigan. First we examine the ancient bedrock, then discuss the Ice Age and its impact on the landscape. Next we detail assemblages of plants and highlight characteristic animals. Finally, we discuss human occupants, from the earliest Ice Age hunters to European settlers.

The second part of the book provides seven highway adventures that indicate sightings likely to be observed along major routes. We outline numerous short diversions. (Needless to say, the book is meant to be in the hands of passengers rather than the drivers of vehicles.)

This book should be an invaluable companion for anyone traveling through the state of Michigan, whether a native Michiganian, a tourist, or a person on a business venture. It is written for the layperson, and a list of easy-to-use field guides is provided on pages 297–301. Being teachers, both of us hope that some readers will want to go to the next level of knowledge. Thus we have included a detailed bibliography at the end of the book.

We hope that your trip through the Great Lakes State is enhanced by what you read here.

ACKNOWLEDGMENTS

First and foremost we thank the staff of the University of Michigan Press for producing and editing this work. The Press went far beyond the call of duty, not only in their help in the organization of the book but in the procurement of extra illustrative material for it. We are grateful to all of you!

We are also grateful to James H. Harding for providing an abundance of photographs of Michigan animals and scenes and to Allen Kurta for the use of photographs of Michigan mammals. We thank all of the other persons acknowledged in the book for the use of images they provided. We sincerely thank James H. Harding and two anonymous reviewers of the manuscript for their very helpful comments.

CONTENTS

PROLOGUE TO TRAVEL

SEVEN MICHIGAN HIGHWAY TRIPS

PROLOGUE TO TRAVEL

PROLOGUE
TO TRAVEL

INTRODUCTION

We want to make your journey in Michigan an interesting and enjoyable learning event rather than merely a trip from "point A to point B." This book is not intended to be a field guide in itself for the identification of specific geological formations, rocks, fossils, plants, animals, or archaeological artifacts. On the other hand, the reader can learn to recognize some broad geological and vegetational features and concepts, some common Michigan animals and their habits, and some archaeological history of the state. Most importantly we hope to instill a curiosity about the natural wonders of the Great Lakes State that will encourage the reader to further explorations of the subjects.

Before You Start

1. Get a Michigan highway map out of your glove box. If you don't have one, inexpensive Michigan highway maps are usually on sale at gas stations and at bookstores for a little more. We like best the free Michigan highway maps that one can get at welcome centers along the major freeways.

2. Get a transparent yellow marker and mark the route of your travel from start to finish. This will make things easier to find along the way. Then you might want to mark blue lines dividing the state into the four regional landscape ecosystems (fig. 1) or the Mason-Quimby line dividing the state into two ancient regions (see fig. 18). This will give you a general sense of where you are and where you are going from each of these standpoints.

3. Then read through the chapters on geology, plants and animals, and archaeology as background for the forthcoming trip. Of course you won't remember all of it, but it should help you to figure out what

Fig. 1. Map of Michigan divided into four regional landscape ecosystems

you might be looking for on the road and questions that might come up along the way.

4. If you have some experience identifying natural objects, don't forget to take your field guides along. If you do not have these, you might want to get some of the ones we list on pages 297–301, either at your public library or local bookstore.

5. Take along a small notebook to record interesting things you see or questions to be asked about them.

6. Do take your camera along, but we have learned that it is death-defying to try to take pictures along any busy roadside in the state. If you want to take photos, get your car and yourselves well off the road. We mention rest stops and scenic lookouts along the major routes, and

these are also indicated in many state maps, including the ones provided at major Michigan rest stops.

7. Field glasses and binoculars are often useful, but only for the passengers, not the driver!

8. Prepare to take a few of the short diversions discussed in "Seven Michigan Highway Trips," the second part of this book. They not only will be relaxing but will allow you to park and see natural objects closer at hand.

9. Rather than stopping only at fast food places for your meals, plan to turn off the highway onto the main streets of towns along the way. Find yourself a mom-and-pop coffee shop or small restaurant and enjoy the atmosphere and ambience of the local community.

10. Or take a small ice chest along with your favorite sandwiches packed in and have a meal at Michigan rest stops. Many have tables under shady trees and most are in nicely wooded areas where you should see birds and squirrels and possibly other forms of wildlife.

11. Plan to play "car games" related to natural objects. Locate an isolated white cloud ahead (front cover) and let each person in the car guess how many minutes it will take to drive under it. Or, guess how many miles it is to any natural object ahead, be it a tree on the top of a hill or the first sighting of one of the Great Lakes. Award points to members of the car for each turtle, opossum, porcupine, rabbit, raccoon, or deer (etc., etc.) spotted along the road—two points for live ones, one point for dead ones. Points can also be awarded for bedrock outcrops, glacial features, or rivers (if they can be named before the signs appear).

12. Finally, consider the fact that taking an hour or so longer to reach your destination will not only make your drive much more enjoyable, but it will be safer and allow you to arrive at your destination with a more relaxed mind and body.

Regional Landscape Ecosystems in Michigan

D. A. Albert, S. R. Denton, and B. V. Barnes of the School of Natural Resources of the University of Michigan have (1986) recognized four regional landscape ecosystems in Michigan (see fig. 1). These four major regions have, in turn, been divided into various districts and subdistricts, but for the purpose of this book we shall characterize only regions I–IV. The four units are recognized on the basis of climate and physiographic features, which in turn are related to soil development and structure, as well as the occurrence of plant and animal communities. Two regions (I and II) are recognized in the Lower Peninsula and two (III and IV) in the Upper Peninsula. Highway trips in this book traverse all of these major regions.

REGION I

Region I is warmer throughout the entire year than the other three regions, and it has a plant growing season that is longer and less changeable than in the other three units to the north. It is characterized by extensive lake plains of sand and clay, ground and end moraines, and various end features left by the ice sheets. The ridges in region I are lower than those in the northern three regions and range from about fifty to one hundred feet high. The dominant soils are loams and clays; sands are less common. The vegetation in region I includes many southern plant species, resulting in plant communities more diverse than in the more northern regions. Many animal species that occur in region I are absent in the more northern regions.

REGION II

Region II has a decidedly different climate than region I. First, it is a more northern latitude; second, it is surrounded on three sides by the Great Lakes; and third, upland areas are more extensive and higher than in region I. The high upland areas contribute to a cooler and more variable climate in region II than in region I, and there is a greater chance for frost in the plant growing season. Moreover, precipitation is not only influenced by the more extensive upland areas, but by the bordering lakes as well. Soils are also more sandy in region II, and extensive, thick glacial deposits are abundant. Lowland swamps and bogs are more common and often more acidic than in region I. The lack of southern species of plants decreases the diversity of plants in region II.

REGION III

Region III, which comprises the eastern part of the Upper Peninsula, is characterized by relatively low elevation and relatively young Paleozoic bedrock consisting of patches of Devonian (just north of the Straits) and more extensive Silurian and Ordovician rocks. The plant growing season is quite similar in length (120–140 days) to region II. The three Great Lakes that surround region III (Superior, Michigan, and Huron) tend to modify extremes in temperature and to reduce the severity of thunderstorms. Soils are poor and composed mainly of poorly drained sand and clay, with a presence of bedrock relatively near the surface in some areas. Northern coniferous trees occur in low, moist areas, and upland areas are dominated by mixed hardwood-coniferous forest.

REGION IV

Region IV comprises the western portion of the Upper Peninsula. Here the oldest Paleozoic rocks (Cambrian) and a very complex system of Precambrian rocks are the important bedrock structures. Frequent outcrops of these rocks occur, and there are many uplands in the region as well as low mountains. The upland topography controls the composition of the vegetation, and the growing season may be as short as sixty days. The temperature in region IV is the most continental of all four of the Michigan regions. The climate is warm during the growing season, very cold in the winter, and more extreme than in the other regions, mainly because there is less lake moderation. Northern hardwood-coniferous forests are abundant, and white pine, red pine, and oak dominate the upland forests.

MICHIGAN GEOLOGY AND PALEONTOLOGY

In geological terms, Michigan is a mass of unconsolidated Ice Age sediments, averaging about twenty-five to one hundred feet thick and several thousand years old, lying on consolidated layers of ancient bedrock thousands of feet thick and many millions to more than a billion years old. These units are formed of rocks that may be grouped into one of the three major classes (table 1).

Igneous rocks are formed by the solidification of gaseous or molten material. They may form by cooling at great depths in the earth (as in granitic rocks); or they may flow out on the surface in a molten state (as in lava) and then solidify; or they may be blasted into

TABLE I.   Some Common Michigan Rocks

Igneous	Sedimentary	Metamorphic
Ash	**Clastics**	Gneiss
Basalt	Boulders, cobbles, and pebbles	Marble
Felsite	Sand and sandstone	Phyllite
Gabbro	Clay and shale	Schist
Granite	Silt and siltstone	Slate
Obsidian	**Chemical and biological**	Quartzite
	Chert and flint	
	Coal	
	Gypsum	
	Dolomite	
	Limestone	
	Salt	

the air as gas or fragments from volcanoes. Common kinds of igneous rocks are basalt, granite, obsidian, and volcanic ash. Igneous rocks exist in massive amounts only in the bedrock formations of Michigan.

Sedimentary rocks are formed when the older rocks are broken up by the action of water, ice, or wind (**clastic rocks**) or by **chemical or biological** agents. The Michigan Ice Age sediments are mainly composed of clastic rocks; the bedrock formations contain both clastic and biologically and chemically formed rocks. Common unconsolidated clastic rocks include cobbles, pebbles, sand, silts, muds, and clays. Consolidated clastic rocks include cobblestones, sandstones, siltstones, and claystones. Biologically or chemically produced rocks include limestones, chalk, and coal (biologically produced) and salt and gypsum (chemically produced). Of the three classes of rocks, sedimentary rock beds are most likely to contain fossils because they have been least altered by geological processes.

Metamorphic rocks form when igneous or sedimentary rocks are changed by great heat or intense pressures or by infiltration of other material at great depths in the earth. Metamorphic rocks tend to be flaky like slate, schist, or gneiss, or nonflaky like marble, which is metamorphosed limestone. Metamorphic rocks are common in the bedrock layers of Michigan and include slate, schist, gneiss, and marble.

Landscape features formed by Ice Age clastic sediments are by far the most common ones seen in Michigan (fig. 2). Bedrock exposures are not abundant in the Lower Peninsula and are mainly exposed in rock quarries, but they may also be seen in occasional road cuts, deep stream channels, and sometimes as massive chunks or **erratics** carried by the glaciers (fig. 3). In the Upper Peninsula of Michigan, however, exposed bedrock formations are more abundant. Granitic rocks may be seen in the form of boulders and large cobbles that were carried by the Ice Age glaciers all over Michigan, or they can be seen in surface bedrock exposures in some areas in the western part of the Upper Peninsula (fig. 4).

Minerals are the principal constituents of rocks. Minerals may be defined as naturally occurring solid elements or compounds exclusive of biologically formed solids. Minerals are composed of geometrical crystals. Although minerals are usually not observed in pure form from a car whizzing through the countryside, one does see outcrops of the rocks that are composed of a single or various combinations of minerals, as well as the commercial mines and quarries where rocks are

Fig. 2. Road cut through the crest of an end moraine of the Port Huron ice advance about 13,000 B.P. (Missaukee County, northern Lower Peninsula)

extracted principally for their mineral content. A few commercially important Michigan minerals are listed in table 2.

Lets discuss some geological terms now that will be frequently used later. The **geological cycle** consists of the natural processes of **uplift, erosion,** and **deposition.** These processes have been repeated endlessly since the earth first cooled billions of years ago and may be recognized in rock strata throughout the world. Consider the simplified diagram of the geological cycle in figure 5. In nature, erosional processes move sediments from uplifted highlands to lowlands or basins. It is in these basins that deposition of these sediments take place until processes within the earth cause uplift to occur again and the cycle is repeated. The breaks that occur between rock strata (layers) because of erosional intervals in uplifted areas are called **disconformities.** If long periods of time have passed between the deposition of one layer of rocks upon another, the fossils and other parts of these layers may be very different from one another. In Michigan, a huge disconformity exists between the Ice Age sediments and the Paleozoic bedrock. This disconformity is associated with what is called the **lost interval,** which will be discussed later.

The **geologic timescale** (fig. 6) was set up in Europe, mainly in England and Wales, and there has been an attempt to include all of the rock strata in the world in this system. This time scale was originally based on **relative chronology,** which is based on the relation-

Fig. 3. Large section of thin-layered Paleozoic rock perched on the crest of an end moraine of the Port Huron ice advance about 13,000 B.P. (Missaukee County, northern Lower Peninsula). This erratic was transported by the ice from the Upper Peninsula to its present location.

Fig. 4. Outcrop of Precambrian granitic rock in Dickinson County in the Upper Peninsula. (Photo courtesy of James H. Harding.)

ship of rock beds to one another and upon the fact that fossil assemblages change from one bed to another. Establishing a relative chronology is based on the geological principle of **superposition,** that is, that younger beds lie upon older beds; and on the geological principle of **faunal succession,** that fossil assemblages change from older beds to younger beds.

Absolute chronological techniques enable geologists to date rock units within the geological timescale. At present, absolute chronology is mainly based on the fixed rate of loss of radioactive materials from natural substances. For beds over about 50,000 B.P. (B.P. = years before the present), most dating is based on the constant radioactive

TABLE 2.   Some Important Commercial Minerals in Michigan

Name and Chemical Composition	Occurrence and Uses
Native Copper (Cu)	From the Keweenaw Peninsula: used to produce brass, bronze, coins, hardware, and wire.
Quartz (SiO_2)	In many rock types: used to produce abrasives, building stone, dishes, electrical instruments, glass, grindstones, jewelry, mortar, optical instruments, scouring instruments.
Hematite (Fe_2O_3)	From Precambrian rocks in the Upper Peninsula: mainly used in the production of iron ore but pigments for paints and jewelry are also important.
Magnetite (Fe_3O_4)	Also from Precambrian rocks in the Upper Peninsula: used in the production of iron ore.
Gypsum ($CaSO_4.2H_2O$)	Occurs in Michigan sedimentary rocks along with salt and limestone: its principal use is in the production of plaster.
Calcite ($CaCO_3$)	From limestone formations in many places in Michigan: used in the production of cement, building stone, as a flux in the steel industry, and in road surfaces.
Dolomite ($CaMg[CO_3]_2$)	Abundant in several areas in Michigan: used as a building stone or a source of commercial magnesium.
Halite (NaCl)	Commercial salt of Michigan: many uses

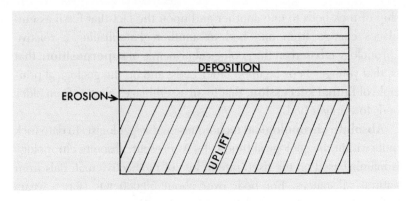

Fig. 5. The geological cycle. In sedimentary basins, uplift occurs, and erosion transports the uplifted sediments to lower areas. When the land is worn down again, deposition occurs. The geological cycle has repeated itself endlessly throughout the history of the earth.

decay that occurs in some minerals in igneous rocks after they become solid. If the rate of radioactive decay is known, then the ratio between the original substance and the product of the decay will tell how long the "radioactive clock" has been ticking. Forms of this method have been used for dating the ancient bedrock formations in Michigan.

For beds under 50,000 B.P. the carbon 14 method has often been employed. Carbon 14 is reduced by one-half in fixed periods of time, but the half-lives are so short that accuracy dwindles dramatically after about fifty thousand years. Carbon 14 studies are usually done on the organic material collagen, a protein that may be taken from plant fiber, wood, seeds, shells, and bones and teeth of Ice Age plants and animals.

The **geological formation** is the basic rock unit mapped by geologists; thus geological sightings in this book will be frequently referred to by their formational names. A formation usually results from a sedimentary event in a basin or other depression or by the building up of a coral reef. Each formation has characteristics by which it may be distinguished from other formations. Formations may occasionally transcend the established geological time units.

Formations are named after the geographic locality where they are well exposed and where they were first adequately described. Thus the Marshall Formation was described at Marshall, Calhoun County, in the southern part of the Lower Peninsula and the Schoolcraft Dolomite is a formation named for an exposure in the town of School-

TIME IN MILLIONS OF YEARS BEFORE PRESENT	ERAS	PERIODS	EPOCHS
— .1 —	CENOZOIC	QUATERNARY	HOLOCENE
— 1.9 —			PLEISTOCENE
— 5 —		TERTIARY	PLIOCENE
— 25 —			MIOCENE
— 35 —			OLIGOCENE
— 55 —			EOCENE
— 65 —			PALEOCENE
— 140 —	MESOZOIC	CRETACEOUS	
— 210 —		JURASSIC	
— 250 —		TRIASSIC	
— 290 —	PALEOZOIC	PERMIAN	
— 320 —		PENNSYLVANIAN	
— 360 —		MISSISSIPPIAN	
— 410 —		DEVONIAN	
— 440 —		SILURIAN	
— 500 —		ORDOVICIAN	
— 550 —		CAMBRIAN	
— 4550 —	PRECAMBRIAN		

Fig. 6. The geologic timescale

craft, Schoolcraft County, in the Upper Peninsula. If a formation is composed of several kinds of rocks, no rock type is included in the name (e.g., Marshall Formation); but if a formation consists of a single kind of rock, the rock type is included in the name (e.g., Schoolcraft Dolomite).

The Bedrock

Bedrock formations in the state (fig. 7) mainly accumulated as sedimentary rocks in a feature aptly named the **Michigan Basin** (fig. 8). The basin is a roughly circular structure, the center of which lies in just about the middle of the Lower Peninsula. About fourteen thousand feet of sedimentary rocks are deposited in the deepest part of the basin. The rocks of this basin may be roughly divided into four main units: (1) the sandstone formations of the late Precambrian and Cambrian, (2) the carbonate and evaporite sequences in the Ordovician, Silurian, and Early and Middle Devonian, (3) the shales and sand-

Fig. 7. Bedrock distribution in Michigan. Abbreviations: *PC*, Precambrian; *C*, Cambrian; *O*, Ordovician; *S*, Silurian; *D*, Devonian.

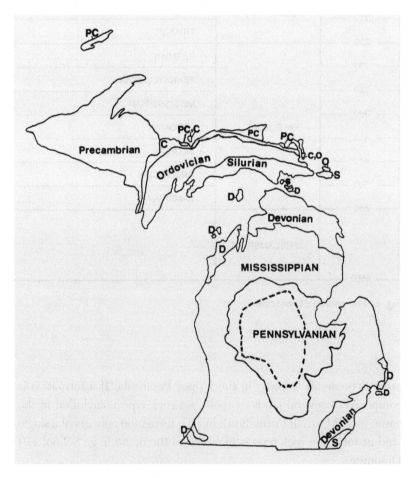

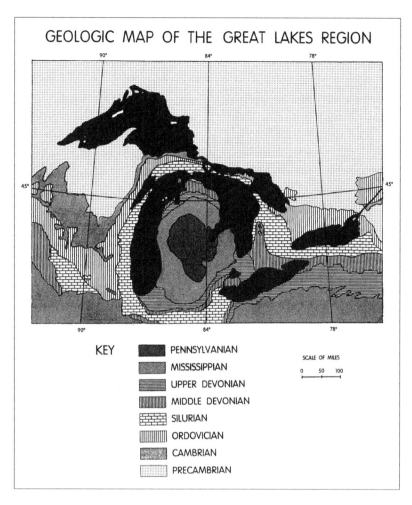

GEOLOGIC MAP OF THE GREAT LAKES REGION

KEY

■ PENNSYLVANIAN
▨ MISSISSIPPIAN
≡ UPPER DEVONIAN
▥ MIDDLE DEVONIAN
▦ SILURIAN
▥ ORDOVICIAN
▨ CAMBRIAN
▢ PRECAMBRIAN

SCALE OF MILES
0   50   100

Fig. 8. Bedrock map of the Great Lakes basin. The center of the Michigan Basin is at about the center of the Pennsylvanian rocks in the Lower Peninsula.

stones of the Late Devonian and Mississippian, and (4) the coal-bearing strata of the Pennsylvanian.

In the circle-shaped Michigan Basin the youngest formations occur near the center of the circle and get progressively older toward the outer edge. This is because as the successive rock layers formed, they sagged downward into the crust of the earth in the form of a series of "superimposed bowls." When subsequent erosion occurred (after the uplift that produced the "lost interval") the rims of the bowls were cut away. For example, Pennsylvanian deposits are found at Grand Ledge in northern Eaton County near Lansing in south central Michigan; Mississippian deposits occur at Marshall southwest of Lansing in Calhoun County; and Devonian deposits occur near the surface at New Buffalo in Berrien County in extreme southwestern Michigan.

The Precambrian Era. The Precambrian (see fig. 6) includes that vast time between the origin of the earth and the Cambrian period, when life on earth first became abundant. Thus it lasted from about 4.5 billion to about 550 million B.P. In Michigan, Precambrian rocks occur near the surface only in the western part of the Upper Peninsula. During the Precambrian the geological cycle repeated itself countless times. Mountain building occurred, sedimentary rocks were formed and deposited, and folding and metamorphosis took place; in fact much of the original structure of the rocks has been changed by metamorphic processes.

Outcrops of granite (see fig. 4), often intruded by younger granitic rocks, are rather common in the western part of the Upper Peninsula. There is even indication in the middle part of the Precambrian that an ancient ice age occurred. The youngest Precambrian rocks in Michigan form the Jacobsville Sandstone. Nice exposures may be seen at Presque Isle just north of Marquette (fig. 9). These rocks are reddish brown in color and are used locally as building stone. Iron and copper in Precambrian rocks have been an important source of the regional economy in the Upper Peninsula. Iron ores were mined and carried by Great Lakes ships to the steel mills in Chicago and Pittsburgh. Pure copper exists in gas bubble spaces in ancient lavas and also as a form of sulfide in the Nonsuch shale at White Pine, in the Upper Peninsula of Michigan.

Fossils of simple life forms have been recorded in Precambrian deposits in Australia from 3.5 billion years ago in the form of bacterial cells called cyanobacteria (formerly called *blue-green algae*). These earliest life forms, composed of one or a few cells, fed on organic wastes or were able to synthesize their own food. A few of these simple forms of life have been detected in Precambrian rocks in the Upper Peninsula.

The Paleozoic Era. Fossils of several kinds of complex organisms were abundant at the onset of the Paleozoic, an era that lasted from about 550 million to about 250 million B.P. During the Paleozoic the interior of North America stood high on land that was composed of

Latest Precambrian Jacobsville Sandstone

Earlier Precambrian Rocks

Fig. 9. Late Precambrian Jacobsville Sandstone overlying Precambrian granitic rocks (under dotted line) at Presque Isle just north of Marquette on the Lake Superior shore of the Upper Peninsula. (From J. A. Dorr Jr. and D. F. Eschman, *Geology of Michigan* [Ann Arbor: University of Michigan Press, 1970].)

rocks that had been through billions of years of geological changes in the Precambrian. During this era this central region was very stable compared to both coastal regions. But this central region subsided from time to time, and shallow seas moved inland into the basins that formed, including the Michigan Basin previously discussed.

The Cambrian period, the first period of the Paleozoic era, lasted about fifty million years from about 550 million to about 500 million B.P. Although fossils are not common, these rocks are associated with some of the most spectacular scenery in the state. Cambrian near-surface rocks occur only in a very narrow belt in the Upper Peninsula (see fig. 7). The rocks are mainly represented by sandstones deposited by stream erosion of Precambrian rocks, or by later sandstones deposited by invading seas.

Lovely Cambrian sandstone formations occur in the Lake Superior borderland of the eastern part of the Upper Peninsula of Michigan. These sandstones occur in the Munising Formation and may be seen in scenic tourist attractions along the Pictured Rocks area east of Munising along the Lake Superior shoreline. Miners Castle (figured later) and Chapel Rock (fig. 10) are two examples. Pretty falls such as Laughing Whitefish Falls, Miner's Falls, and Munising Falls are all in the area, and all contain Cambrian sandstones. Moreover, Upper and Lower Tahquamenon Falls near the western shore of Whitefish Bay farther east contain Cambrian sandstones.

An inland sea was present in the Michigan Basin during much of the **Ordovician period,** which lasted from about 500 million to about 440 million B.P. Ordovician near-surface rocks in Michigan occur only in the Upper Peninsula as a wide band about 160 miles long mainly south of the Cambrian bedrock area. Michigan Ordovician rocks consist mainly of marine dolomite, sandstones, and shales. Marine fossils are more common in Michigan Ordovician rocks than they are in rocks of Cambrian age.

Fine exposures of Ordovician rocks occur in the southern Upper Peninsula in the Stonington Peninsula and in the Escanaba River valley. Ordovician rocks can also be viewed as a thin layer above the

Fig. 10. Layered Late Cambrian sandstone forming the Chapel Rock tourist attraction east of Munising in the Pictured Rocks area of the Lake Superior shore of the Upper Peninsula. (From J. A. Dorr Jr. and D. F. Eschman, *Geology of Michigan* [Ann Arbor: University of Michigan Press, 1970].)

Cambrian rocks of Laughing Whitefish Falls, and as a dolomite layer capping Cambrian rocks of Munising Falls. West of Grand Island, where the Ordovician wedges up to the shore of Lake Superior between the Cambrian rocks, beautiful Au Train Falls (fig. 11) flows over middle Ordovician rocks of sandstones and dolomite.

The Silurian period is known for its shallow, landlocked seas, great reef formations, and deposits of salt and gypsum. Fossils are abundant in some areas. The Silurian is a rather short period that occurred from about 440 million to about 410 million B.P. Silurian rocks are near the surface in the Upper Peninsula of Michigan and on Bois Blanc Island, where they form the southernmost band of Paleozoic bedrocks (see fig. 7), beginning in the west at the level of the north shore of Big Bay De Noc and continuing eastward to the tip of the peninsula at the south shore of Munuscong Lake. A mixture of Silurian and Devonian rocks occurs on Mackinac Island. They come near the surface in the Lower Peninsula only in the southeastern corner of Monroe County in extreme southeastern Michigan (see fig. 7).

Outcrops of Silurian rocks are rather common in the southeastern part of the Upper Peninsula (fig. 12), where they may be seen near highway road cuts. In fact, one sees fine exposures of Silurian rocks in

Fig. 11. Lower Au Train Falls west of Grand Island in the Upper Peninsula. Here water flows over Middle Ordovician dolomite and sandstone. (From J. A. Dorr Jr., and D. F. Eschman, *Geology of Michigan* [Ann Arbor: University of Michigan Press, 1970].)

Fig. 12. Silurian dolomite in a quarry in Schoolcraft County in the Upper Peninsula. Note the resemblance of the top thin-layered rocks to the Lower Peninsula erratic (see fig. 3) perched on the glacial moraine. (Photo courtesy of James H. Harding.)

the road cuts shortly after crossing the Mackinac Bridge. After this, occasional exposures continue to occur as one travels westward along U.S. Highway 2. The Silurian in the Upper Peninsula has provided commercially important limestones and dolomite used for making cement, road aggregates, building stone, and agricultural lime. One of the world's largest dolomite mines is located near Cedarville northeast of the Straits. Beautiful exposures of Silurian rocks also occur in Lake Michigan bluffs on the northwest side of the Garden Peninsula southwest of Manistique.

Although salt and gypsum deposits are not seen in surface rocks in Michigan, extensive deposits of these materials are found deep beneath the surface. Salt and gypsum were formed by the process of evaporation in shallow Silurian seas. Massive commercial salt deposits may be found near Midland and in southeastern Michigan. In fact, in the 1970s, Michigan supplied between 20 and 25 percent of salt used in the United States. Extensive reef formations, often associated with gas and oil deposits, are other Silurian subsurface features in Michigan.

Near the end of the Silurian the seas withdrew from the Michigan Basin. Thus the **Early Devonian period** saw a period of erosion, or at the least a lack of deposition in the area. The Devonian period was a long one that lasted from about 410 million to about 360 million B.P. Devonian rocks occur near the surface in the Upper Peninsula in the Straits area (fig. 13), and rocks representing both the Silurian and the Devonian occur on Mackinac and Bois Blanc Islands in the Straits of Mackinac. In the Lower Peninsula, Devonian rocks are found near the surface in the northern part of northern Michigan, in extreme south-western Michigan as part of a Silurian/Devonian complex, and in southeastern Michigan (see fig. 7). By the middle of the Devonian period the Michigan Basin was again occupied by seas that remained in Michigan throughout the remainder of the period. Many kinds of fossils occur in Devonian sediments and because of the abundance and variety of fossil fishes the period has been called "the age of fishes." Commercially important salt again formed in evaporative seas in the middle part of the Devonian. The Upper Devonian in the state is dominated by black shales. This material was carried into Michigan from uplifted areas in the Appalachian region.

Mississippian period rocks are found near the surface only in the Lower Peninsula, where they encircle the Pennsylvanian rocks of the

Fig. 13. Outcrop of Devonian Mackinac Breccia one mile north of the Mackinac Bridge. (Photo courtesy of James H. Harding.)

state (see fig. 7). In Europe, the Mississippian and Pennsylvanian periods are combined as a single period called the **Carboniferous** that is known for its coal beds. But in North America, the Mississippian is best known for its limestone formations and the Pennsylvanian for its coal beds. The Mississippian lasted from about 360 million to about 320 million years B.P. Fossils of marine invertebrates may be found in Michigan Mississippian rocks.

Many commercially important Mississippian limestone formations lie south of the Great Lakes region. In the Michigan Basin, the rocks of this period consist mainly of shales, siltstones, and sandstones. Views of Early Mississippian crossbedded sandstones may be seen along I-94 near Battle Creek and at Napoleon on M-50 southeast of Jackson. These beds are in the Marshall Formation, a unit that has yielded marine invertebrate fossils. In the late Mississippian the Michigan Basin was uplifted, the seas retreated, and part of the earlier marine sediments were eroded away. During the interval of time between the Mississippian and the following Pennsylvanian period an extensive time of uplifting and folding occurred in the area.

The **Pennsylvanian period** lasted from about 320 million to about 290 million B.P. and was the last geological period before the great "lost interval" in Michigan. The Pennsylvanian corresponds to about the last one-half of the European Carboniferous period. Although the Pennsylvanian is known for its coal-bearing formations, coal has been of limited commercial importance in Michigan. Pennsylvanian rocks in Michigan, as well as in the entire Great Lakes drainage system, occur nearest the surface in the center of the Lower Peninsula of Michigan and are surrounded by Mississippian rocks (see fig. 7).

During the Pennsylvanian a low area in the present Appalachian region filled with sediments, and almost all of the northeastern part of the United States alternated between terrestrial and marine environments as the seas came in and went out again. During a part of each cycle there were times when great coal-producing swamps existed. Evidence of ancient plants and fishes have been found in Pennsylvanian sediments exposed by the Grand River at Grand Ledge, near Lansing.

Mesozoic era rocks (see fig. 7) are known only on the basis of the **Jurassic** period sediments that are scattered among the Pennsylvanian rocks in Michigan. This evidence of Jurassic rocks in Michigan mainly comes from plant pollen samples in well cores. Thus, little is known about the "life and times" of the Jurassic period in the state.

The Lost Interval—or Why No Dinosaurs Have Been Found in Michigan

The great "lost interval" in Michigan geological time occurred from late in the Pennsylvanian period to late in the Pleistocene (Ice Age) (see fig. 6). This is a time span of about 290 million years! The only records of an intervening geological period during this interval consist of evidence of Jurassic rocks occurring within and scattered among the Pennsylvanian rocks in Michigan as discussed directly above.

Uplift late in the Pennsylvanian not only produced the Appalachian mountain chain but warped the entire Great Lakes region upward. Thus the entire region, including Michigan, was transformed from a sedimentary basin to an upland area where the major geological process was erosion for the next 290 million years.

Dinosaur bones have never been found in Michigan, much to the disappointment of many avid rock and fossil hunters. Why not? The answer is not complex. Dinosaur bones have been found only in the Triassic, Jurassic, and Cretaceous rocks of the Mesozoic era ("Age of Reptiles") (see fig. 6). Since Triassic, Jurassic, and Cretaceous rocks do not occur in Michigan (with the exception of Jurassic rocks from well cores, which have yielded no bones), no dinosaurs have been found either. This, by the way, is also the situation in the entire Great Lakes Basin. This is not to say that dinosaurs could not have occurred in Michigan or the Great Lakes region, just that we do not have a record of the life of these uplands during the lost interval.

The Ice Age

The present topography of Michigan is the result of the so-called Ice Age (Pleistocene epoch) (see fig. 6). The Ice Age (which really is the last one of many such cold periods dating back to the Precambrian) began about 1.9 million years B.P. and ended 10,000 B.P. with the worldwide extinction of many large mammals. This includes the huge, elephant-like mammoths and mastodonts that were very numerous in Michigan. Michigan is a microcosm for the study of the extinction of these large mammals as well as for studies of the reoccupation of formerly glaciated areas by plants and animals. Characteristic areas where mammoths and mastodonts might be found or have previously been found will be pointed out in the trip sections to follow.

During the Ice Age massive ice sheets called glaciers advanced and retreated in North America. Time periods associated with general glacial advances and cold climates are called **glacial ages.** Time periods associated with general glacial retreats and more temperate climates are called **interglacial ages.** The classic names for glacial and interglacial ages in North America are given in table 3. The only well-documented classic North American glacial ages are the Wisconsinan (last glacial) and to a lesser extent, the Sangamonian (last interglacial) and Illinoian (glacial previous to the Sangamonian). In fact, many geologists have ceased to use the classic glacial and interglacial age terms previous to the Illinoian. Almost all of the surficial sediments that lie over the bedrock in Michigan are products of the Wisconsinan glacial age (table 3).

How Did the Glacial Ice Shape the Topography of Michigan? Figure 14 is a diagram based on a photograph of the leading edge of the Greenland ice sheet. The edge of the ice forms a sheer cliff. In front of the cliff is a glacial outwash area with braided streams. In between the streams are other glacial features. Similar conditions existed for thousands of years in the Pleistocene of Michigan.

Glacial ice changes the landscape in several ways. Mainly it erodes away the land that it moves over and transports rocks and debris that it has plucked from the surface of the land and deposits this material either directly by melting in place or by meltwater systems that spread the material over the countryside. Most of the material carried by the ice is held in suspension within. However, almost all of the suspended

TABLE 3.   Classical Names for North American Glacial and Interglacial Ages, with Comments

Wisconsinan Glacial (lasted from about 110,000 B.P. to 10,000 B.P., the end of the Ice Age).
Sangamonian Interglacial (thought to have lasted from about 150,000 B.P. to 110,000 B.P., but this chronology is still somewhat questionable)
Illinoian Glacial (chronology not fully documented but term still widely used)
? Yarmouthian Interglacial (poorly documented, if it actually exists)
Kansan Glacial (chronology not fully documented but term still widely used)
? Aftonian Interglacial (poorly documented, if it actually exists)
? Nebraskan "Glacial" (most sites previously assigned to the Nebraskan are now considered to be Late Pliocene, and probably did not represent glacial intervals)

Fig. 14. Schematic diagram of the final withdrawal of the great ice sheet in Michigan at the end of the Ice Age. As the sun comes up in the east, the leading edge of the ice sheet is seen as a sheer cliff. Glacial meltwater floods the newly exposed land in various patterns. Streams erode the top of the ice as well.

material occurs near the bottom of the ice. The Pleistocene ice sheets were so thick that there appears to be practically no limit to the size of particles that could be carried. In western Canada, huge pieces of land called **megablocks** that were over a mile wide and hundreds of feet deep were carried for up to two hundred miles by the ice sheet. On a smaller scale, large granitic boulders and even large sections of Paleozoic sedimentary rocks (see fig. 3), both termed erratics, have been carried by the ice all over Michigan, often far south of their pre-Pleistocene origin.

The sediments carried by ice sheets are either called **till** or **outwash** deposits (fig. 15). Till comes directly from the ice and consists of particles of all sizes and shapes mixed together. Till forms structures called **moraines. End moraines** form at the end of the ice lobe, **lateral moraines** form at the side of the ice lobe, and **ground moraines** form when the ice moves across the land surface rapidly. Most of the big hills in northern Michigan are portions of end

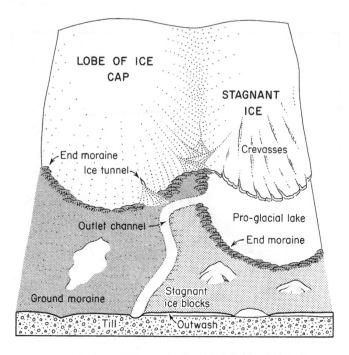

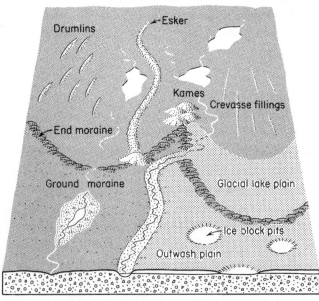

Fig. 15. Generalized diagram to show relationships between glacial ice and glacial topographic features before *(above)* and after *(below)* the retreat of the ice. (From J. A. Dorr Jr. and D. F. Eschman, *Geology of Michigan* [Ann Arbor: University of Michigan Press, 1970].)

moraines. Other types of moraines are **terminal moraines** that indicate the ultimate end points of major glacial advances and **recessional moraines** that indicate temporary stops during glacial retreats.

Most areas of Michigan have additional glacial features called **drumlins, eskers, kames,** and **kettle holes** (see fig. 15). Drumlins are elliptical hills that are composed of glacial till that was left over when the glacier retreated. The direction of the ice flow is indicated by the long axis of drumlins. Narrow, snakelike ridges that originate from deposits laid down in tunnels in or under retreating ice are termed eskers. Kames are isolated rounded hills of glacial outwash sand and gravel. Kettle holes, rounded depressions where remains of mammoths and mastodonts are often found in Michigan, arose from rounded ice blocks that melted after the ice withdrew.

The succession of basins that have contained the **Great Lakes** mainly developed in soft limestones and shales of Paleozoic age. These basins were time and again eroded out of the preglacial valleys that at one time drained midcontinental North America. In Michigan, each glaciation removed most of the sedimentary and fossil evidence of the preceding one, so that the main record comes from the last glacial event, the **Wisconsinan** (see table 3). The scouring effect of these ice sheets must have been huge, as indicated by the fact that the present floors of Lake Huron and Lake Michigan are well below sea level. The effect of the Paleozoic bedrock topography on the flow of the glacial ice in southern part of the Great Lakes region is indicated by the looping positions of the end moraines.

The Wisconsinan Glacial Age. Almost all of the present surface topography of Michigan reflects the glacial events of the Wisconsinan, the last age of the Pleistocene (see table 3). This is because the Wisconsinan topography was neither as highly weathered as those of previous Pleistocene ages nor scoured out by a later glacier. On the other hand, the Wisconsinan itself scoured so much of the evidence of previous glacial events in Michigan that good evidence of pre-Wisconsinan stages is yet to be found in the state. The Wisconsinan did not consist of a single glacial advance and withdrawal but had several advances and retreats during its extent.

The Wisconsinan glacial age is thought to be about the same length as the Devensian glacial age in Britain. Both of these ages lasted about one hundred thousand years, from about 110,000 to 10,000 B.P. The end of the Wisconsinan age corresponds to the end of the Pleistocene (see table 3). Most Michigan Wisconsinan deposits date between about 12,500 and 10,000 B.P. But much older Wisconsinan sediments and fossils occur in the base of a stream channel at Mill Creek in St. Clair County, and Wisconsinan sediments about 35,000 years old have been found in water wells in Kalkaska County. Moreover, a 25,000 B.P. fossil duck bone site was found in an organic layer from water well diggings near Casnovia in Muskegon County, and a mammoth site about twenty-four thousand years old was found near Coleman in Midland County.

Michigan Landforms. As we have emphasized, events of the geological past, especially the activity of the ice sheets, have provided Michigan with its landforms. Michigan is blessed with highlands, hilly uplands, upland plains, lowland plains, and lake-border plains. The low, level, lake-border plains were relatively recently flooded. These landforms together form a very complex meshwork of features in Michigan, and even a short drive in the state is likely to take the traveler through hilly moraines, till plains, glacial outwash plains, and lake plains, as well as other geological features previously mentioned.

The highest lands in Michigan are found in the Upper Peninsula, where elevations of eighteen hundred feet can be found. Features well over one thousand feet are not uncommon in the northern part of the Lower Peninsula. The ski resorts of the state are associated with the steep slopes of the glacially produced "mountains" of northern lower Michigan. But other highlands are found in the north central part of the Lower Peninsula and farther south in Hillsdale and Lapeer Counties. The largest areas of lake plains are to be found in the eastern part of the Upper Peninsula, the area around Saginaw Bay west to Midland and in southeastern Michigan (fig. 16). Other large areas of lake plains are in the northwestern part of the Upper Peninsula and in the northwestern part of southwest corner of Michigan.

Origin of the Great Lakes of the "Great Lakes State." The Great Lakes are said to be the only glacially produced structures that can be seen from the moon. They occupy ninety-five thousand square miles of the earth's surface and have over eight thousand miles of shoreline. Michigan is surrounded by four of the five great lakes, two more than any other state in the United States!—Lake Superior in the north, Michigan in the west, Huron in the northeast, and Erie in the southeast. Superior is coldest and deepest, Erie is warmest and shallowest, and Michigan and Huron are intermediate. The native fish faunas of these lakes reflect these differences.

Fig. 16. Generalized map of surface formations in Michigan. *Shaded,* ancient lake (lacustrine) plains; *unshaded,* glacial surface formations (moraines, till plains, outwash plains).

These lakes are products of (1) the bedrock formations that were produced during the Paleozoic era (2) the erosion of these rocks during the lost interval, and (3) the glacial processes of the Pleistocene. Geologically they are infant lakes, but like all lakes they will eventually fill in with sediments and disappear. At present they are tremendously important to us, as among other features, they hold one-sixth of the earth's freshwater!

Before the Ice Age, the basins that hold the present Great Lakes were stream valleys in the various landforms of the lost interval. When the ice sheets came, they tended to move along these valleys, following the path of the least resistant rocks. Finally, melting icewater filled in the eroded structures. The Great Lakes began to fill up in earnest in the late part of the Wisconsinan, somewhat before 13,300 B.P., and these early lakes were given different names than the modern ones. But by 4,000 B.P. the lakes were nearly in their present state of development. Needless to say, the Pleistocene Great Lakes had various shapes caused by fluctuating shorelines that reflected the various glacial advances and retreats.

The modern lakes all drain in an easterly direction, as Lake Superior drains into Huron at Sault Ste. Marie and Lake Michigan drains into lake Huron at the Straits of Mackinac. In turn Lake Huron drains southward along the St. Clair River into Lake Erie and Lake Erie drains into Lake Ontario. At long last, Lake Ontario drains into the Atlantic Ocean by way of the St. Lawrence River. These huge inland lakes, a product of the Ice Age, have provided habitats for aquatic life and a water supply for terrestrial animals and plants, and they have had a marked effect on the climate of Michigan.

Smaller Bodies of Water. Other than the Great Lakes, Michigan has over thirty-five thousand officially mapped lakes and ponds. Twenty of these are very large inland lakes, including Higgins, Burt, Mullett, Black, and Torch Lakes in the Lower Peninsula and Manistique, Indian, Fletcher, and Portage Lakes in the Upper Peninsula. Many major rivers occur in Michigan, as twenty-four occur in the Lower Peninsula and sixteen in the Upper Peninsula. The Grand River in the Lower Peninsula has the most major tributaries, including the Rouge, Flat, Maple, Looking Glass, Red Cedar, and Thornapple Rivers. Of course, countless smaller streams are part of each of these river systems.

Wetlands, including various bogs, fens, and swamps are very important features of Michigan. Ironically, the early explorers found that large areas of Michigan were poorly drained and swampy. Thus, early on, many of the original wetlands were drained by both surface drains and buried tiles for agricultural purposes and urban development. With Michigan's expanding population, recent drainage of wetlands for commercial building sites and housing projects has taken a remarkable toll on the remaining wetlands.

Waves and Currents. The shores of the Great Lakes and other larger lakes in Michigan are greatly affected by the action of waves and currents. Waves derive their energy from winds, which derive their energy from differences in the heat produced by the sun. When waves approach the shallows, they become breakers and expend energy that moves sediments along on the bottom. The extent to which the wave moves up the beach depends on the point at which the energy is used up against the shore. As the water runs back down the beach, it expends potential energy that moves material back toward the lake.

This all means that wave action energy is expended in a relatively narrow band along the shore, but a great deal of work is done in this band. Waves can not only drag materials back and forth, but they can move objects along the shore when the water strikes the shore at an oblique angle. This action slowly rounds and diminishes the size of boulders, cobbles, and pebbles, until they finally become grains of sand.

These sedimentary rocks tend to be sorted by size by wave action, with the cobbles and pebbles remaining near the beach where the wave action is weak and the finer sand grains are carried back into deeper water. Thus, when waves cut into cliffs composed of glacial till, the boulders, cobbles, and pebbles form a rocky beach. But when waves cut into cliffs that have developed in dune sand, a sandy beach is formed, but the finest particles still end up offshore.

During storms very large rocks may be thrown up on the beach, and during violent storms, not only may sandy cliffs be knocked down and dissolved, but masses of solid rock may be torn away. Obviously beach and cliff erosion are serious problems for owners of houses and cottages near the lakes. On the other hand some of the most beautiful sites in Michigan are shore features such as wave-cut cliffs, arches, caves, and vertical stacks of rock.

Dunes. Michigan is a state replete with dunes (fig. 17). Dunes occur not only along the coast, but inland as well in many areas of the state. Inland dunes tended to form in the past when the climate of Michigan was warmer and drier. Dunes are structures formed by windblown sand. The three situations that are necessary for the formation of coastal dunes that have been present in Michigan since the origin of the Great Lakes in the Pleistocene are (1) relatively stable winds across large bodies of water, (2) sandy beaches along these bodies of water, and (3) a downwind area where the sand can be deposited.

A sand dune that is formed without the impact of vegetation is asymmetrical with a quite gentle windward side and a much steeper leeward slope. Since the wind comes off the lakes, the side near the lake has a gentle slope, and the side away from the lake is steep. Thus climbing a high dune to get a view of the lake may be a strenuous task. These kinds of dunes tend to **migrate** inland. But if a dune is covered with vegeta-

Fig. 17. Coastal dunes in Emmet County, northwest Lower Peninsula

tion, it may become stabilized. However, the destruction of vegetation may reactivate the dune, and often **blowouts** occur, especially on the windward side. Sometimes blowout dunes even become steeper on the windward side than on the leeward side. The coastal dunes in Michigan are younger than the inland dunes, some of which formed over ten thousand years ago. Our present coastal dunes began to form less than forty-five hundred years ago when the coasts became similar to what they are today. There are generally two kinds of coastal dunes. **Foredune ridges** are relatively low (twenty-five to fifty feet high) and **high dunes** are usually over one hundred feet high. High dunes are usually located somewhat inland behind the foredunes.

Some ancient high dunes consist of sand that was deposited on top of high glacial features such as moraines that were near the beach when ancient Great Lake levels were higher. These are called **perched dunes.** The great Sleeping Bear Dune northwest of Traverse City is a perched dune that stands about 450 feet higher than Lake Michigan.

Inland dunes are usually the most ancient dunes in the state. These structures formed along the margins of the ancient lakes when lake levels were much higher. They are up to about thirteen thousand years old. These ancient dunes are no longer growing because they have been stabilized by vegetation for thousands of years. Large areas of inland dunes occur northeast of Holland, southwest of Saginaw Bay, near the northern tip of the Lower Peninsula, and in the eastern part of the Upper Peninsula.

The Mason-Quimby Line. Looping convexly across the state at about the middle of the Lower Peninsula of Michigan is a line drawn on maps called the Mason-Quimby line that divides Michigan into two distinct ancient areas (fig. 18). The Mason-Quimby line had its origin in studies of Pleistocene archaeology and geology. R. J. Mason (now of Wisconsin) and G. I. Quimby of Michigan are scientists who were interested in Pleistocene Indians in the state and how they procured food for themselves. Mason questioned why there were no fluted spear points (see fig. 18) (similar to the ones that were used by Paleo-Indians in the West to kill mammoths) north of the counties in the southern third of the Lower Peninsula of Michigan. Quimby noted the relationships between humans, vegetation, and mastodonts; and both Mason and Quimby believed that the Paleo-Indians of the entire Great Lakes region were mastodont hunters. This was because the fluted spear points in southern Michigan and other parts of the region were very similar to the Clovis spear points used by mammoth hunters in the West. Later, Quimby stated that the distribution of fluted points and known mastodont remains in the state (all south of the Mason-Quimby line) was related to the probability that Paleo-Indians hunted these animals.

It has been suggested recently that another important feature of the Mason-Quimby line is that *all* of the valid records of large extinct Pleistocene vertebrates, not just mammoths and mastodonts, lie south of the line. This is probably because of the position of the ice margins in Michigan during the last episodes of glaciation. Fourteen thousand years ago the leading edge of the ice was about thirty-five miles south of the Mason-Quimby line, and by 13,000 B.P. it had moved to about seventy miles north of the line.

As the ice withdrew between these intervals, it left a mass of sterile mud, sand, and gravel that must have been difficult to recolonize by plants and animals. Thus, biological communities north of the line never became stable to the point that they could support enough large vertebrates to contribute significantly to the fossil record. It would seem that human hunters in the Pleistocene stayed in the southern Lower Peninsula because that was where the big game was.

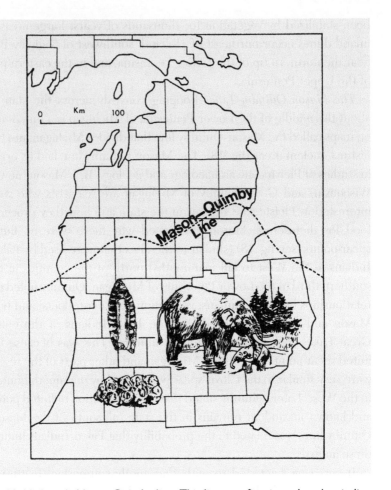

Fig. 18. Michigan's Mason-Quimby line. This line was first introduced to indicate the northernmost occurrences of mammoth and mastodont remains in the state as well as most Paleo-Indian artifacts. Now it indicates the northernmost occurrence of all large extinct Ice Age vertebrates as well. The object in the upper left below the line is a Paleo-Indian fluted spear point; upper right, a female mastodont and its baby; lower left, a mastodont tooth in surface view.

Michigan's Fossils. Fossils may be defined as any identifiable evidence of prehistoric life and may be subdivided into actual fossils and trace fossils. Thus a fossil may be the bone of a vertebrate animal, a shell of an invertebrate animal, or some trace of a plant or animal etched in rock. Michigan fossils depict the very simple forms of life that existed in the Precambrian, the strange forms of multicellular life that occurred in the Paleozoic, and the spectacular extinct mammals that coexisted with humans in the Late Pleistocene.

Precambrian fossils are confined to the Upper Peninsula. **Stromatolites** are moundlike, pillarlike, or domelike structures that are layers of sediments built up by the activities of bacteria called **cyanobacteria** (formerly called blue-green algae). Some of these are massive layered structures that may be observed near highways in the Upper Peninsula. These fossils are over two billion years old! Other Precambrian fossils in the Upper Peninsula of Michigan include microscopic threadlike and saclike bodies and various carbon residues that indicate the presence of very simple life.

Paleozoic fossils consist of more advanced forms of life that occur in bedrock of Cambrian, Ordovician, Devonian, Mississippian, and Pennsylvanian age. Most of these fossils represent marine creatures that existed in Michigan's shallow Paleozoic seas, but some spectacular Pennsylvanian coal-swamp plants occurred in lower Michigan. Important Pennsylvanian plants include **lycopods, sphenopsids,** and **seed ferns.**

Important marine invertebrate fossils of the Michigan Paleozoic include **stromatoporoids** and **corals** (including the famous Michigan "Petoskey stone," which is actually a coral!), **brachiopods, gastropods,** and **pelecypods.** Stromatoporoids and corals were very important in building the reef formations of the Paleozoic of Michigan. Brachiopods, gastropods, and pelecypods were bottom-living, shelled animals that fed on particulate matter on the sea floor.

Nautiloids, ammonoids, trilobites, and **echinoderms** were other important invertebrate animals of the Paleozoic seas. Nautiloids and ammonoids had intricately chambered shells. Trilobites were relatively active creatures with a body composed of three lobes of segmented plates. They seem to be everyone's favorite invertebrate fossil. Echinoderms include fossil starfishes, sea lilies, and odd plated creatures called blastoids and cystoids.

Michigan's extinct **vertebrate fossils** occur in two main categories: (1) **Paleozoic fishes** (2) **Ice Age fishes, amphibians, reptiles, birds,** and **mammals.** Paleozoic fishes (fig. 19) include ancient armored jawed fishes called **placoderms** (fig. 19A and B), sharklike **cartilaginous fish** teeth and spines (fig. 19C, D, and E) and spines of strange bony fishes called **acanthodians** (fig. 19F and G).

All of the following extinct **Pleistocene** mammals are found south

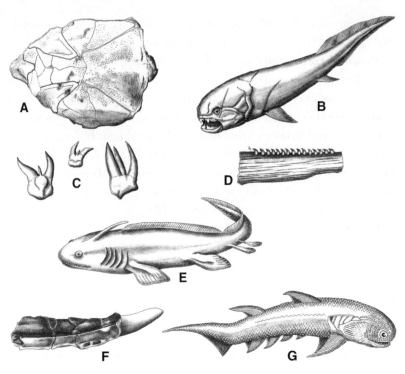

Fig. 19. Ancient fishes of Michigan. A, plate from the head shield of the Devonian placoderm Protitanichthyes; B, artist's reconstruction of *Protitanichthyes*; C, teeth of xenacanth sharks; D, spine fragment of Pennsylvanian xenacanth shark; E, artist's reconstruction of a xenacanth shark; F, end of a fin spine of a Middle Devonian acanthodian fish ("spiny shark"); G, artist's reconstruction of the common acanthodian, *Climatius*. (Courtesy of Michigan State University Museum.)

of the Mason-Quimby line (see fig. 18) in southern lower Michigan. The most important Michigan Pleistocene vertebrates, in fact probably the most important Michigan fossils, are those of the huge, elephantlike **mammoths** and **mastodonts** that existed in the state from about 12,500 to 10,000 B.P. After this time, they became extinct in Michigan as well as all over the world. These mammals were very numerous south of the Mason-Quimby line and probably were hunted by Paleo-Indians who used fluted spear points to kill these behemoths (see fig. 18). It is believed that mammoths and mastodonts were numerous in the area because of the widespread availability of salt licks and shallow saline water in Michigan during the Pleistocene. This idea is based on the fact that, in order to exist, modern African elephants must have an available salt supply.

Many people mistakenly think that the terms mammoth, mastodont (or, incorrectly "mastodon") are different words for the same animal. Actually, these animals are as different from one another as horses are from rhinos. The skull of mammoths is domed on top, and both the skull and the sheaths that hold the tusks are oriented at an almost vertical angle. In the mastodont the skull is flat on top, and both the skull and tusk sheaths are almost horizontally directed.

The teeth or even pieces of teeth of mammoths and mastodonts are easy to distinguish from one another. The surfaces of mammoth teeth are composed of a series of thin, transverse rows of enamel. The surfaces of mastodont teeth are composed of a series of large knobs, usually in two rows from front to back. The differences in teeth were reflected in the food habits of the two animals. Mammoths ground up grasses with the ridges of their cheek teeth, while mastodonts crushed up mast and browse with the knobby surfaces of their cheek teeth. Mastodonts outnumber mammoths about five to one in ancient Michigan, where woodlands that produced trees, shrubs, and mast were much more common than grasslands.

The bodies of mammoths and mastodonts are also very different. The mammoth body skeleton is more lightly built than the mastodont body skeleton, which has a stout, heavy frame. The mammoth has long front legs, the rear end is low to the ground, and the body arches upward to a hump behind the neck. Mastodonts have a somewhat piglike body, with shorter legs and with the rear end at about the same level as the front end. If the animals were alive and we could see them side by side, they would really look quite different from one another,

Four other extinct Ice age vertebrates occur as Michigan fossils. The **giant beaver** was a huge rodent about as large as a black bear. The term "beaver" is really a misnomer, as this animal did not cut down trees or build damns, but was more of a large, clumsy "waterhog" that moved about the Pleistocene lakes and marshes feeding upon succulent aquatic vegetation. Only about ten finds of giant beavers have been made in Michigan, but finds of these interesting extinct rodents are more abundant in Ohio.

The **flat-headed peccary** was a long-legged piglike animal with razor-sharp canines. These animals probably existed in protective groups. **Scott's moose,** often called the stag moose, had longer legs, and the antlers had longer and thinner branches than those of the modern moose. The extinct moose supposedly was an inhabitant of sphagnum bogs. Finally, the **woodland musk ox** was taller and slimmer than the modern musk ox and had a pitted basin between the horns that is not present in the modern animal. The woodland musk ox is thought to have been a grazer that inhabited both woodlands and plains.

The mystery surrounding the fact that all of the above Michigan Ice Age mammals (as well as many other large mammals elsewhere in the world) became extinct about 10,000 B.P. at the end of the Pleistocene is one of the most hotly debated issues in science. There are two main hypotheses. One is that environmental changes at the end of the Pleistocene somehow interacted to cause the death of these large mammals. The other is that overkill by ancient human hunters caused this major extinction.

MODERN MICHIGAN PLANTS AND ANIMALS

Plants exist together in assemblages called **plant associations** that are part of larger units termed **biotic communities.** A biotic community may be defined as an assemblage of plants and animals that interact (usually in a harmonious way) with one another and with the physical environment. This definition is meant to be a broad one. Thus the term could pertain to a one-acre pond or the deciduous forest community of a large part of the United States. As the physical environment changes, so does the composition of biotic communities, and this was an especially important aspect of life in the Ice Age.

Reestablishment of Plant Associations in Michigan after the Ice. The redevelopment of Late Pleistocene and post-Pleistocene plant associations in Michigan is not only important in its own light, but also as it relates to the reinvasion of animal species into the area after the retreat of the last ice sheet. These events have been particularly well studied in southern Michigan, where numerous fossil pollen studies have been done. When the ice sheet retreated, it left a mass of sterile mud, sand, and gravel. In order to establish biological communities, plants and animals had to gain a foothold in these areas.

Records of plant life during a temporary withdrawal of the ice about 40,000 B.P. in Kalkaska County and about 25,000 B.P. in Muskegon County indicate a boreal or sub-boreal climate with open forests that were dominated by spruce and pine. Tamarack and probably white cedar were prominent in the swamps, with sedges, cattails, and herbaceous plants characteristic of disturbed ground found in marshy and well-drained areas.

The earliest records in southern Michigan indicate evidence of tundra vegetation when the ice sheet began its final withdrawal about 14,000 B.P. Marshes and muskegs were characteristic of the lowlands and wetlands. By 13,000 B.P., about half of the Lower Peninsula was deglaciated. Almost all of the well-drained areas had scattered stands of pioneer trees such as juniper, aspen, ash, spruce; and sun-tolerant shrubs such as willow, silverberry, and crowberry.

From 12,500 to about 11,000 B.P. southern Michigan had a boreal forest that was dominated by spruce trees, but with areas of open woodland or boreal parkland. Between 11,000 and 9,900 B.P. there were marked changes in the pollen record. At about 10,600 B.P. jack pine and red pine began to replace spruce in southwestern lower Michigan. By 10,000 B.P. the forest communities in southern Michigan had become diverse, with mixed forests of white and red pines, yellow birch and paper birch, aspen, oak, white ash, red and white elm, and blue beech.

Glacial ice was gone from Michigan except for the northern edge of the Upper Peninsula by 9,900 B.P., and in the southern part of the state, a mixed hardwood forest existed dominated by birch, ash, blue beech, elm and oak, with lesser amounts of hickory, walnut, butternut, and basswood and small amounts of white pine. In central lower Michigan, however, a poorly defined pine-spruce hardwood forest was present, with spruce especially abundant in the "thumb" area. For some reason, spruce-pine forests persisted longer in the thumb than elsewhere at similar latitudes. Actually, the pine period ended between 9,800 and 9,000 B.P. in southern Michigan and not until about 8,000 B.P. in the thumb.

The **Holocene** (see fig. 6) comprises the period of time between the end of the Pleistocene and the present, and during this interval more important changes took place in the plant communities of Michigan. During the early to middle Holocene new plants invaded the state. Hemlock reached North Manitou and Beaver Islands by 7,000 B.P. and Sault Ste. Marie by 6,400 B.P. Hemlock reached central lower Michigan by about 5,800 B.P. and the interior of the Upper Peninsula by 5,000 B.P. It is believed that American beech probably entered Michigan from Ontario. This tree arrived in Lapeer County in the thumb area by about 8,000 B.P. and the interior of the Upper Peninsula by 5,000 B.P.

Vegetational changes in Michigan have been used to suggest temperature changes in the Holocene of Michigan. There was an increase in temperature from 9,000 B.P. to at least 2,500 B.P. However, cyclic changes in the vegetation, which consisted of dry oak forests being replaced by moister forests and vice versa, occurred in southern Michigan during this interval. Based on both plant and animal evidence, most scientists recognize that a **hypsithermal** or "warmest Holocene period" occurred about 5,500 B.P.

After about 2,500 B.P. the climate became moister and cooler again, and this produced changes in the vegetation. In southern Michigan beech-maple forests expanded, while oak-hickory and prairie-oak grassland retreated. Moreover, white pine forests expanded southward into central lower Michigan. Several climatic fluctuations occurred between 1,500 B.P. and the present as warm and cool periods alternated. Obviously when European settlers came to Michigan, some major changes took place, as the pollen record indicates that forest tree pollen decreased and "weed pollen," especially ragweed, increased.

In summary, vegetation began to develop in Michigan about 15,000 B.P. when the last ice sheet began to retreat for the final time. By 13,000 B.P. about half of Michigan was deglaciated, and tundra communities existed in the southern part of the state. From about 12,500 to 11,800 B.P. boreal forest communities had become established in southern Michigan. By about 10,000 B.P. the ice was gone except for some in the northern part of the Upper Peninsula, and hardwood forests had reached southern Michigan. The Holocene epoch from 10,000 B.P. until the present saw fluctuations between beech-maple and oak-dominated vegetation in southern Michigan. About 5,500 B.P. an important "warmest period" or hypsithermal occurred in the state.

Reinvasion of Vertebrate Animals in Michigan after the Ice. The timing of the reinvasion of vertebrate animals (fishes, amphibians, reptiles, birds, and mammals) into deglaciated Michigan is not known as precisely as that of plants. Nevertheless suggestions have been made about the recolonization of amphibians, reptiles, and mammals based on the fossil record and the type of vegetational communities they presently prefer.

The first **amphibian** to reinvade southern Michigan after the ice was probably the **wood frog** (fig. 20), which presently extends northward into the subarctic tundra. Wood frogs could have arrived in the state between 14,800 to 12,500 B.P. They are the commonest true frogs of moist woodland floors in Michigan today and are able to freeze solid during the winter without harmful effects. Other amphibians that tolerate boreal forests probably arrived in southern Michigan about 12,500 to 11,800 B.P. These include the **blue-spotted salamander, spotted salamander** (fig. 21), **eastern tiger salamander, four-toed salamander, mudpuppy, eastern newt, red-backed salamander, eastern American toad** (fig. 22, Michigan's most widespread toad), **gray treefrog** (fig. 23, one of two Michigan species), **northern spring peeper, western chorus frog, bullfrog, green frog** (fig. 24, Michigan's commonest true frog), **pickerel frog, northern leopard frog,** and **mink frog** (fig. 25, has a minklike odor and is found only in the Upper Peninsula today).

How long did it take amphibian species to move northward as new communities developed after the withdrawal of the ice sheet? Pleistocene bullfrogs, green frogs, leopard frogs, and wood frogs moved from southwestern Indiana to northwestern Ohio at a rate of about sixty-six miles per one thousand years in the late Pleistocene. This roughly approached the mean rate of the withdrawal of the ice at the time.

The first **reptiles** to invade Michigan also probably arrived during the time boreal forests became established. These include the **snapping turtle** (fig. 26, Michigan's largest turtle), **painted turtles** (fig. 27, Michigan's "state reptile"), **wood turtle** (fig. 28, one of Michigan's most endangered turtle), **Blanding's turtle** (fig. 29, a very frequent roadkill in some areas in the spring), **five-lined skink lizard** (fig. 30, Michigan's only widely distributed lizard), **northern ring-necked snake, western fox snake, northern water snake** (fig. 31, Michigan's common water snake, sometimes mistaken for a cottonmouth), **eastern smooth green snake** (fig. 32), **northern red-bellied snake,** and **eastern garter snake** (fig. 33).

Secondary amphibian invaders probably entered southern Michigan when the mixed coniferous/broadleaf plant communities became established about 10,000 B.P. These amphibian species were the **Blanchard's cricket frog, Fowler's toad** (fig. 34, a toad with a haunting mating call), and **Cope's gray treefrog.** Secondary reptile invaders were probably the **spotted turtle** (fig. 35), **common map turtle, eastern box turtle** (fig. 36, a deciduous woodland species), **spiny softshell turtle, blue racer** (fig. 37, glides quick and fast across the road, as do many snakes), **eastern fox snake, eastern hog-nosed snake** (fig. 38, a harmless snake that flattens its neck like a cobra), **eastern milk snake, queen snake, brown snake, Butler's garter snake, northern ribbon snake,** and **eastern massasauga rattle-snake** (fig. 39, Michigan's only venomous snake; does not occur in the Upper Peninsula).

Tertiary amphibian invaders probably began to enter the state after 9,900 B.P. as mixed hardwood vegetational communities began to become established in southern Michigan. These species are the **marbled salamander, small-mouthed salamander,** and **western lesser siren salamander,** all extremely rare in Michigan today. Tertiary reptiles include the **common musk turtle** (fig. 40, a small, lake-bottom crawler), **red-eared slider turtle, six-lined racerunner lizard, Kirtland's snake, black rat snake,** and **northern copper-belly snake.** Except for the common musk turtle and black rat snake these tertiary reptiles are very rare in Michigan today. The red-eared slider may be a modern introduction into the state after having been here once before during a somewhat warmer time in the Holocene.

Many species of **mammals** living today are tolerant of tundra conditions and probably began to invade Michigan between 14,800 to 12,500 B.P. when tundra vegetation became established. These species probably included such familiar mammals as the **black bear, mink, northern river otter, coyote, gray wolf, red squirrel, American beaver, meadow vole, muskrat, common porcupine, snowshoe hare,** and **moose.**

Additional mammal species, including the **large extinct species,** probably invaded Michigan during the 12,500 to 10,000 year interval when, first, boreal forest communities dominated, spruce trees developed, and later the communities became more diverse by the addition of hardwoods. These **secondary** invaders would have included the **eastern mole, northern short-tailed shrew, common raccoon, American badger, striped skunk, common gray fox, bobcat, extinct giant beaver, woodchuck, eastern gray squirrel, eastern fox squirrel, white-footed mouse, eastern cottontail, extinct flat-headed peccary, extinct Scott's moose, extinct woodland musk ox, mammoth, mastodont,** and **white-tailed deer.**

Fig. 20. Wood frog. The black patch through the eye is a good field mark. (Photo courtesy of James H. Harding.)

Fig. 21. Spotted salamander. The double row of distinct yellow or orange-yellow spots is a good character for the identification of this species. (Photo courtesy of James H. Harding.)

Fig. 22. Calling male eastern American toad. This toad has usually one but no more than two large warts in each of the largest dark spots. (Photo courtesy of James H. Harding.)

Fig. 23. Calling male gray treefrog. The expanded, disklike toe tips are good field marks for this species. The expanded throat pouch indicates this specimen was calling. (Photo courtesy of James H. Harding.)

Fig. 24. Green frog. This large green frog has a ridge-like lateral fold that extends down the side of the body. (Photo courtesy of James H. Harding.)

Fig. 25. Mink frog from Iron County. This somewhat shiny, mottled frog has a peculiar minklike odor. It occurs only in the Upper Peninsula in Michigan. (Photo courtesy of James H. Harding.)

Mammalian **tertiary** invaders probably began to enter the state after about 9,900 B.P., when mixed hardwood forests began to become dominant in southern lower Michigan and some prairie vegetation became established. The tertiary invaders probably were the **least shrew,** the **Indiana bat,** the **evening bat,** and the **prairie vole.** All of these species are presently confined to the southern part of the Lower Peninsula, and the shrew and the bat are rare. Several mammalian species presently continue to move northward. As an example, the **Virginia opossum** (fig. 41) invaded Michigan during recent historical times, crossed the Mason-Quimby line during the last fifty years, and only recently invaded the Upper Peninsula.

Modern Plant Associations of Michigan. In general terms, plant associations in Michigan may be grouped into three broad biotic zones (fig. 42). The Carolinian Biotic Province in the lower part of the Lower Peninsula is dominated by deciduous hardwood forests. The Canadian Biotic Province, which is located in the upper part of the Lower Peninsula and occurs throughout the entire Upper Peninsula, is dominated by a mixture of deciduous hardwood and coniferous forests (fig.

Fig. 26. Nesting snapping turtle. The flattened dark shell and long spiked tail identify this large turtle. The specimen in this photo is digging its nest. (Photo courtesy of James H. Harding.)

Fig. 27. Midland painted turtle. The combination of red and yellow markings on the head and red marks on the shell are good field marks for this common turtle. This individual is digging a nest. Unfortunately many painted turtles nest near the highway and are killed by cars. (Photo courtesy of James H. Harding.)

Fig. 28. Wood turtle eating a strawberry. The fact that its shell looks like it has been sculptured from wood accounts for the name of this turtle, and it is also a good field mark. This turtle is illegal to possess in Michigan. (Photo courtesy of James H. Harding.)

Fig. 29. Blanding's turtle sunning itself on a partially submerged log by the road. The bright yellow chin is the best field mark for this species. (Photo courtesy of James H. Harding.)

Fig. 30. Five-lined skink. The five light lines are a very good field mark. The only other lizard in the state has six light lines on the body and occurs only in a single population in the thumb area (Lower Peninsula). (Photo courtesy of James H. Harding.)

Fig. 31. Northern water snake. This snake, always found in or near water, has a pattern of dark blotches on a rather dull-colored body. It is not poisonous, but it will bite if you grab it. (Photo courtesy of James H. Harding.)

Fig. 32. Smooth green snake, the only all-green snake in Michigan. (Photo courtesy of James H. Harding.)

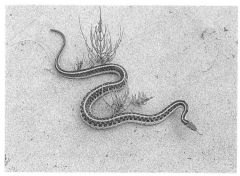

Fig. 33. The eastern garter snake is the most common snake in Michigan. The snake in the picture is from the Upper Peninsula, where populations with yellow spots, a distinct black body color, and bright yellow stripes seem to be rather common. In other populations in Michigan a variety of color patterns occur. (Photo courtesy of James H. Harding.)

Fig. 34. Fowler's toad. This toad, which occupies the western part of the Lower Peninsula only, can be distinguished on the basis of having more than two large warts within the large dark blotches on the body. (Photo courtesy of James H. Harding.)

Fig. 35. Spotted turtle. Many think the spotted turtle is the most beautiful turtle in Michigan. Its bright yellow spots and lack of a yellow chin will distinguish it from other turtles in the state. (Photo courtesy of James H. Harding.)

Fig. 36. Female eastern box turtle. This woodland turtle is easily distinguished by the fact that a hinge in its lower shell allows the animal to completely close the shell around the body parts. It is illegal to possess this turtle in Michigan. (Photo courtesy of James H. Harding.)

Fig. 37. Blue racer. The shiny, dark blue color distinguishes the blue racer, an alert, very active snake, from other serpents in the state. (Photo courtesy of James H. Harding.)

Fig. 38. Eastern hog-nosed snake. This chubby snake with an upturned snout is harmless, but spreads the head and hisses in a way that alarms people. When molested, it turns on its back and feigns death. Please do not harm this nonpoisonous snake, which is not as common as it used to be in Michigan. (Photo courtesy of James H. Harding.)

Fig. 39. Eastern massasauga rattlesnake. This is Michigan's only poisonous snake, and it occurs only in the Lower Peninsula and on Bois Blanc Island. No other Michigan snake has a rattle on the end of the tail. (Photo courtesy of James H. Harding.)

43). In between lies a vegetational transition zone between the Carolinian and Canadian Biotic Provinces. The transition zone is much more extensive in the western part of the Lower Peninsula than it is in the eastern part due to the warming effect of Lake Michigan and the prevailing direction of southwest winds.

The most common trees in the Upper Peninsula are birch (see fig. 43), maple, hemlock (fig. 44), aspen, spruce, and fir; and the most common ones in the Lower Peninsula are beech, maple, birch, aspen, and pine. Elms, common elements of the vegetation of presettlement days, are largely gone due to the Dutch elm disease; and in northern Michigan, many early pine forests have been replaced by birch and aspen.

In essence, however, all of Michigan is a zone of transition between broadleaf deciduous forests to the south and the boreal conifer forests of Canada. Moreover, the mixture of plant species in any given area may be complex due to local factors. This has led to a more complex vegetational picture in Michigan than is shown on many vegetational maps covering North America.

Fig. 40. Common musk turtle from Barry County. This small turtle with two thin stripes on the side of its relatively large head has a very musky odor. As in the individual in the photograph, this turtle often has much algae growing on its shell. (Photo courtesy of James H. Harding.)

Fig. 41. Virginia opossum. This primitive mammal is frequently killed on the road during the warmer months of the year. (Photo courtesy of James H. Harding.)

Tree species common to the boreal forests generally occur on acid boggy soils or on sandy uplands. Many deciduous broadleaf species, however, prefer more fertile clay or loamy soils. One must remember that presettlement vegetational associations have been greatly modified by human settlement and agricultural and industrial development.

In the Carolinian Biotic Province (see fig. 42) the **presettlement** forest consisted of deciduous hardwood forests except for the wettest, most acid areas. Dry, well-drained uplands supported stands of black oak, white oak, red maple, and shagbark hickory. Moister uplands with

Fig. 42. The biotic provinces and the transition zone between them in Michigan. All of the Upper Peninsula is in the Canadian Biotic Province.

finer soils, however, supported stands of beech, sugar maple, basswood, and red oak. Lake plain and lowland areas support different tree complexes. In areas near Lake Michigan, beeches and maple were more common than in other places because of the relative lack of drought in this environment. On the other hand, the lake plain muck soils of the Saginaw Bay lowland supported ash, American elm, red and silver maples, as well as swamp oaks.

North of the Carolinian Biotic Province the climate is cooler, the growing season is shorter, and coarse sandy soils are widespread. Moreover, soils are more acid. Thus, boreal plants occur more widely than in the south. Here beech and sugar maple mixed in with hemlock, and pine and yellow birch occur, especially in the northwest part of the Lower Peninsula, where there is a relatively large amount of rainfall.

Fig. 43. Typical trees that occur in woodlands in the north-central part of the Lower Peninsula. Red pines are to the left, and white pines and paper birch trees are to the right. The scene is near the entrance of Hartwick Pines State Park. Wheels are from an old big wheel logging wagon.

Spectacular white and red pine forests were spread over the lowland sandy soils of the northern part of the lower peninsula. These forests formed the heart of the lumber industry in Michigan and provided timber for the buildings in emerging industrial cities such as Chicago and Detroit. A small, uncut remnant of white and red pine forest is found in Hartwick Pines State Park (see fig. 43), not too far north of the Mason-Quimby line (see fig. 18) in central Michigan.

Similar forest associations developed in the Upper Peninsula during presettlement times. Pines generally developed on acid, sandy soils; but the cooler summer climate allowed more hemlock, yellow birch, balsam fir, and white spruce in the uplands than in northern lower Michigan. This was particularly true in the cool Keweenaw Peninsula. Moreover, bog associations of black spruce and larch were common in the cold, acid, poorly drained areas of the Upper Peninsula.

Michigan's forests have changed drastically since the appearance of European settlers. The changes were most profound in the relatively low areas of northern Michigan that were dominated by white and red pine. In this region the massive logging operation and fires that

Fig. 44. Eastern hemlock tree. Eastern hemlocks occur from well-drained situations to intermittent wetlands in the Canadian Biotic Province.

occurred in its aftermath changed the commercially desirable pine forests to those of jack pine (fig. 45) and scrub oaks on poor soils and aspen and white birch on somewhat better soils. But logging on good upland soils where beech, yellow birch, sugar maple, and hemlock were the dominant trees had much less effect on composition of the forests that were to follow.

Since so much of the poor sandy soil in northern Michigan was subject to logging and resulting fires, forests of oak, aspen, and white birch are the most common there. This habitat supports large deer populations that flourish on young aspen trees. Ironically for deer-hunting enthusiasts, these trees are not shade tolerant and ultimately will be replaced by sugar maple or red maple. In other northern Michigan areas disturbed by logging, jack pine is dominant. The endangered Kirtland's warbler is restricted to young stands of jack pine. Here one faces the dilemma of keeping young jack pine forests from maturing in order to save this rare bird.

Because of its position between the deciduous forests to the south and the pure coniferous forests to the north, as well as its diversity of

Fig. 45. Jack pines along U.S. 131 in Kalkaska County, northern Lower Peninsula. Defoliated paper birch trees on the right were decimated by a gypsy moth outbreak in the 1990s.

topographic features and soils, Michigan has (or at least had) several plant associations, some quite large, with quite localized distributions. These distinctive forest associations occur both in the Lower and the Upper Peninsula of Michigan (fig. 46). Scattered through about the lower half of the Lower Peninsula were large areas of elm-ash-cottonwood forests, which in many areas (e.g., the thumb area) have been replaced by agriculture. In the upper central part of the Lower Peninsula one finds an area where pine, oak, and aspen were dominant, at least until the logging days. Finally, in the Upper Peninsula, large areas of spruce-fir are widely scattered about.

In the southwestern part of the Lower Peninsula, a few spotty areas of prairie with grasses similar to those of prairie areas in Illinois and Iowa exist. These were more extensive in presettlement times where they significantly interrupted the forest pattern. These prairie relicts are thought to be left over from the warm, dry mid-Holocene hypsithermal time.

Dune habitats (fig. 47) in Michigan occur along significant parts of the coasts of Lake Michigan and Lake Superior. These habitats have unique assemblages of grass, trees, and herbaceous plants that have fascinated botanists for over one hundred years. Acid soils support blueberry patches (fig. 48) in both northern and southern Michigan.

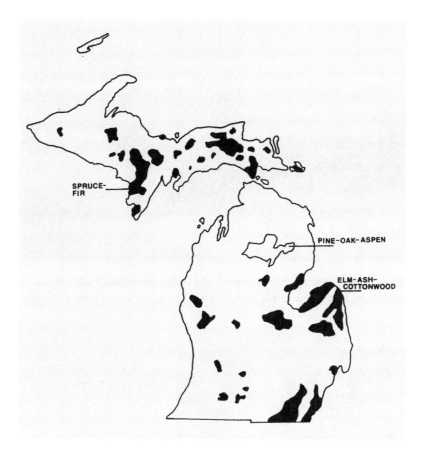

SPRUCE-
FIR

PINE-OAK-ASPEN

ELM-ASH-
COTTONWOOD

Fig. 46. Distinctive forest associations in Michigan. In the Lower Peninsula, elm-ash-cottonwood associations are shaded, and pine-oak-aspen associations are enclosed by a heavy line. In the Upper Peninsula, spruce-fir associations are shaded.

In the north they are found in boggy areas as well as in sandy pine stands, but in the south they are more common in boggy areas. Morel mushrooms are sought after in both the northern and southern parts of the Lower Peninsula of Michigan, but the most popular morel hunting area is in the northwestern part of the Lower Peninsula.

Wetland Habitats and Ecological Succession. Wetlands may be simply defined as natural areas of low-lying land that are either submerged or periodically inundated by fresh or saline water. Wetlands are among the most interesting and yet fragile habitats in Michigan. Wetlands are in the process of continuous change because of the nat-

Fig. 47. Typical low, shrubby vegetation of a typical dune habitat adjacent to Lake Michigan in Manistee National Forest, Manistee County, Lower Peninsula

Fig. 48. Blueberries. (Photo courtesy of Tal Margalith.)

ural process of ecological succession, but added to this is the immediate destruction brought on by human drainage and development.

The most common wetlands in Michigan are **marshes** and **bogs.** A marsh may be defined as an area of a more or less continuous waterlogged soil dominated by emergent plants, but without a surface accumulation of peat. On the other hand, a bog may be defined as an area with a peaty substrate, rich in organic debris but low in mineral nutrients; and with a vegetation of shrubs, sedges, and mosses (such as sphagnum). Bogs are much more acidic than marshes. A grassy bog habitat with scattered, stunted conifers is called a **muskeg. A fen** is an organically rich mire that is usually dominated by grasses and that has a winter water table at or above ground level.

All aquatic habitats tend to be in the lower areas of any given region. Since low areas tend to fill in with sediments, **ecological succession** of plant communities occurs. The succession of wetland communities tends to proceed until a stable **climax forest** occurs as the terminal stage of the process. **Climax dominant** species are the dominant species of the climax community. American (blue) beech and sugar maple trees are climax dominant species in a beech-maple climax community. On the other hand, white oak and shagbark hickory are climax dominant species in oak-hickory climax communities. The different communities that occur during ecological succession leading to a climax community are called **seral stages.**

In general, more temperate areas usually (whether these be due to local effects or latitudinal changes) have different seral stages than cooler areas. For instance, in more temperate areas, large lakes may become smaller lakes, small lakes may become ponds, ponds may become marshes, marshes may become marsh thickets, and marsh thickets eventually become climax forests. In less temperate areas, bogs and subsequent bog thickets tend to develop in open lakes, and these thickets finally give way to climax forests.

In the more temperate areas, ponds support such species as water lily, pond weed, and duckweed that give way to marshes that support such species such as cattail, bulrush, wild rice, and saw grass. As the marsh fills in, a marsh thicket appears with such species as buttonbush, alder, swamp rose, and cottonwood. The marsh thicket eventually gives way to the climax forest of the particular region.

In cooler areas, the bogs and subsequent bog thickets that develop in open lakes foster sedges, grasses, and sphagnum mosses that develop as floating masses of vegetation in concentric rings of plant growth that gradually advance to the center of the lake. These raftlike floating mats (often called quaking bogs) build up from the top toward the bottom and gradually add roots and debris that can support a bog forest dominated by larch, spruce, and arbor vitae. A bog forest may last a very long time before it is finally replaced by a climax forest community.

Characteristic Vertebrates of Michigan. Many vertebrates (fishes, amphibians, reptiles, birds, and mammals) are particularly characteristic of this state. Many of these have been listed and figured in the section on the reinvasion of Michigan after the withdrawal of the glacier, and some will be referred to again here. Since many of these animals are secretive and are not likely to be seen by most people, we shall include only those that are likely to be observed by the users of this book in their travels through the state.

The **brook trout** is the state fish of Michigan, but it is obviously not likely to be seen by automobile travelers. Persons traveling to Michigan Great Lakes ports where commercial fishing is done, or especially where large charter boats are returning with customers with fish, are likely to see several characteristic food and game species. The most common fish caught on large charter boats is the **yellow perch,** which averages about eight or ten inches long and is often caught by the bucketful on these boats. The yellow perch is a wonderful food fish with a sweet, flaky texture. The native **lake trout** and the introduced **coho salmon** are cherished food and game fish that most often come in on smaller chartered boats as well as commercial fishing boats. Favorite "smokehouse" fish caught by commercial fishermen are the small **chubs** (or ciscos) and the delicious **whitefish.** Lake trout and coho salmon are also smokehouse favorites.

Many Michigan amphibians and reptiles are so secretive that they will probably not been seen by the travelers that use this book. Among the amphibians, the **wood frog** (see fig. 20) and the warty **eastern American toad** (see fig. 22) may be seen hopping through the woods or fields in many areas, and the **green frog** (see fig. 24) is likely to be seen in shallow, well-vegetated areas of almost any still body of water in the state. Sometimes hundreds of small, spotted **northern leopard frogs** (fig. 49) cross Michigan highways during rainstorms, but these amphibians are not as common as they once were.

Several kinds of turtles may be seen crossing Michigan highways, especially during the first warm spring weather and in the early summer. Unfortunately many of them become highway casualties. Others bask on logs, rocks, and mats of vegetation in ponds, lakes, and slow-moving rivers and streams, and may be easily identified with binoculars. Three very characteristic Michigan turtles are the dull-colored, long-tailed **snapping turtle** (see fig. 26), **Blanding's turtle** with its bright yellow chin (see fig. 29), and the **painted turtle** (see fig. 27) with red and yellow stripes on its head and neck and red marks on its pretty olive shell. The painted turtle is by far the most abundant turtle in the state and occurs in almost every shallow, quiet body of water, where it often basks on logs or mats of vegetation (fig. 50). The painted turtle has recently been officially designated as the "state reptile" of Michigan. The **eastern box turtle** (see fig. 36), presently a protected ("special concern") species, has a hinge that allows it to close its dome-like shell around all of the body parts. This species is occasionally seen walking through the woods or crossing highways in the southwestern part of the Lower Peninsula.

The most abundant snake in Michigan is the **eastern garter snake** (see fig. 33), which may be seen at almost any stopping place in the countryside where there is vegetation or ground cover present. This snake has three yellowish or whitish stripes, one on each side and one in the middle of the back. The beautiful, gentle little **eastern smooth green snake** (see fig. 32) may occasionally be seen crossing the road in Michigan in the northern part of the state, especially in areas where grassy meadows or wide grassy road shoulders are present. The chubby **eastern hog-nosed snake** (see fig. 38) has an upturned snout and a blotched or solid-colored body. When alarmed it may hiss and spread its neck, but it is completely harmless and should be left alone! Hog-nosed snakes are partial to sandy areas in the Lower Peninsula. Only one venomous snake, the massasauga or swamp rattler (see fig. 39), occurs in Michigan, and that snake is confined to the Lower Peninsula. These snakes are rather infrequently seen because of their secretive habits.

Birds are so plentiful in Michigan that we include only a few large species that are particularly characteristic of the state. Incidentally,

Fig. 49. The northern leopard frog was very abundant in the state until a few years ago, when the population crashed. It seems to have been replaced by the green frog (see fig. 24). (Photo courtesy of James H. Harding.)

Fig. 50. A basking midland painted turtle. These turtles can be identified in the field by their low, rounded, rather shiny, dark olive shells, red and yellow markings on the head, and the lack of a solid yellow chin. They prefer quiet water where areas that are choked with vegetation are available. The painted turtle is Michigan's state reptile. (Photo courtesy of James H. Harding.)

the **American robin,** common in many states in the eastern United States, is the state bird of Michigan. The **common loon** is a summer resident of the northern part of the state and is most often seen as it flies over or circles around lakes. It makes several characteristic calls, but the most easily recognized one sounds like high-pitched, hysterical laughter. Loons on the water are the size of a small goose and have a black head, a white neck, and a checkered back.

The **great blue heron** (often incorrectly called a crane) is a very large wading bird about four feet tall that is most often seen standing in the shallow water of lakes, ponds or marshes waiting to catch fish, frogs, or snakes with its sharp bill. Its large size and blue-gray color separate it from other water birds. **Canada geese** are very abundant in Michigan and may be seen in large numbers in lakes and ponds as well as in fields where they forage for food. These birds are familiar to most people, as they are very often seen flying overhead in V formation honking vigorously.

The **bald eagle** is once again holding its own in Michigan. In the northern part of the state, this great bird is often seen circling high in the air over lakes. Its great size, white head, white wing tips, and white tail are unmistakable field marks in the adult birds. Occasionally bald eagle nests are built near enough to the highway to be seen from passing cars. These huge nests are usually at the top of the tallest tree in the area.

Michigan is one of the states where, in certain areas, **sandhill cranes** may be commonly seen. This bird is usually seen slowly wading around in marshes or flooded areas; or flying, with its neck fully extended and with a characteristic strong upward beat of its wings. This huge bird is larger than a great blue heron and has a distinctive red head.

Kirtland's warbler is a small bird with a twitchy tail that primarily breeds in Michigan in about a fifty- by seventy-mile area of jack pine forest in the northern Lower Peninsula. It may have also bred in Wisconsin at one time. The bird has a yellow breast, spotted sides, and a striped grayish back. The habitat consists of areas where there are stands of small jack pines between about five and twenty years old. When the jack pines get older and larger, Kirtland's warbler disappears. Managed burning of mature forest and planting of new jack pine stands have been used in Michigan in an attempt to save this little bird.

Michigan is home for a variety of mammals. Some of the most interesting ones are northern species that occur mainly above of the Mason-Quimby line, but the widespread **white-tailed deer** (see fig. 63) is Michigan's "state mammal." The white-tailed deer is presently more abundant in the northern part of the state than it was in presettlement days because stands of aspen that the deer forage on have largely replaced the lumbered-out pine forests. White-tails also thrive in the farming and suburban areas of southern Michigan.

An amazing number of white-tailed deer are killed on Michigan highways. It is not unusual to see two or three at a time leap from the road shoulders onto the road. A collision with a deer not only causes damage to the car but is dangerous for its occupants; thus drivers should be alert at all times for deer on or near the highways.

Now we turn to the primitive marsupial (pouched mammal), the **Virginia opossum** (see fig. 41), a creature that has been moving steadily northward in Michigan and has recently been reported from the Upper Peninsula. Opossums existed with the dinosaurs over sixty million years ago and are true living fossils. These flat-footed mammals have a waddling gait, sparse fur, and a naked tail, and appear to some people to resemble "giant rats." Baby opossums spend their very early life in their mothers pouch and later are carried about on her back. Road-killed opossum are commonly seen south of the Mason Quimby line and somewhat less commonly observed in the northern part of the Lower Peninsula and in the Upper Peninsula.

Two common Michigan water mammals, the **American beaver** and the **muskrat,** are sometimes mistaken for one another. The beaver is larger, with a body about thirty-five to forty-five inches long and weighing up to about fifty-five or sixty pounds. It has a tail that is flattened from top to bottom. The muskrat is much smaller, with a body about twenty to twenty-five inches long and a weight of only about three pounds. A muskrat tail is flattened from side to side.

A beaver lodge (fig. 51) is very large. It is built of sticks, logs, and mud and is up to ten feet high and twenty-five feet wide. Beavers dam up small streams and create significant bodies of water, called beaver ponds (fig. 52) that are characterized by dead trees killed by flooding. A muskrat house (fig. 53) is smaller. It is built of mud and plants such as cattail and bulrush and is up to four feet high and six feet wide and is almost always seen in open water. Beavers are practically never seen dead on the road, but muskrats are common roadkills all over the state.

The **common porcupine** (fig. 54) is the most characteristic Michigan "north woods" mammal to many travelers because of the significant number of these robust, spiny rodents that are seen dead on the highways north of the Mason-Quimby line. One of the reasons so many porcupines are killed on the road is that they tend to lick up the salt spread on the highways for deicing purposes. Porcupines occupied all of southern Michigan at one time, but became extinct there when the woods were turned to farmlands. Porcupines are covered by literally thousands of barbed quills. When attacked, porcupines lash out with their tails, which are studded with these easily detached quills. The quills that attach to the would-be predator are pulled inward by muscular contractions and often prove fatal if they pierce a vital organ or blood vessel. So keep your dog on a leash at all times when in porcupine territory!

Black squirrels are common in many parts of Michigan, and visi-

Fig. 51. Beaver lodge in Kalkaska County, northern Lower Peninsula, near Fife Lake. Beavers build lodges by piling logs, sticks, and mud on an island or in a shallow pool.

Fig. 52. Beaver pond. Beavers dam up streams to form ponds. These activities create new habitats for creatures like painted turtles and green frogs that prefer standing water. On the other hand, trees in the flooded area die (see also fig. 100).

Fig. 53. Muskrat house (mound in foreground with Blanding's turtle on top) built mainly of cattail leaves. The bird on the cattail plant is a female red-wing black-bird, which is nondescript compared to the male of the species. (From a diorama in the Michigan State University Museum [courtesy of Michigan State University museum].)

tors from south of the state are quite intrigued by these animals, which are not as common farther south. Actually, the black squirrel is a color phase of the **eastern gray squirrel** (fig. 55), which has silvery tips on the hairs of its gray coat. In some areas in the state, the black phase is most common in urban settings and the gray phase most common in woodland settings. Black squirrels are frequent roadkills, especially in urban areas.

The **snowshoe hare** (fig. 56) is a characteristic animal of the north woods and occurs mainly north of the Mason-Quimby line in Michi-

Fig. 54. Common porcupine. (From A. Kurta, *Mammals of the Great Lakes Region*, rev. ed. [Ann Arbor: University of Michigan Press, 1995]; photo by James F. Parnell.)

Fig. 55. Eastern gray squirrel. (From A. Kurta, *Mammals of the Great Lakes Region*, rev. ed. [Ann Arbor: University of Michigan Press, 1995]; photo from the Roger W. Barbour Collection, Morehead State University.)

Fig. 56. Snowshoe hare. (From A. Kurta, *Mammals of the Great Lakes Region*, rev. ed. [Ann Arbor: University of Michigan Press, 1995]; photo by James F. Parnell.)

gan. This hare is particularly well suited to survive winters in areas with deep snow cover, as the large hind feet act as snowshoes and the white winter coat tends to conceal them from predators. In the summer the snowshoe has a brownish coat with a darker band running down the back. The snowshoe is larger than the cottontail and has much bigger feet, as well as lacking the rusty brown patch on the back of the neck that occurs in the cottontail. The snowshoe eats grasses, clovers, herbaceous plants, young tree leaves, and even ferns in the summer; and bark, buds, and twigs in the winter. Because of its secretive nature, the snowshoe hare is not nearly as likely to be seen by the traveler as the cottontail rabbit. However, sometimes one may see snowshoes in open rows in pine plantations at dawn or dusk.

Coyotes (fig. 57) are often confused with either gray wolves (fig. 58) or feral dogs in Michigan. Actually, the only reported occurrences of wolves in the state are from the Upper Peninsula, where most of the animals have recently been reintroduced from Wisconsin. (A now-small colony of wolves has existed on Isle Royale for many years.) Coyotes are smaller than wolves, weighing about 40 pounds, whereas a healthy gray wolf weighs about 120 pounds. Moreover, the coyote has larger ears and a slimmer muzzle than the gray wolf. Coyotes may be distinguished from dogs on the basis that they hold their tails below the back when running, whereas dogs hold their tails raised or straight out. Coyotes are sometimes seen slinking from the road shoulders into the woods, especially north of the Mason-Quimby line and in the Upper Peninsula. These animals are now increasingly seen in the south and are even seen in suburban areas near Lansing. Their characteristic nocturnal yelps and howls are sometimes heard in open areas. Coyotes appear to be "car smart" and are seldom seen dead on the road.

Black bears (fig. 59) are found in forests north of the Mason-Quimby line. They are moderately abundant, but are rather infrequently seen by travelers, as they tend to stay in thick woodlands composed of either deciduous or coniferous trees or mixtures of both. Forests with a thick understory are preferred. Look for bears in openings near dense woods at dawn or dusk. Female black bears are often seen with their one to three cubs close by. Black bears stick to the woods so much that they are seldom seen as roadkills.

Black bears feed upon a variety of vegetable and animal material and are particularly fond of fruits and berries of all kinds. Acorns form a staple diet late in the season. Black bears store up fat in the late summer and sleep through the winter in a den made under a large treefall, stump, or pile of brush. This sleep is a type of semihibernation where their heartbeat slows down and their temperature drops. The two tiny, rat-sized cubs are born late in the winter in January or February and nurse until the mother wakes up in April.

Bobcats (fig. 60) are found in Michigan in all but the thumb area and the southern portion of the Lower Peninsula. They prefer large hardwood forests but also live in mixed coniferous/deciduous woodlands and in coniferous forests. Bobcats have a spotted coat and a bobbed tail and are almost three times the size of a house cat. Also look for bobcats in open areas near woods at dawn or dusk. Bobcats commonly feed upon cottontail rabbits and snowshoe hares but will also eat squirrels, mice, birds, and carrion. Occasionally a young deer is taken.

The **elk** (or more correctly the **wapiti,** fig. 61) occurs both in North America and in Europe, where it is called the **red deer.** Elk once occurred over most of the United States and Canada, but now the only elk in the Great Lakes basin are an introduced population in a restricted area in the northeastern part of the Lower Peninsula. Elk are very large deerlike animals with a shaggy mane on the neck and upper chest and, in the male, an antler that consists of a single beam that bears several tines. The rack can be six or more feet wide. The elk actually avoids dense forests, preferring open meadows or woodlands with grassy clearings. Elk prefer to eat grasses and forbes such as clover and aster. In winter they turn to twigs and bark, but still may rummage through the snow to find grasses and forbes. Elk often graze in open areas at dawn and dusk, which is the best time to observe them.

The **moose** (fig. 62) is the largest member of the deer tribe and is as big as a horse. Its overhanging snout, shoulder hump, a flap of skin called the bell that hangs from its neck, massive antlers, and long legs are its most characteristic features. The moose occurs in northern Europe and Asia as well as in North America. Moose occupy the Upper Peninsula of Michigan and Isle Royale, but are vulnerable to a brain worm (a nematode that lives in the membranes surrounding the brain) brought northward by the white-tailed deer. The moose feeds

Fig. 57. Coyote. (From A. Kurta, *Mammals of the Great Lakes Region,* rev. ed. [Ann Arbor: University of Michigan Press, 1995]; photo by James F. Parnell.)

Fig. 58. Gray wolf. (From A. Kurta, *Mammals of the Great Lakes Region,* rev. ed. [Ann Arbor: University of Michigan Press, 1995]; photo by Jim Wvepper.)

Fig. 59. Black bear. (From A. Kurta, *Mammals of the Great Lakes Region,* rev. ed. [Ann Arbor: University of Michigan Press, 1995]; photo by James F. Parnell.)

Fig. 60. Bobcat. (From A. Kurta, *Mammals of the Great Lakes Region,* rev. ed. [Ann Arbor: University of Michigan Press, 1995]; photo by James F. Parnell.)

Fig. 61. Elk. (From A. Kurta, *Mammals of the Great Lakes Region,* rev. ed. [Ann Arbor: University of Michigan Press, 1995]; photo from the Roger W. Barbour Collection, Morehead State University.)

Fig. 62. Moose. (From A. Kurta, *Mammals of the Great Lakes Region,* rev. ed. [Ann Arbor: University of Michigan Press, 1995]; photo by John and Gloria Tveten.)

Fig. 63. White-tailed deer. (From A. Kurta, *Mammals of the Great Lakes Region,* rev. ed. [Ann Arbor: University of Michigan Press, 1995]; photo by James F. Parnell.)

on tender tree leaves in late spring; aquatic plants such as lilies, rushes, and sedges in the summer; and buds and twigs in the winter. Moose are not likely to be seen from the road unless it is in a relatively remote area with open, vegetated ponds or lakes nearby, and usually at dawn or dusk. Moose are most often encountered on Isle Royale or in remote areas in the Upper Peninsula.

Roadkills

Why do animals cross the road? The obvious answer is to get to the other side. But that is not always the case. Since reptiles cannot produce heat internally, they must find external sources to keep them warm if temperatures drop below comfortable levels. Thus, reptiles often bask on the road when the temperature starts to drop in the evening as roads (especially blacktops) tend to retain heat. In Michigan, snakes, especially those that give birth to living young, will crawl onto the road at night to maintain their body temperatures. On the other hand, when the temperature has been cold at night, the roads are obviously open places for both turtles and snakes to bask in the sun. Unfortunately, basking reptiles are very likely to be killed by motor vehicles. Both basking turtles and turtles actively crossing the road are actually at a disadvantage because of their shells, for when there is a near miss by a car, the tendency is for the turtles to withdraw into their shells and "wait it out." Since several turtle species reproduce very slowly, road casualties can slowly decrease their numbers toward the point of extirpation.

Blanding's turtle (see fig. 29) as well as other turtles, especially snapping turtles (see fig. 26) and painted turtles (see fig. 27) cross roads to find proper nesting places, and sometimes nest right on the road shoulders. This means that there are two good chances (coming from and back to the water) for them to get run over. We have pulled many turtles off the road to save them from cars, but we wonder how many of them crawled right back out across the road again to look for nesting sites.

Other reptiles in Michigan occupy different habitats in different times in the year, and this leads them to cross roads to get from one habitat to the other. A prime example of this is the massasauga (see fig. 39), Michigan's only venomous snake. Massasaugas tend to hibernate in places like chimney crayfish burrows in wetlands but move into upland areas in the summer to feed on mice and voles. They may become roadkills on roads and highways during these movements.

Drought also causes reptiles to wander in search of new aquatic habitats. When the bog in back of our cottage in the Kalkaska area dried up, painted turtles came through our yard in numbers for several days, heading for the lake in front of our place. Unfortunately, many were killed crossing a blacktop that separated the bog from the lake.

Amphibians often cross the road in the spring, sometimes in large numbers, to get to their favorite breeding pond. Sometimes very many are killed during this annual migration. In Europe, in several countries, special tunnels have been built to allow frogs and salamanders to reach their breeding ponds by going under, not over the roadways. Actually, this has worked very well as the animals have preferred the tunnels to the roadways. We have seen frog crossing and even turtle crossing signs in Europe.

Amphibians also tend to cross roads in very large numbers as a result of overcrowding. When leopard frogs (see fig. 49) were common in Michigan, hundreds of young ones could be seen on the road from time to time, moving en masse out of small, crowded ponds. This usually occurred on warm rainy nights. Less commonly, large numbers of tiger salamanders have been seen crossing roads at night in Michigan, presumably either moving to hibernating places or to breeding ponds.

Birds alight on roads mainly to get food. Vultures, crows, and ravens are scavengers that feast on road-killed mammals and sometimes reptiles and amphibians. Other birds such as kestrels alight on wires near the road shoulders to feed on mice and voles on the grassy banks. Birds are highway casualties from time to time, but most adults can effectively dodge cars quite well. But fledgling birds just learning to fly are often killed on the road.

Mammals seem to be the most common animals seen dead on the road. Mammals are much more active than reptiles and wander across roads to get from their shelters to feeding areas, looking for mates during the breeding season, or migrating from one place to the other looking for dry or moist habitats depending what their preferences are and what the season brings. Since most wild mammals are mainly active at night, dawn or dusk, they are often confused or blinded by lights. But even in the daytime, deer have the disturbing tendency to bolt out on the highway from roadside ditches with no warning to the driver. (One should be especially watchful in areas that are marked by deer crossing signs.)

The Most Common Roadkills Seen in Michigan. I once took a colleague from the Netherlands out to see some native Michigan animals and the only live one we saw during a spring morning jaunt was a woodchuck. On the other hand he was able to see numerous roadkills including turtles, opossums, raccoons, and a white-tailed deer (fig. 63), all of which he obligingly photographed. Turtles are the most common reptile or amphibian roadkills seen in Michigan, whereas raccoons are among the most common mammals seen dead on the road in southern Michigan and porcupines are the most common smaller mammals seen in the northern part of the state. Of course, one sees many deer roadkills in all parts of the state.

Roadkills as Resources. For fifty years, I (JAH) have been picking up roadkills for the sake of science; sometimes at risk to health and body; and sometimes causing uneasiness or downright discomfort to my spouse. These animals, mainly amphibians, reptiles, and mammals, have been preserved in fluids ("pickled"), prepared as study skins, or made into skeletons; all deposited in the scientific collections of the biology departments or museums where I have worked. Making skins or skeletons of roadkills is at best a chore that has to be dealt with, or at worst a disgusting experience. These study specimens are used for researches of many kinds. For instance, blood, tissue, organs, and even DNA can be extracted from roadkills for many kinds of scientific studies. This means that live animals are spared, and this in itself justifies the roadkill-gathering occupation.

An entomologist that we both know was fondly nicknamed "Roadkill" by his department; in fact we each have a "Roadkill" T-shirt prepared in his honor by one of his entomological colleagues. Roadkill mainly investigated dead mammals along the highways and byways of Michigan, where he picked up the many kinds of insects (much to the delight of his scientific friends) that were feeding on the dead animals.

Bones by the Roadside

Often the dry bones of unfortunate animals killed by cars may be found by the roadside or in adjacent woods and fields. Many of these bones are easy to identify. Turtles are often highway casualties. The high-domed, rounded shells of dead box turtles (fig. 64, top left) may sometimes be seen along road shoulders or woodland paths in southwestern Michigan. The flatter shells of road-killed or predated painted turtles (fig. 64, top right) may be seen almost anywhere in the state if wetlands are nearby. Snapping turtle shell remains may also be found statewide, and these shells are very rough and flat (fig. 64, bottom).

Rabbit, squirrel, and muskrat skeletal remains are also abundant in rural areas. The lower jaws of all of these animals are quite characteristic. Raccoons and opossums are very abundant in the state, especially in the agricultural part of the Lower Peninsula. These animals are very frequently killed by cars, and their lower jaws are also easy to identify. The cannon bones of deer are also commonly found along road shoulders.

Spotting and Identifying Live Animals from the Car

Spotting and identifying animals from a moving car is an art that must be learned. First one must be aware that there are living (or dead) things out there on the road as well as on the road shoulders, road embankments, fence posts, telephone wires, and in the air. Many people just do not notice things any smaller than a dog or maybe a rabbit on the road, and we have watched many folks run over small animals, such as turtles, snakes, and chipmunks, who seemingly had no idea that they were doing so. Thus, the first thing to do is to be observant. For example, turkeys are commonly seen along roadsides in Michigan, especially in the northern part of the Lower Peninsula because they like to feed in these situations. A turkey would be easy to see from a car window if you were looking for such things. But if you were listening to a tape, reading the paper, or just thinking about getting to the place where you were heading, you would undoubtedly miss the sight of a big bird on the roadside.

Fortunately, many roadside animals have markings or habits that will identify them even if one gets only a fleeting glimpse of them. To get you started, we will mention a few common Michigan animals with obvious markings and habits. Then you can use your field guides, many of which point out obvious field marks and habits, to work on more difficult identifications.

Turning to turtles, if you see a greenish-brown, spotted pancake crossing the road under its own power it's a softshell turtle (fig. 65). It is probably on its way to a nesting site, or its former pond or stream dried up and it is looking for a new one. Painted turtles have smooth, gently rounded rather than domed, shiny black or olive shells with red and yellow marks on them (see fig. 27). On the other hand, Blanding's and box turtles (see figs. 29 and 36) have domed shells. Blanding's turtle shells are larger, darker, and more elongate than those of box turtles. If you can see the head of the Blanding's turtle, it has a bright yellow chin that is a dead giveaway to that particular species. Snapping turtles (see figs. 26 and 64, bottom) are very big turtles with large heads and with flattened, dark, rough-looking shells. Moreover, they have long tails with a row of flattened spikes on the top like a miniature dinosaur.

Some people cannot tell snakes from sticks or fan belts on the road. Snakes are almost always curved and they usually have their heads elevated above the road unless they are dead. Telling individual snake species at a glance is more difficult, but if you see a large, shiny, bluish black snake moving very rapidly across the road, you can be almost certain that it is a blue racer (see fig. 37). The state's only venomous snake, the eastern massasauga (see fig. 39) is a thick, dark-colored snake with a very visible rattle on the end of the tail. There are three species of garter snakes in Michigan and all have yellowish, light greenish, whitish, or orangish stripes running down their bodies. Two of these, the eastern garter snake (see fig. 33) and ribbon snake, cross the road by making controlled and graceful lateral undulations like most snakes. But the third, the little Butler's garter snake, cannot negotiate road surfaces very well and rather than graceful undulations makes uncontrolled, spasmodic wiggles, "going nowhere fast" as the saying goes.

Very large birds soaring overhead with flat wings and with white heads, wingtips, and tails are bald eagles, not as uncommon as they used to be in the northern parts of the state. Very large all-blackish birds soaring (with wings in a shallow V and without periodic wing beats) are turkey vultures. Sometimes (mainly on smaller roads) one sees them feasting on dead deer or other mammals, then one notices that they have naked heads covered by wrinkled skin. Some think the reason that vultures are much more common than they used to be in Michigan is because of the increased number of deer in the state and other road-killed mammals such as raccoons on the highways.

Very large, long-legged birds flying overhead with the neck extended and with the main stroke of the wing beat being the upstroke are undoubtedly sandhill cranes. On the ground, standing in marshes or fallow fields, sandhill cranes are by far the tallest birds in Michigan. Various herons, including the very large great blue heron, fly with the neck curved back. Great blue herons are commonly seen standing in the shallow water of marshes and lakes, where they are waiting to

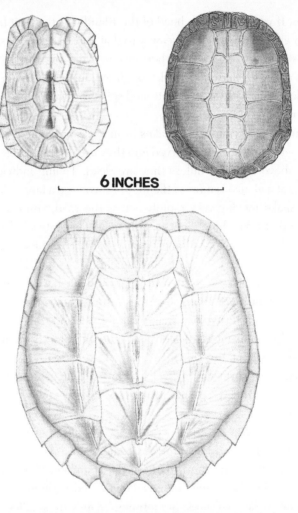

6 INCHES

Fig. 64. Shell of eastern box turtle *(top left)*, midland painted turtle *(top right)*, and snapping turtle *(bottom)*. Shells of dead turtles may be found on the road shoulders, in the woods, and on beaches. (Drawings by Robin Ross.)

catch fishes, frogs, snakes, and even small mammals. Canada Geese, which are presently very common in Michigan, fly in V-shaped formations with much honking going on as the group flies overhead.

On road shoulders and on the highway, crows characteristically come to feed on the remains of just about any vertebrate that has been run over. In portions of the Upper Peninsula one finds common

Fig. 65. Spiny softshell turtle. The soft, leathery, pancakelike shell and snorkel-like nose easily distinguish this turtle from others. The spiny softshell is not uncommon in the southern part of the Lower Peninsula. This odd turtle is seldom seen near roads and highways but it sometimes may be seen sunning on muddy or sandy banks of sloughs or slow-flowing rivers. (Photo courtesy of James H. Harding.)

ravens doing the same thing. Ravens are larger than crows, but one way to surely tell the difference between the two is that ravens always take two or three hops before they become airborne. Usually in March, often while snow is still on the ground, redwing blackbird males begin to station themselves on the edge of cattail marshes. These shiny black birds with their bright red wing patches are characteristic species seen from the car window where cattail ditches or marshes are near the road shoulder.

Several types of raptorial birds are commonly seen along Michigan highways. Red-tailed hawks are large hawks that commonly station themselves along the roadsides in dead trees or on fence posts waiting for prey up to rabbit size to capture in their talons. Marsh hawks are streamlined hawks that characteristically fly very low over marshes and grassy meadows looking for their prey. In open woodlands look for gray-colored hawks about the size of crows streaking under the woodland canopy looking for prey ranging from small birds to squirrels. These may be either sharp-shinned hawks or Cooper's hawks. Kestrels are small birds of prey formerly called sparrow hawks. These birds characteristically hover above the ground with rapid wing beats looking for small prey such as grasshoppers and mice.

MICHIGAN ARCHAEOLOGY

People have been in Michigan for nearly twelve thousand years (fig. 66). During this time, they experienced conditions that ranged from cold to temperate climates, adjusted to dramatic changes in water levels of the Great Lakes, and witnessed great changes in plant and animal communities. Technology was developed by these people to help them live in these different settings. Evidence of ancient technological change includes adzes and axes for working wood, netsinkers, plummets, and hooks for fishing, bows and arrows for hunting, pottery for cooking, and pits for storing food. Charred remains of domesticated plants indicate the onset of horticulture to supplement wild foods. People interacted with their neighbors through ties of kinship, peaceful trade, and sometimes even with hostility. There were also times when new people migrated into Michigan, including Europeans who traded with the Indians for valuable furs and made alliances with different tribes in the French and British wars for control of North America. Finally, the tribes ceded their lands to Americans who created farms, settlements, and industry in Michigan.

Most of our knowledge of human cultures in Michigan comes from archaeology, which seeks to understand the past by systematically recovering and examining the physical evidence people left behind. There is much that is lost to us forever. We do not have oral traditions covering all twelve thousand years, and we have only incomplete written records of the past three hundred years. The only hard evidence of the past is archaeological evidence, that is, remains of the materials people used in their daily lives. The results of over a century of work by Michigan archaeologists have expanded our knowledge, and ongoing studies continue to raise intriguing questions about Michigan's

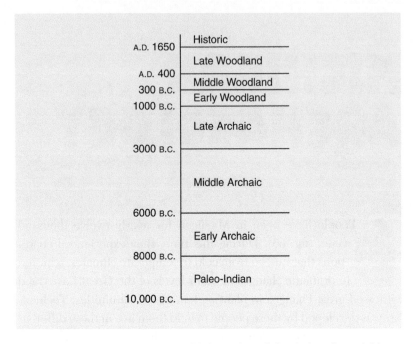

Fig. 66. Archaeological sequence in Michigan from Paleo-Indian through Historic periods

people. The following narrative about Michigan archaeology draws upon their work as well as our own. The references in the "what to take along" section at the end of this book include general works about Michigan archaeology. In addition, at the end of the book we have included references for people interested in learning more about particular topics or sites.

Paleo-Indians Colonize Michigan

The first people in Michigan, known as **Paleo-Indians,** probably arrived sometime around 11,500 or 12,000 years ago and encountered a very different world from the one with which we are familiar. Paleo-Indians lived in a late Pleistocene/late glacial environment with large ice sheets covering the northern parts of the state. The water levels in Lakes Michigan and Huron were higher than they are today and the two lake basins together formed one lake (Lake Algonquin) that joined at the Straits of Mackinac. Northern portions of Lake Algonquin were sometimes covered with ice. As the ice retreated, various unique forest communities became established.

Pleistocene animals in Michigan during the Paleo-Indian period included the now extinct mammoths, mastodonts, woodland musk oxen, giant beavers, Scott's moose, and flat-headed peccaries. Additionally, a number of animals were present that do not live here today, such as caribou, boreal lemmings, jumping mice, and ermine. These animals would have been found in various habitats such as woodlands, wetlands, bogs, and grasslands. Some of these animals would have been hunted by Paleo-Indians.

Paleo-Indians were hunters of large game. In the western United States their artifacts have been found with mammoth and bison bones. In the Midwest, Paleo-Indian materials occasionally co-occur with the bones of mastodonts, although the extent to which they hunted these elephant-like creatures is a matter of some debate. It is clear that caribou were an important prey of Paleo-Indians in the Great Lakes and northeast, including Michigan, where a caribou was identified at a Michigan site known as **Holcombe Beach.** Although Paleo-Indians hunted these large animals, they also obtained a variety of other foods. Sites from the Paleo-Indian period in the Great Lakes region and the northeast have yielded the remains of elk (wapiti), arctic fox, hare, and fish. Fruit seeds and nut shells have also been found.

Few Paleo-Indian sites are known in Michigan, but many distinctive early Paleo-Indian fluted spear points have been found in the state. These points are distinguished by a groove or **flute** that goes down the center of the projectile from the base toward the tip (fig. 67). Michigan fluted points are very similar to fluted points used in the western and eastern United States at about the same time. Later Paleo-Indians made points very similar to the fluted ones in outline and workmanship but with no flutes or only one.

It is very difficult to identify sites from this early period because fluted points are the only artifacts that we can be certain were left by Paleo-Indians. Other kinds of artifacts are often found at Paleo-Indian sites, however, including hide scrapers with projections for engraving bone or wood (spurred scrapers), large triangular scrapers, and lunate-shaped knives (fig. 67). While similar kinds of artifacts may have been used in later times, the above tools, especially if found together, strongly indicate a Paleo-Indian occupation. Another difficulty in recognizing Paleo-Indian sites is that the same places were often occu-

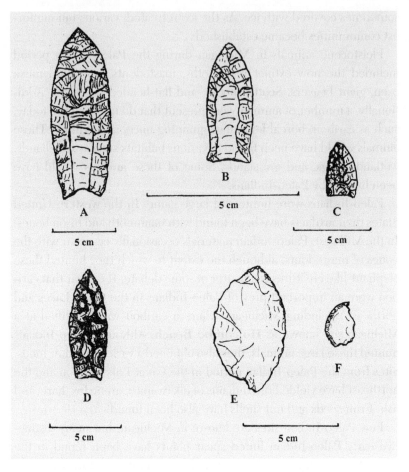

Fig. 67. Paleo-Indian fluted points and artifacts. A, Gainey; B, Barnes; C, Holcombe; D, Late Paleo-Indian Samels Lanceolate; E, Lunate knife; F, Spurred scraper.

pied by later people whose artifacts are mixed with those deposited earlier (multicomponent sites). Thus, it is difficult to distinguish the Paleo-Indian artifacts from later ones.

Paleo-Indians made their living by moving from place to place, stopping temporarily at locations where they expected to find food. They did not stay long in any one location, but traveled with only the things they could carry, including the artifacts they needed. Moreover, Paleo-Indians lived in relatively small groups. Under circumstances where a few people stayed at one site for short periods of time and conserved their resources, it is not surprising that their sites are not only hard to identify but are difficult to find.

Michigan archaeologists often speak of Paleo-Indians as being "ridge-runners" because the sites that are known are usually located on high glacial features such as moraines or old high-water lakeshores. These settings might have been selected by Paleo-Indians because they were surrounded by diverse habitats where a variety of food could be obtained, but many of these locations created a good opportunity for spotting and intercepting caribou as they migrated between their winter and summer feeding grounds. Paleo-Indian sites with diverse surrounding habitats occur in Michigan and Ontario. The southeastern Michigan **Gainey site** was on a moraine that would have been in a spruce parkland type of forest. There was a considerable diversity of vegetation that included hardwoods as well as spruce, and a swamp or bog was nearby.

A **spruce parkland** such as that at the Gainey site would have been unlike the modern northern (boreal) spruce forests. At the present time, spruce forests in relatively high latitudes are dense and uniform so that there is not much food for herd animals such as the barren ground caribou (tundra reindeer) who live there only in winter. Large animals such as moose, woodland caribou, or elk can be found in today's boreal forests, but they are solitary animals and relatively few in number. Unlike northern peoples of today, Michigan's Paleo-Indians could exploit a rich environment with boreal forest and at times tundra, cold-tolerant deciduous woodlands, grasslands, and wetlands with no forest cover. Such a mixed environment would have contained a relatively broad spectrum of plants and animals.

One puzzle about Paleo-Indians in Michigan has intrigued archaeologists for nearly forty years. The problem concerns the observation by archaeologists Ronald Mason and George Quimby that neither Paleo-Indian artifacts nor Pleistocene animal remains were found north of a line between Bay and Newaygo Counties. The question raised by the **Mason-Quimby line,** or MQ, is why this apparently sharp boundary should exist (see fig. 18). By the time Paleo-Indians arrived in Michigan about 11,500 years ago, the glacier was north of the Straits of Mackinac, and some vegetation was established on both sides of the MQ. There was no obvious barrier to keep Paleo-Indians or animals south of the Mason-Quimby line.

Recent research combining archaeological, paleontological, and paleobotanical evidence suggests that to the south of the MQ the boreal forest was a unique mosaic of vegetation that was attractive to a variety of animals. Thus, the land south of the MQ provided exactly the biological diversity upon which Paleo-Indians relied. In contrast, soil development was slow north of the MQ, and vegetation was probably relatively sparse and poor in the nutrients needed by game animals. Since Mason and Quimby's pioneering studies of the late 1950s, a few early Paleo-Indian fluted points have been found north of the MQ. Points of a later style are more common however, indicating people began to occupy the north more frequently later in the Paleo-Indian period. This northern movement seems to have taken place about 10,500 to 10,300 years ago, when the forests could support more animals and the people who hunted them.

This distribution of fluted points and Paleo-Indian sites in the Lower Peninsula suggests a pattern of colonization from south to north (fig. 68). Most early components are reported from the southern third of the Lower Peninsula, particularly the southwest and southeast but with some components in the central counties as well. But since fluted points found in the southwest and southeast include all types from the earliest to the latest, it appears that these areas were the most commonly used "entrances" into Michigan. The earliest Paleo-Indians entering the lower peninsula from the southeast made their artifacts of Upper Mercer chert, which comes from eastern Ohio. The fluted points from this early intrusion are known as **Gainey points** after the Gainey site in Lapeer County (see fig. 67A). Later fluted points were made of more local materials including Bayport chert, which is found around Saginaw Bay. These points, which differ somewhat in form and style from the Gainey point, are called **Barnes points** after the Saginaw County Barnes site (see fig. 67B). Finally, the latest in the fluted point series from Michigan are called **Holcombe points** after the Holcombe Beach site in Macomb County (see fig. 67C). Holcombe points are the most common of the Paleo-Indian points found north of the Mason-Quimby line.

A very interesting site in Grand Traverse County, **Samels Field,** was occupied about 10,300 B.P. by late Paleo-Indian/Early Archaic people. Among the artifacts from the Samels Field site are **Samels Lanceolate** projectile points, large blades, heavy scrapers, and gravers indicating that this was not just a hunting camp (see fig. 67D). Rather, Samels Field was used as a base camp where a relatively large

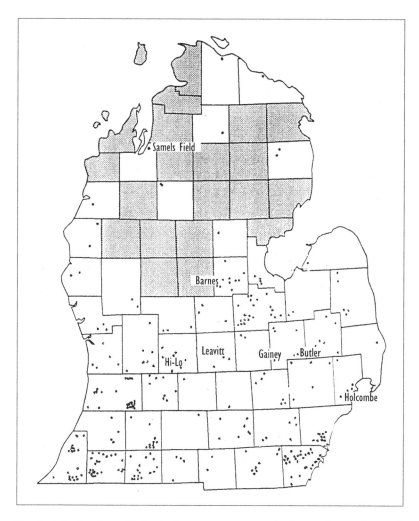

Fig. 68. Distribution of Paleo-Indian components in the Lower Peninsula as of 1995. Most of these are in the southwest and southeast, the "entrances" into the peninsula. Colonization then proceeded from south to north. No Paleo-Indian components have been found in the shaded counties. (After Cleland, Holman, and Holman 1998.)

group prepared hides, worked wood, and made stone tools of local **Norwood chert.** Additionally, **Bayport chert** from around Saginaw Bay was brought to Samels Field as **preforms,** which were preshaped pieces to be made into finished tools at the site itself. This important site has been donated to the Archaeological Conservancy by the property owners and will, thus, be preserved for future study.

In comparison to the Lower Peninsula, Paleo-Indians came some one thousand years later to the Upper Peninsula, and they came from the west, not from the south. The Lake Superior basin and much of the Upper Peninsula were ice covered until 10,700 B.P. when the ice front receded northward. Shortly after 10,000 B.P., the glacier readvanced into the Upper Peninsula, as evidenced by a spruce and tamarack forest that was buried by the ponding of water at the margins of the ice. This most recent glaciation known as the **Marquette Stadial** retreated about 9,500 B.P., and since then the peninsula has been ice-free.

A series of late Paleo-Indian/Early Archaic sites on old shorelines of inland lakes in the center of the Upper Peninsula indicate this area was occupied soon after the final glacial retreat. People who lived here about 9,500 B.P. made beautifully worked projectile points of a style known as **Eden-Scottsbluff** (fig. 69A and B). Such points are associated with late Paleo-Indian sites on the Plains and in the Western Great Lakes region. The Eden-Scottsbluff points in the Upper Peninsula are made of **Hixton silicified sandstone** that outcrops in west central Wisconsin. Archaeologists differ as to whether the people at these Upper Peninsula camps went to the Wisconsin quarry themselves or traded for the Hixton material. It is clear, however, that the material was specially reserved for projectile points, as other stone tools were made from locally available quartzite, quartz, and chert.

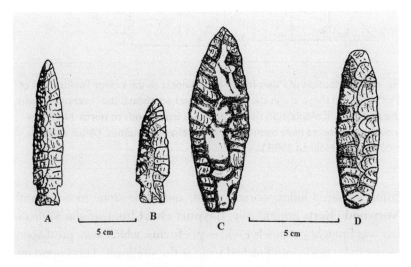

Fig. 69. Paleo-Indian projectile point types found in the Upper Peninsula. A, Eden; B, Scotsbluff; C, Hell Gap; D, Agate Basin.

Some people may have been at ice-free locations in the Upper Peninsula as early as 10,500 years ago, as indicated by one **Hell Gap** and one **Agate Basin** projectile point at inland lake sites (fig. 69C and D). These points, again of more western styles, suggest an early occupation of the area even though the ice was only a few kilometers away and the climate must have been very harsh.

The Archaic

Adjusting to a Postglacial Environment: Early and Middle Archaic. About ten thousand years ago, there were great changes in the Michigan environment. The glaciers were gone from the Lower Peninsula and the Upper Peninsula was ice-free some five hundred years thereafter. Some animals such as the mammoth and mastodont became extinct, while others, such as the cold-adapted caribou and musk oxen, moved north after the retreating ice. Pollen records show that about ten thousand years ago the composition of Michigan forests changed from a dominance of spruce to large amounts of pine along with increasing numbers of deciduous trees such as birch, ironwood, elm, oak, and ash, particularly in the southern Lower Peninsula. Spruce still dominated the eastern Upper Peninsula, but the central Upper Peninsula supported a mixed pine-hardwood forest. The peoples of Michigan were faced with a choice. Should they follow the caribou and the musk oxen north and thereby continue with their Paleo-Indian way of life, or should they adjust to hunting a new combination of animals, and gathering a different set of plants? This choice was not made in one generation. Rather, over several generations some people probably chose to move north, and some stayed. The first period of adjustment to new conditions is the **Early Archaic,** which dates from about ten thousand to eight thousand years ago.

The Early Archaic is tantalizing because we have very little direct evidence of sites of this period. What we do have are projectile points that are very similar to Early Archaic projectiles from other parts of eastern North America, so we date those found in Michigan by comparison with those found elsewhere. We also must make inferences about the Early Archaic ways of life by comparison with Early Archaic sites outside Michigan and on indirect evidence from Michigan.

One of the problems confronting archaeologists about the Early

Archaic arises from the earliest projectile point types associated with this time. In the Lower Peninsula there are two general point types that seem to be contemporary, yet differ significantly from one another. The first of these types is the **Hi-Lo** (ca. 10,500 to 10,000 B.P.) which was named for the Hi-Lo Gun Club in Ionia County. Hi-Lo points are of a shape and form that suggest continuity from late Paleo-Indian times. These artifacts represent a logical transition from one period to another, which in turn suggests that the people who made them were descendants of the Paleo-Indians. The inference of continuity from the Paleo-Indian period to the Early Archaic is strengthened by the fact that Hi-Lo points are equated with the Plano point tradition of the west, which was a stylistic successor of Paleo-Indian fluted points. The other oldest Early Archaic point type found in Michigan, known as **Kirk,** is a notched, often serrated, form that is most similar to points found in the Southeast and Midwest. Kirk points are so different from the lanceolate forms characteristic of Paleo-Indian points that they appear to be evidence of some kind of cultural break between Paleo-Indian and Early Archaic times. Because Kirk points from southeastern Michigan are often made of Ohio chert, some archaeologists believe there was an influx of new people into the region. Alternatively, development of the Early Archaic way of life may have taken place in situ and the new artifact forms may have been adopted from other cultures by a process known as **cultural diffusion.** The fact that many Kirk points are made of Ohio chert does not really answer the question. Groups may have come into Michigan from Ohio, or Michigan groups may have interacted with their Ohio neighbors and thereby acquired Ohio chert. At the same time, they may have found the artifact forms used by their neighbors to be more suitable for their purposes. In any case, inferences about Early Archaic foods suggest that people incorporated a wide range of plants into their diet. While they continued to hunt deer and elk, they also sought small game, birds and, to some extent, fish.

The question of why we find Early Archaic spear points but no sites is intriguing. At one time, it was suggested that much of the Lower Peninsula was abandoned because it was covered with pine forests that would support very little game and would provide few plants for people. At that time, it was recognized that any sites that might exist would have been along Great Lakes shorelines where the environment would have been more productive. Since these shorelines are now covered by hundreds of feet of water, early sites there are not available for study. The idea that the Early Archaic forests were too pine dominated to provide food has largely been discarded because new data indicates some mixed forest communities were present.

The Early Archaic occurred shortly after the Great Lakes water levels dropped dramatically (10,300 B.P.). Lake Superior was about 240 feet lower than it is today and in Lake Huron the waters were nearly 390 feet lower than they are now. Lake Michigan was nearly 350 feet lower. During Paleo-Indian times, the waters of **Lake Algonquin** in the Michigan and Huron basins drained south and west (at Chicago) and south and east (at Port Huron). When drainage was through these southern outlets, the water levels were very high, at 605 feet above sea level. With the retreat of the glacial ice, beginning about 11,000 B.P., lower northern outlets were exposed. Thus, the water drained eastward through what is now the St. Lawrence River system. When the lowest northern outlet was exposed, the fall in lake level elevations was quite rapid. By about 9,500 years ago the water in Lake Michigan, known as the **Chippewa stage,** was at 230 feet above sea level. In Lake Huron, **Stanley stage** water levels were at 190 feet above sea level. Lake Chippewa drained into Lake Stanley through the Straits of Mackinac. During these low water stages, the **Houghton stage** of Lake Superior also drained into Lake Stanley through the St. Marys River.

Although it took some 1,500 years for lake levels to fall to their lowest point, they did not again rise to 605 feet above sea level until about 5,000 years later (ca. 5,500–4,700 B.P.). This rise to former levels, known as the **Nipissing stage,** occurred when the northern land that had been depressed by the great weight of the glacier "bounced back" through a process known as **isostatic rebound.** This uplifting of the land raised the northern outlet of the lakes to a point where the southern outlets at Chicago and Port Huron were again the lowest ones, and so the lakes again drained to the southwest and southeast. The waters of the lakes reached their present level of about 580 feet above sea level when the outlet at Port Huron was downcut to 580 feet while the one at Chicago remained at 605 feet.

If Early Archaic peoples were following a seasonal round similar to that of the Late Archaic, they would have spent warmer seasons along the lakeshore and moved along the river systems from fall through spring. The winter would have been spent in upland areas where deer and other game could be found. The uplands are upstream in the branching headwaters regions of the rivers. These headwaters cover a wide area. People would not necessarily go to the same place every year, nor would they have to pass through on their travels back and forth as they would at major confluences of a river system. During the winter, people would be spread out over the landscape, they would occupy temporary camps, and they would have only necessary equipment with them. Furthermore, because the lake levels were so low, there was simply a great deal more land that people could use. The reason we don't find sites is not that people were not here but that we are observing only the artifacts left behind in the winter when people were scattered across the landscape and when they were the most mobile.

Archaeological evidence from the Upper Peninsula indicates that a late Paleo-Indian way of life persisted beyond ten thousand years ago as evidenced in Marquette County by Eden-Scottsbluff projectiles made of Hixton silicified sandstone (see fig. 69). This continuity of lifeways should not be too surprising, as the glaciers retreated later from the Upper Peninsula and boreal forests were present in many areas. Furthermore, the people with whom Upper Peninsula groups were in contact lived in northern Wisconsin. In the Upper Peninsula, unlike the Lower Peninsula, the exchange of ideas and materials was with the west, not the south.

In the **Middle Archaic** (ca. 8,000 to 5,000 B.P.), artifacts are relatively rare, and there are few known sites. In all probability, as in the Early Archaic, many sites were near the lakeshores and along streams now covered by water. In the past two decades a few sites have been found on buried land surfaces that were occupied during the Middle Archaic but were later covered by **alluvium** (water-deposited soil) resulting from the rise in water levels leading to the Lake Nipissing stage. Our picture of the Middle Archaic, however, is still far from complete.

Middle Archaic peoples lived during a climatic period known as the **hypsithermal** (ca. 8,500 to 5,100 B.P.), when the temperatures were warmer and conditions drier than today. By this time, there were deciduous forests in central Michigan that included American beech and hemlock in addition to oak, elm, and ironwood. A mixed deciduous-coniferous forest became established first in southern Michigan and then, progressively farther north.

Environmental conditions in the Middle Archaic were illustrated by discoveries at a paleontological site that was exposed by the removal of a layer of peat in central Michigan near Lansing. The site, known as the **Harper site,** was radiocarbon dated to 5,840 +/–80 B.P. The remains of a variety of animals were found, including elk, or wapiti, white-tailed deer, a mallard, a largemouth bass, a spotted turtle, a painted turtle, a Blanding's turtle, and a musk turtle. These creatures lived around a mucky lake with open water with areas of dense aquatic vegetation and boggy spots around the edges. The lake has since filled in so that the bones, wood, and pollen that record the environment of this earlier time were preserved.

The **Weber I** site on the Cass River near the town of Frankenmuth provides good information on life near the end of the Middle Archaic (ca. 6,200 to 4,500 B.P.). Weber I was buried under alluvial soil deposited by the Cass River during the rise of Lake Nipissing. People visited this location from time to time in the late summer and early autumn to hunt animals, especially elk (wapiti) and deer, but also raccoons, muskrats, geese, fish, and turtles. Additionally, Middle Archaic people at Weber I harvested nuts, berries, and mustard. The animal bones and antlers along with the plant remains indicate a late summer, early fall occupation, as all of the identified species were available at this time of year. The antlers and nuts are particularly strong seasonal indicators.

Wood charcoal from Weber I shows a mixed forest in the vicinity with beech and maple being the most common but with relatively large numbers of pine and other conifers as well. During the Middle Archaic, Weber I probably also had open grasslands nearby and certainly was adjacent to wetlands. At the time Middle Archaic people were at Weber I, the site was at the edge of an embayment that covered much of the land south and west of the city of Saginaw, an area now known as the Shiawassee Flats.

The occupation at Weber I shows that Middle Archaic people chose to live at locations where they could obtain a wide variety of plant and animal foods nearby. The embayment and wetlands and the mixed forest and grasslands were sources of many foods that varied with the seasons. Not only were there different foods available, but people could divide up tasks so that the animals, fish, birds, and plants could be procured and processed at the same time.

Another Middle Archaic site in the Saginaw Valley, the **Bear**

Creek site, shows that people moved through the landscape as the seasons progressed. At Bear Creek there are the remains of mammals, birds, fish, and turtles, indicating that a group of people were there during the spring. The same site was occupied again in the fall, as shown by the hickory nuts, walnuts, and acorns found there.

People were mining copper in the western Upper Peninsula by at least seven thousand years ago. This mining continued through the Late Woodland period. Indian miners belonged to several different groups over all this time, but the implements they made were traded widely. Lake Superior copper is often found in Middle Woodland Hopewellian sites and in Mississippian sites. Both of these archaeological cultures are associated with areas far to the south of the Upper Peninsula, such as Ohio and Illinois.

Adapting to Modern Environmental Conditions: Late Archaic. Perhaps the hallmark of the **Late Archaic,** which began about five thousand years ago, was the perfection of a subsistence system based on a wide variety of foods in an environment where forest composition was essentially as it was in the nineteenth century before vast amounts of land was cleared by settlers. People had a varied diet of plant and animal foods obtained from a variety of habitats such as wetlands, forests, rivers and streams, and grasslands. The amount and kinds of food available varied with the seasons of the year, and different foods might be available in different locations. For example, nuts were abundant in the autumn, but places where they could be found in quantity varied from year to year. One solution to the problem of finding wild resources was to move to the resources when and where they were available. Such movement was not haphazard but was highly systematic and flexible.

The Saginaw Valley enabled patterned seasonal movements of people during the Late Archaic. The radial drainage system of this region provided the habitat variety sought by Late Archaic peoples along with a transportation network composed of the Saginaw River with its four tributaries, the Cass, Flint, Shiawassee, and Tittabawassee Rivers. Each of these rivers coursed in a different direction, and each had smaller tributaries that could be followed. Thus, people could move seasonally along these watercourses while keeping their options open as to which direction to go. While food was abundant and diverse in the Saginaw Valley, environmental contingencies could be met by using a flexible system of movement. In the center of the network near the Shiawassee Embayment, critical wetland resources could be exploited around the embayment. But water levels there fluctuated in unpredictable cycles, and in order to offset the risk at these central wetlands people could move to more interior areas where wetlands were stable, and they could also hunt in the forests and grasslands.

Another critical season was autumn, when both plants and animals were not only taken for immediate consumption but were preserved for the winter and early spring. In addition to tasks of getting and processing food, tools had to be refurbished (fig. 70) and hides had to be prepared to make into clothing. The autumn was usually spent in the center or middle parts of the drainage system. By passing through the center, people could accomplish the many autumnal tasks as well as have more choices where to go in the winter when food was limited. Additionally, people were more likely to encounter other groups who could provide information about environmental conditions to be expected in the coming cold season. Given that a variety of food was sought, groups often chose camping locations in places where several

Fig. 70. Stone tool making, flint-knapping. Here, flakes to be made into tools are struck from a chert core using a stone hammer. The core is placed on an anvil. (Courtesy of Michigan State University Museum.)

habitats were nearby. Groups then could explore areas where specific resources were likely to be found.

The Weber I site is a good example of a site used by people practicing an economy based on varied resources. After Lake Nipissing receded, Weber I (at 3,000 B.P.) was located at about the middle of the Cass River drainage system. The Late Archaic occupation at Weber I was separated from the Middle Archaic occupation at the same site by several meters of sterile soil and was around two meters below the modern surface, so the materials from these two occupations are not mixed.

The animal and plant remains from the Late Archaic occupation at Weber I are not substantially different from those from the Middle Archaic, as deer and elk (wapiti) were important game animals hunted and nuts and berries were collected. There are differences between the two occupations however, because during the Late Archaic, Weber I was occupied during the warm seasons. Tubers were collected and lake sturgeon caught in the early spring. Blackberries, blueberries, and elderberries were picked in the summer. People at Weber I hunted deer and processed a great deal of nuts in the early fall. Thus, Late Archaic people resided at the site for at least portions of three seasons, whereas Middle Archaic people were there mainly for short-term fall hunting.

The Late Archaic diet at Weber I was diverse and included plants and animals obtained from open areas (elk and berries), from forest edges (deer), and from wetlands and the river (fish, turtles, tubers). Wood from the site shows that the environment was essentially modern with many varieties of nut-producing trees and much less maple, beech, and pine than in earlier times.

The food remains at Weber I, particularly those from the autumn, reflect the importance of having different members of a group get different foods at the same time. Some people hunt or fish while others collect berries or nuts; some members make or refurbish stone tools, while others prepare hides and make clothes, and prepare or preserve food for later use. Hunting and gathering peoples of the world divide such tasks on the basis of gender and age, although most members of the group have the skills to perform most tasks as needed.

Late Archaic people lived and traveled in small groups, but their social contacts were widespread. In the case of the Saginaw Valley, and surely in other places, the smaller groups living in the same region were closely related and would regularly meet one another to gain information and to be sociable. In the Late Archaic, however, there is evidence that social contact was more widespread than in just the immediate region. This evidence consists of chipped stone artifacts made of raw material from distant places such as Indiana (Hornstone/Wyandotte chert) and Ontario (Onondaga chert) as well as Upper Peninsula copper implements and southeast gulf coast marine shells. Similar occurrences of "imported" raw materials throughout the eastern woodlands are considered to be evidence of **reciprocal exchange** with neighboring groups whereby goods of roughly equal value were traded, often between regular trading partners. In similar societies throughout the world, such exchange did not serve the purpose of creating personal profit, as private wealth was not valued. Among people who worked together as relative equals and who moved frequently, gift giving, generosity, and sharing were prized. Thus, trade of this kind strengthened social relationships with people who might then be counted upon in cases of economic hardship. The archaeological contexts in which the Late Archaic imported items were found support this idea, for in many cases such items were included as grave goods accompanying a burial, or as separate caches. Thus, these artifacts were not used in everyday activities but were treated as objects with value as "gifts" for the dead. Artifacts of exotic raw materials were relatively unusual at Late Archaic campsites. Unlike tools made of locally available materials, tools made of the unusual materials were cared for and reused until they were completely worn out.

The Woodland

Early Woodland: Sunflower and Squash Are Planted and Pottery Is Used in the South. The appearance of pottery in the eastern woodlands of North America marks the end of the Archaic and the beginning of the Woodland period that encompasses the most recent three thousand years of prehistory. Many archaeologists have wondered why Michigan people started using vessels made of clay about 500 B.C. Since this early pottery was not used in the north but was confined to southern areas where hickory and other nut-bearing trees could be found, it was suggested that these vessels were used to render nut oil.

More recent evidence casts doubt on the nut oil hypothesis for pottery use, but in any case pottery certainly signals new methods of preparing food.

Early Woodland (1000 B.C. to A.D. 1) pottery is very thick and is tempered with large angular pieces of granite (grit). Vessels are marked on the exterior and interior by cord impressions produced by striking the vessel with a paddle wrapped with cord. As the millennium progressed, the vessels became thinner, but potters continued to cordmark both the interior and exterior. Even later, many interiors were plain and so were some exteriors. These pots were made by adding coils or rolls of clay on top of one another so that when the pots broke, they often fractured along the lines of the coils. They were usually shaped like a flowerpot with flat bases and straight walls (fig. 71A). Some Early Woodland vessels had lugs riveted near the rim to make it easier to lift and carry the vessels. Because lug handles are characteristic of similar pottery found in Ohio, it is probable that the idea of lugs came from that region. In fact, the shape of Early Woodland pots is directly comparable to vessels made of steatite (soapstone) in the northeast, and steatite vessels also had lug handles. Except for these lug handles, Michigan Early Woodland pottery is most like that found in Illinois known as Marion Thick. This similarity indicates strong cultural contact with that region.

Relationships among various Early Woodland peoples in Michigan, Illinois, Ohio, and Ontario are shown in the styles of projectile points made at the time and in the raw materials from which these points were made. The most common projectiles on Michigan Early Woodland sites are **Kramer points,** which are distinguished by stems that are long and straight with flat or squared bases (fig. 71C). Kramer points are also found in Indiana and Illinois, but Michigan Kramer points are normally made of materials found locally. **Meadowood points** are thin forms with small side-notches that mark the transition between Late Archaic and Early Woodland (fig. 71B). In New York, Meadowood points are made of Onondaga chert from that region. Although some Michigan Meadowood points are made of Onondaga chert, many are made of the Pipe Creek and Ten Mile/Dundee cherts found in northern Ohio and Michigan or of other local materials. **Adena points,** like Kramer points, have long stems but differ from Kramer points in their lobate stem form and convex bases (fig. 71D). Adena points are widespread, and when they occur in Michigan sites

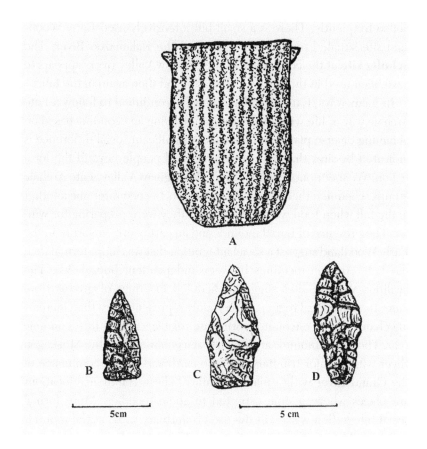

Fig. 71. A, Early Woodland pot (note the "flower pot" shape, lug handles, and cordmarked surface); B, Meadowood; C, Kramer; D, Adena

are often made of Indiana Hornstone/Wyandotte chert, which outcrops in southern Indiana.

In addition to using pottery, Early Woodland peoples of southern Michigan supplemented wild foods with domesticated squash and sunflower. It has been suggested that squash may have been used for containers as well as for food. The presence of squash (ca. 800 B.C.) and sunflower (ca. 1000 B.C.) shows that some attention was paid to gardening, but people continued to rely on hunting and gathering wild foods. In southwest Michigan for example, most sites represent small residential camps where people obtained seasonally available foods from nearby river floodplains, such as the St. Joseph. There is evidence that the interior portions of river drainages were also used but not so frequently. There is a small but intensively used Early Woodland site situated on a bluff overlooking the Kalamazoo River. The **Schultz site** at the confluence of the Saginaw Valley rivers appears to have been used in the early warm season and then again in the fall.

In many ways, Early Woodland peoples continued to follow a Late Archaic way of life with small groups practicing an economy based on obtaining diverse plants and animals. A significant social difference is indicated by sites that may have integrated people beyond the local region. We mentioned earlier that in the Saginaw Valley, Late Archaic groups scheduled their seasonal movements to encounter one another in the fall when food was abundant and they were preparing for winter. The presence of burial mounds and an earthwork enclosure in the Early Woodland suggest a social integration that was more formal than the Late Archaic meetings between independent households. The facilities at these sites suggest scheduled meetings of groups from more than one local region and certainly represent more than increasing chances of an encounter with close relatives during the economic year. The burial mounds are situated at a confluence of the Muskegon River with a major tributary, and the earthwork is at a confluence of the Grand River with a major tributary. These confluence locations are places where people expected to come together. More formal social integration is seen in the use of mortuary ritual at the mounds and probably ritual at the earthwork, which is divided by a ditch and embankment. Raw materials at the earthwork came from different regions and included various Michigan, Indiana, and Ohio cherts.

Middle Woodland: New People in the South? and Continuity of Lifeways in the North. In the first century B.C., people in parts of southern lower Michigan participated in the prehistoric **Middle Woodland** cultural expression known as **Hopewell.** Hopewell is associated in the Midwest with burial of the dead in large and complex artificial mounds. Grave goods accompanying the dead included fine imported and locally made pottery, conch shell containers and beads from the gulf coast, copper tools and beads from the Upper Peninsula, finely made projectile points of nonlocal raw materials, and carnivore fragments such as wolf jaws and teeth.

In Michigan, Hopewell mound groups occur along the St. Joseph River, the Grand River, and the Muskegon River. About twenty-nine Hopewell mounds, the **Converse Mounds,** existed in what is now downtown Grand Rapids, but they were destroyed by development of the city in the nineteenth century. Recent excavations undertaken by the Commonwealth Cultural Resources Group prior to relocation of the S curve on U.S. 131 in Grand Rapids uncovered encampment debris near the Converse Mounds but no trace of the mounds themselves. Originally there were seventeen **Norton Mounds,** also near U.S. 131 in Grand Rapids. At least six of the Norton Mounds were also destroyed, but controlled excavations were done at Norton. The destruction of the Converse Mounds by later development and the fact that some Norton mounds no longer exist is not uncommon for highly visible archaeological features such as these. Many mounds were destroyed by the end of the nineteenth century by looters and by antiquarians.

Although Hopewell mounds are found throughout the Midwest with major centers in Illinois and Ohio, those in Michigan are particularly similar to mounds found in the **Havana Hopewell** culture of the Illinois River valley. This close similarity to Havana Hopewell (fig. 72A) is not surprising given earlier ties to the Illinois region and the ease by which both people and ideas could come to the Lower Peninsula via the river systems beginning at the Illinois River and going to the Kankakee and the St. Joseph.

Michigan participation in Hopewell mortuary practices is evidenced only along the St. Joseph, the Grand, and the Muskegon Rivers. It has been suggested that these rivers were most suitable for a way of life that relied on the resources of broad floodplains. Hopewell groups also used the Kalamazoo River system, which lacked these broad floodplains, but these groups were probably there only at certain times of the year. Havana Hopewell subsistence-settlement practices are the subject of current research in Michigan. These studies are important for understanding Michigan Middle Woodland life. While Illinois and Michigan Hopewell mortuary practices were quite similar, it is not at all certain that Illinois and Michigan subsistence practices were so nearly the same.

Hopewell-related Middle Woodland sites and artifacts are found in the Saginaw Valley. Although there was a circular facility, probably for ritual events, at the **Schultz site** where the rivers meet, apparently there were no Hopewell mound groups in the Saginaw Valley. Further, the pottery is not from Illinois. Instead the form and style of the Saginaw pottery indicates that it is a local variant of Illinois Hopewell. Thus, Saginaw Middle Woodland peoples did not participate in the extensive trade networks involved in Hopewellian interaction but were clearly familiar with some aspects of Hopewell that were incorporated into their own way of life.

Aside from sites along the river systems of southwest Michigan and the Saginaw Valley, the Middle Woodland in the southern Lower Peninsula is elusive, for without distinctive Hopewellian sites and artifacts, it is very difficult to identify sites from this time period. Thus, the non-Hopewellian of southern Michigan is not well known.

Prehistoric cultures from the Middle Woodland time period in the Canadian Biotic Province are referred to variously as **Lake Forest Middle Woodland, Northern Tier Middle Woodland,** or **Initial Woodland.** Regardless of how they are classified, the years from about 100 B.C. to A.D. 600 mark the adoption of pottery in the north. This pottery has broad similarities across the northern Great Lakes, but there is regional variation as well. Northern Michigan **Laurel ware,** which was made by the coil technique, had a conoidal shape (fig. 72B). It was decorated over much of the rim and body in rows or panels. The decoration was produced by using a tool such as the edge of a notched shell or stick to stamp the clay around the pot.

The largest Laurel sites are located along the north shore of Lakes Michigan and Huron and the south shore of Lake Superior. These sites are situated on points of land, at the mouths of streams, and along shallow bays where a variety of lake bottom conditions present the

Fig. 72. A, Havana Middle Woodland pot; B, Laurel Middle Woodland pot. (Courtesy of Michigan State University Museum.)

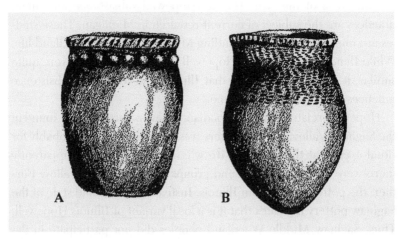

opportunity to catch fish preferring different habitats. Spring-spawning fish, suckers, were particularly important after the long winters in the north when food became scarce. Sturgeon were caught at Laurel lakeshore sites, where people also hunted and picked berries during the warm season. Fishing gear found at Laurel sites includes togglehead harpoons made of antler, fishhooks of copper, and netsinkers of stone. Wild rice was probably gathered in the autumn, and winter was devoted to hunting in the interior. Because environmental conditions varied from year to year, Laurel households were flexible in their choices of site location and were prepared to hunt, fish, or gather a variety of foods in season.

While Laurel peoples were not Hopewellian, they did supply **copper** to southern Hopewellian groups. While none of the prehistoric copper mines on Isle Royale have been directly associated with Laurel activities on the island, Laurel camps there have yielded copper nuggets and scrap as well as copper tools. A Middle Woodland site on the Keweenaw Peninsula has been interpreted as a place where native copper was collected and fabricated into finished pieces. A cache of thirty pounds of copper was found in a leather bag at this site. A second bag of woven milkweed contained a crescent-shaped knife, awls, a triangular projectile point, and unfinished copper beads. This second bag may have been a woman's bead-making kit, as implements in the bag, particularly the crescent-shaped knife, were typically used by women. Such knives, known as *ulus*, or "women's knives," as well as awls were commonly associated with women's domestic tasks.

In addition to pottery and copper, Laurel peoples made stone tools of local materials such as pebble chert, quartz, and quartzite. Many of their tools were made using the bipolar technique; that is, flakes were removed from either end of a stone core while the opposite end rested on an anvil.

Late Woodland: Living along the Southern Rivers and Fishing the Northern Great Lakes. The Late Woodland period began as an outgrowth of the preceding Middle Woodland. Until about A.D. 1000, there is little evidence of migration of new peoples into Michigan. Rather, people who were already here lived on various resources of their local region within the broad biotic zones we see today. They relied mainly on wild plants and animals for food and raw materials, although in some areas domestic plants supplemented the food supply. These necessities of life were obtained by rather complex systems of movement through local territories that followed the cycles of the seasons. In most of the Lower Peninsula territories were organized around river basins, as evidenced by the distribution of early Late Woodland pottery. Ceramics with distinctive characteristics are found along the drainage of particular rivers or groups of rivers. For example, pottery known as **Spring Creek ware** is associated with west Michigan sites along the Grand and Muskegon Rivers and north to the Manistee River. The makers of Spring Creek ware followed a pattern of seasonal movement through these drainage basins at the northern edge of the Carolinian Biotic Province and in the transition zone between the Carolinian and Canadian Biotic Provinces (fig. 73).

While the early Late Woodland peoples of Michigan lived in par-

Fig. 73. Distribution of early Late Woodland phases and traditions in the Lower Peninsula and eastern Upper Peninsula ca. A.D. 800 to 1000. (After Holman and Kingsley 1996.)

ticular areas, these territories were not formally bounded and defended but were regarded as theirs because of regular use by the same group of people. It is very likely that boundaries to these territories were easily crossed by neighbors who were recognized as kin by "blood" or marriage and were frequently welcomed as visitors. Being neighborly would have been a very important kind of "insurance" for people in cases when the food supply in their own territory was low. Winters, especially, could be very harsh and unpredictable. It was critical for groups to have sources of emergency aid. Such a use of territories is commonly seen among northern and other hunter-gatherer groups.

Archaeological evidence for this view of territory and neighbors in the early Late Woodland comes from the distribution of differing types of pottery. In our example, Spring Creek ware is *very similar* to other pottery types from the same time in most of the Lower Peninsula. However, it is only through the study of slight differences in the frequency of rim and lip treatments, including decoration, or surface treatments that Spring Creek ware can be recognized by an archaeologist. The widespread distribution of pottery that is so similar, yet slightly different in different regions, suggests that the makers of these ceramics were good neighbors, probably marriage partners and kin. They all made their pottery in roughly the same style, and the consistent differences were likely the result of habit and proximity to other potters. There was no need or inclination for Spring Creek potters to distinguish their ceramics from other wares in the Lower Peninsula.

Pottery called **Mackinac ware,** unlike the pottery found along the Lower Peninsula rivers, is consistently different from other ceramic wares. The makers of Mackinac ware were peoples from the Upper Peninsula and northern Lower Peninsula who unlike others south of them in the Lower Peninsula did not move through river systems during their subsistence cycle. Instead the makers of Mackinac ware placed great reliance on fish from the Great Lakes. This inland shore fishery was intensively focused on lake trout and whitefish that are abundant in northern waters, including the Straits of Mackinac region, in the fall. These fish could be dried and stored as important supplements to winter hunting. Because Mackinac ware was found at sites outside its normal range of distribution, in areas that apparently were frequented by the makers of other ceramics, it seems that the makers of this pottery were also good neighbors.

Cultural Change in the Late Woodland. Early Late Woodland peoples were closely related groups who regularly moved through a territory, such as a river system, but they also freely moved back and forth through the territories of other groups. Later, after about A.D. 1000, this use of territories and relationships between groups began to change. Evidence pointing to cultural change includes the fact that not all later pots look alike. It is easy to distinguish a later Late Woodland **Juntunen ware** pot from the northern Lower Peninsula or the eastern Upper Peninsula from a **Traverse ware** pot from the northwestern Lower Peninsula. These ceramics differ in decoration, shape, and surface treatment. The kinds of differences in pottery are comparable to the differences between plastic or Styrofoam cups that have fast-food company logos printed on them. Thus, ceramic evidence from the later Late Woodland period implies more marked social boundaries between groups (fig. 74).

Fig. 74. Distribution of later Late Woodland phases and traditions in the Lower Peninsula and eastern Upper Peninsula ca. A.D. 1000 to 1650. Note Mississippian and Upper Mississippian in southwestern Michigan.

Later period burials also contrast with those in the early Late Woodland. Earlier burials from southeastern Michigan show that people were honored and remembered in ways appropriate to their age, their sex, and their personal achievements. Later however, when **ossuary burial** (groups of people placed in the same pit) became more common, individual achievement was obscured. On the other hand, ossuary burial emphasized the importance of the membership in a community group.

Other evidence of more formal social boundaries in the Lower Peninsula comes from **earthwork** sites, at least some of which occur at potential territorial boundaries. These circular or horseshoe-shaped earthworks often had a surrounding ditch or "dry moat" that was topped by wooden posts (palisade). Some earthworks that have been investigated had domestic debris next to the wall with a center area that was free of debris. There are a number of suggestions as to the function of these sites, which mainly date to about A.D. 1450. They may have been defensive, as they are often in defendable locations. They may have been ceremonial, as evidenced by the central area that could have been used for a dance circle. They may have been locations where trade between groups took place. Evidence for trade in one earthwork site is seen in pottery from the northeastern Lower Peninsula along with pottery from the southeastern Lower Peninsula (pottery with two different "logos"). Each of these possibilities implies social identity that is more formal and more marked than was the case earlier in the Late Woodland.

Another indication of changed social relationships comes from animal remains from late sites. This evidence indicates a trading system in the Late Woodland like that known later in the Historic period. Historically, people such as the Huron in western Ontario traded corn (maize) for meat and hides supplied by the Chippewa who lived in the Upper Peninsula. The Huron needed meat and hides because game was not plentiful in their territory. The Chippewa needed corn because they lived so far north that they could not rely on horticulture. The Ottawa who lived between these two groups were the "middlemen" in the trade; that is, they conveyed the corn to their Chippewa kin and the meat and hides to the Huron. The Ottawa themselves were fishermen who raised some corn but lived far enough north that the corn harvest was not always productive. All of these groups benefited from the trade because they could supplement their own food supply. Although all Late Woodland groups hunted, fished, and gathered, it is probable that after about A.D. 1000, some people in southern Michigan placed more emphasis on planting corn and other crops, while others near the Straits of Mackinac concentrated on fishing, and still others in the Upper Peninsula were more reliant on mixed hunting, gathering, and fishing. Thus, later Late Woodland peoples had the same reasons to trade as did Historic Indian groups.

Understanding the importance of domesticated plants such as corn is a continuing endeavor in Michigan archaeology because remains of this crop are not often found in archaeological sites. Corn has been found at some northern sites along the Lake Michigan coast in the Lower Peninsula and on Bois Blanc Island in the Straits of Mackinac. Whether this maize was grown or obtained through trade is problematic. Corn has also been found in southwestern lower Michigan, where it would be expected, but here, maize was rare and occurred only at sites along the St. Joseph River, after about A.D. 1100. So-called garden beds (ridged fields; see fig. 93) recorded in the area may have been fields for Upper Mississippian people, but there is no direct evidence for this. These features were destroyed by nineteenth-century settlers who farmed in the same locations, and the nineteenth-century Potawatomi in the area did not know who made them.

In the Saginaw Valley maize was frequent only after about A.D. 800–1000. Corn was planted along with tobacco, squash, beans, sunflower, and chenopodium after about A.D. 1100. Earlier Late Woodland people in the Saginaw Valley foraged along the radial network of rivers and streams there. Wetland resources were important at sites located next to channels and wetlands in the central basin of this river system. This is in contrast to later peoples who had small "farmstead" sites near well-drained soils where they could plant crops and obtain wild foods as well. Likewise, in southeast Michigan after circa A.D. 1000–1100 site location shifted to settings with well-drained arable soils.

In the Straits of Mackinac region, fall-spawning fish were the most important food source throughout the Late Woodland. After about A.D. 1200, during the Juntunen phase, corn was probably obtained from some local plantings and by formal exchange of fish for corn with people farther south and east. This exchange would have been similar to that seen historically.

Ridged fields found near the Menominee River in the western

Upper Peninsula are being investigated by archaeologists from Northern Michigan University. It is probable that people here spent the summer in fishing camps and went to satellite sites for other activities. They could have harvested wild rice in the autumn before leaving for their winter hunting camps. The mixture of various pottery styles in the western Upper Peninsula indicates this area was open to several groups, many of whom probably obtained copper there (fig. 75).

At least one of the several groups in the western Upper Peninsula were part of an archaeological culture known as **Upper Mississippian.** Upper Mississippian materials have been found in many midwestern states, including Wisconsin and Illinois. While there is a great deal of regional variation in Upper Mississippian, this archaeological culture is normally associated with corn horticulture and with shell-tempered pottery. In contrast, Late Woodland pottery is tempered with crushed granite (grit). Some Michigan examples of Upper Mississippian pottery have both shell and grit temper, and others have only grit temper.

Fig. 75. Distribution of Late Woodland phases and traditions in the Upper Peninsula

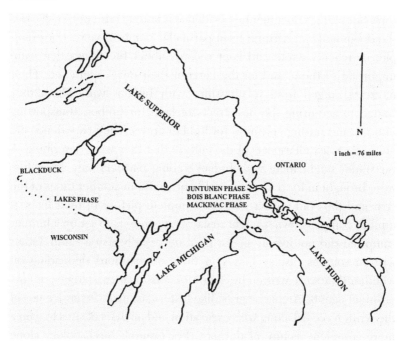

In the Lower Peninsula, Upper Mississippian pottery is found in southwestern Michigan dating to about A.D. 1050 and continuing to about A.D. 1600. This pottery overlaps with Late Woodland pottery for a time at sites along the Kalamazoo River, but the relationship between Upper Mississippian and Late Woodland is unclear. Late Woodland appears to end here about A.D. 1250. Late Woodland peoples may have been displaced, relationships may have been hostile, or one of these prehistoric cultures may have been assimilated into the other. Sites with Upper Mississippian materials have been found along the Grand River in central Michigan and in the Saginaw Valley. The nature of the Upper Mississippian presence in these locations is unknown.

Historic Period

Michigan archaeologists actively study sites of the Historic period. The very word *history* means that there are written records describing life and events in the past. Why not just read about these things? While written records are valuable for helping us to understand the past, there are many reasons why they do not present a complete picture. Sometimes documentary evidence is simply rare, but in all cases the documents are written from particular points of view. For example, merchants wrote and kept records about the things that were important to them, and on the basis of their own experience. Their interests ranged from relationships with Indians with whom they traded to acquiring the best tracts of land for timber, transporting lumber, and setting up camps for lumber crews. Their experience did not encompass all aspects of the culture that they were describing. A fur trader might meet with Indian trading partners only when furs were brought in for trade but would not see them at other times of the year and thus did not have a very complete picture of their lives. A lumber company owner might make arrangements to set up a lumber camp but did not live in one or even necessarily visit a camp. Other written sources display biases in their observations depending on whether they were written by explorers, missionaries, soldiers, or government agents. Archaeologists, like historians, make extensive use of the written record along with excavation and analysis of sites to gain a more complete picture of the past. For example, archaeology along with documents written by Europeans, and Indian oral history can answer questions about Indian life that cannot be answered entirely by either documents or oral histories alone. Archaeology can answer questions about life in lumber camps where workers' lives were recorded in songs and stories, sometimes perhaps in letters or diaries, but whose view of this era was quite different from that of the companies who employed them. Archaeology can answer questions about how women and children contributed to the life of past groups. Questions about gender and age as answered through archaeology illuminate the lives of people who were often ignored in historic documents. Historic period archaeology then, is important for understanding how the various parts of past cultures fit together.

Indians, Europeans, and the Fur Trade. Historic sites archaeology of the seventeenth to mid-eighteenth centuries is focused on the first Europeans in the Great Lakes region, the French missionaries and traders, and on the Indians with whom they lived and traded. The French generally followed Michigan's lakeshores and rarely went to the interior. Particular locations were considered crucial for purposes of controlling trade with the Indians and for converting them to Christianity (fig. 76). The **Straits of Mackinac** is one of these key locations, as this is a crossroads between Lake Huron and Lake Michigan, and between the Lower and Upper Peninsulas. Anyone traveling north, south, east, or west must pass through the Straits of Mackinac. Furthermore, the Indians whom the French wished to encounter had regularly gathered at the Straits for hundreds of years, especially during the fall fishing season. The French were drawn to this area where large groups of people were likely to be found and furs could be accumulated for shipment to Montreal. Similarly, the rapids of the Saint Marys River (**Sault Ste. Marie**) was a place where the Saulters, or "People of the Sault," came in great numbers every fall to fish. The Sault, like the Straits of Mackinac, is at a crossroads, in this case between Lakes Huron and Superior. In fact, the first mission in Michigan was built at Sault Ste. Marie in 1668.

Locations such as the Straits of Mackinac and Sault Ste. Marie were crucial for another, related reason. The seventeenth and eighteenth centuries were periods of empire-building for the European powers. Control of the Great Lakes and trade in furs was desired by both the French and the British. Indians too were involved in these political struggles as allies of one or the other European power. Additionally,

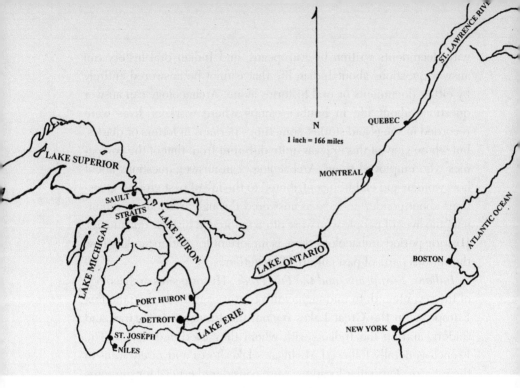

Fig. 76. Map of key locations for controlling trade in the Great Lakes and for defense. Centers of greatest importance are at Straits of Mackinac and Detroit.

various Indian groups vied for positions as brokers between Europeans and other Indian groups. The French and, later, the British followed by the Americans, built forts to maintain a military presence at the same locations.

Historic sites archaeology of the seventeenth century has been most productive at the Straits of Mackinac at the restored **Fort Michilimackinac** in Mackinaw City and in the vicinity of the **Marquette Mission** in St. Ignace. The archaeological importance of this area cannot be underestimated. Much can be learned here because the archaeological remains are well preserved and because the various groups in the region are represented at the mission site, the forts, and the Indian villages. The first French sites were on the north side of the Straits at St. Ignace, where Father Marquette established his mission in 1671. Ottawa and Huron Indians had villages near the mission, and there was a fort, Fort Dubaude, which has yet to be located by archaeologists. Most archaeological work in St. Ignace has been in the area of the mission and at the nearby Tionontati Huron village. In 1715, activity moved to the south side of the Straits with the building of Fort Michilimackinac and the development of private land around the fort. Continuous work has examined questions such as the extent to which Indians adopted European technology such as guns and metal kettles and how this affected their lives.

The Tionontati Huron retained their traditional subsistence base of planting maize, beans, and squash and hunting animals. The abundance of fish bones in their village is not surprising given the long-time importance of fishing at the Straits. Archaeology has shown that the French, like the Indians, ate many wild foods. This too is not surprising because the French at the Straits of Mackinac were relatively isolated and did not receive supplies of food from their eastern settlements such as Montreal. Archaeology also documents how the French occupation at the Straits grew from a modest outpost and mission into a trading settlement of central importance in the Great Lakes region.

The waterways at Port Huron and Detroit were other key areas for anyone who desired to command the route between Lake Huron and Lake Erie. For a time, the Iroquois prevented the French and their Indian allies from using Lake Erie to bring their furs east. In 1668, near the end of a twenty year peace with the Iroquois, a fort was erected at Port Huron. This temporary stronghold, Fort St. Joseph, was to block the British from using the waterway to engage in the fur trade at the Straits of Mackinac. In 1701, again at time of peace, Antoine de la Mothe Cadillac, governor of New France (Canada) established a colony and trading center at Detroit which was protected by **Fort Pontchartrain.** Cadillac persuaded many Indians to move to the Detroit area including some Ottawa, Huron, Chippewa and Miami groups. Additionally, the settlement was populated by French farmers each of whom had land fronting the river and extending back from the river in long narrow lots, or "ribbon farms." The **long lot** system provided every farmer access to the river in order to send and receive goods by water. The French long lots of southeast Michigan are still recorded on Michigan maps along with the mile square section lines established by the American system of measuring from an east-west base line and a north-south meridian. Like the Straits of Mackinac, Detroit was a location that brought together military men, traders, farmers and tribes but there are few hints of this important settlement in the archaeological record. Fort Pontchartrain was located in what is now downtown Detroit, so later activities have largely obscured or destroyed the eighteenth-century remains. Similarly, a small amount of material has been recovered from Fort de Repentigny (1754–62) at Sault Ste. Marie. The earlier fort was superseded by the American Fort Brady.

When the British took Canada from the French in 1760, Michigan came under the British flag. The British expanded Fort Michilimackinac and garrisoned the fort at Detroit. It was the British policy at the time not to open the Great Lakes region to settlement by people from the eastern colonies. French farmers and property owners around both forts remained and continued to own their land. Fort Michilimackinac was captured by the Chippewa during Pontiac's war against the British in 1763. At the same time, Fort St. Joseph in southwest Michigan was taken by a force of Potawatomi warriors and the fort at Detroit was besieged. The British were able to withstand the siege at Detroit with supplies and reinforcements brought in by boat through Lake Erie.

Most British period archaeology, like that of the French period, has been conducted at the Straits of Mackinac. Archaeology at Fort Michilimackinac indicates that the fort was enlarged after it was retaken in 1764. This enlargement was made necessary largely because the French at Michilimackinac retained ownership of their row houses within the fort and of their land outside the fort. The French continued to eat wild foods, but the British occupants of the fort were regularly supplied with domestic animals to eat. During the British period at the Straits, a sawmill and grist mill were built at Mill Creek east of Fort Michilimackinac. The British moved their fort to Mackinac Island in 1780.

American Settlers. Before American settlers moved into Michigan, the U.S. government negotiated treaties with various Indian groups who ceded their land in exchange for annuity payments, cash, and goods, as well as farming implements and instruction in agriculture. In addition, Indians were to receive the services of a blacksmith. In some cases reservations were established and hunting and fishing rights were secured. Land was ceded first in the southern Lower Peninsula, which was also the first to be surveyed and settled.

Michigan was surveyed according to the requirements of the Northwest Ordinance of 1785. North-south measurements were taken from a base line and east-west measurements were taken from a meridian. Land was divided into townships that were six miles square. Townships in turn were divided into sections of one square mile. As they moved over the land to take their measurements, surveyors made note of natural features, soil types, vegetation, and streams they encountered. These surveyors' observations are extremely useful to archaeologists because lumbering, farming, and other activities that have taken place since they were made have substantially changed vegetation and drainage patterns. For example, information about habitats that would have been found around a prehistoric site suggests what kinds of resources might have been available there in different seasons. This in turn provides a clue in determining how a site was used that can be checked against any plant and animal remains found at the site. Were there berries nearby? Were berry seeds found at the site? When would these berries have been available? If no berries grew nearby, might those found at the site been part of a reserve of stored foods? A second use of the survey records of the presettlement environment is to construct a picture of the regional availability of foods in different places during each season. This can provide an understanding of how people might have scheduled their seasonal movements throughout the region.

Michigan was opened for settlement in 1818 when a government land office was established in Detroit. Michigan was not the first choice for easterners moving to the Northwest Territories, however. Among several reasons why the region was settled late was the fact that there were difficulties in reaching Detroit, which was the starting point. Overland travel meant crossing the "Black Swamp" at the east end of Lake Erie, and travel by ship across Lake Erie to Detroit was dangerous. Travel was made easier when the Erie canal was built and steamships were available. It was only after about 1830 that Michigan became a popular destination for people from the northeastern states, who arrived by ship at Detroit or Monroe. Other people came by the roads built by the federal government, including one across the Black Swamp. Roads built across the interior to connect the east and west sides of the territory made it easier for people to move to their new lands.

Questions about patterns of American settlement are interesting to archaeologists who recognize the opportunity to examine changes from early locally oriented settlement to the integration of Michigan into the national system. Early settlers lived in a "frontier" setting where inadequate transportation limited most of their contact to the local community and where products usually were shipped by river. Most of the first farms were relatively self-sufficient. People grew a variety of food, including corn, and they usually raised hogs that could be fed not only on corn but could forage for wild food such as acorns. In addition to raising crops and keeping hogs, farmers supported themselves by hunting and fishing. They also picked wild fruits, made maple syrup, and gathered honey. Indian neighbors would trade venison and maple syrup for flour and other items. Farmers would take their grain to a nearby settlement where it would be ground into flour at the local mill, and there was normally a blacksmith in the settlement as well. Lumber was cut at the settlement sawmill. Early settlements also had churches, a school, and a general store. In some cases, there were doctors, lawyers, and a local newspaper.

Many of the settlers came to Michigan as individual families, but in several cases people from ethnic or religious groups would join together to establish life in a new land. These groups established "colonies" or covenanted communities that were organized according to rules agreed upon ahead of time. The Mayflower Compact signed by the Pilgrims before they landed at Plymouth in 1620 is an example of such a covenant. The town of Holland is a well-known example of a community of this type in Michigan. Holland was settled by a Dutch congregation, and as historian Willis Dunbar notes, the town government was closely allied with the governing body of the church. Archaeologists are interested in studying the differences between the development and organizations of communities organized by covenant and communities made up of people with a variety of ethnic and religious affiliations.

A second characteristic of the Michigan territory of interest to archaeologists is the military posts built along the Canadian border during the nineteenth century. These forts were established about the time of the War of 1812, when conflict between Britain and the new United States included the Great Lakes and the international border. Like the French and British before them, Americans positioned these forts at key locations commanding the flow of traffic through the lakes (see fig. 76). For example, forts at Detroit and Port Huron guarded the passage between Lake Erie and Lake Huron. Detroit was the major port and commercial center of Michigan territory, as it is today. The fort at Port Huron, **Fort Gratiot,** was a post of secondary importance in relation to Detroit. Examination of the archaeological data from excavations at Fort Gratiot has shed light on the relative status of officers and soldiers at the fort and on the mutually beneficial relationship between the military and the growing community at Port Huron.

Lumber and Mines. Michigan's rich natural resources formed the basis for a series of business ventures financed by easterners. By the time Michigan became a state in 1847, people began to look to lumber, copper, and iron as a source of profit. During the years before the Civil War, when communities and farms were being established in Michigan, most communities had a sawmill. These mills were local businesses where people could bring their lumber to be processed for building their houses, barns, and other buildings. The timber cut at these mills was usually obtained locally. Many people had woodlots on their own land that they could use.

Lumbering on a commercial scale became one of Michigan's most important industries during the mid–nineteenth century as America required increasing supplies of wood for construction. About the same time, it was clear that the supply of timber in northeastern states such as Maine and New York was not enough to meet the growing demand for construction lumber. Commercial enterprises turned to Michigan's northern forests in order to profit from this high demand. **White pine** was the preferred choice for construction material because it was soft and, thus, easy to work with. White pine was also chosen for its beauty. It is not surprising that lumber companies invested in Michigan forest land because white pine was so abundant, particularly in the northern Lower Peninsula. White pine **stumps** can still be seen in northern Michigan forests.

Michigan's **river systems** were another reason why lumbering became important here. Between the late 1840s and the 1870s, the rivers provided the means for transporting lumber from the forests to the mills for sawing into construction pieces and for shipping from ports on the lakes. The **Saginaw** River valley was the first Michigan location chosen by lumber companies because it had the necessary access to the forests, river transport, and a Great Lakes port. The Saginaw River system is a radial network consisting of the Saginaw River itself and major tributaries, including the Shiawassee, the Tittabawassee, the Cass, and the Flint. These tributaries flow from various directions to join the Saginaw River at Green Point in the city of

Saginaw. Logs could be floated down these streams to mills in Saginaw and in Bay City. The Saginaw River empties into Saginaw Bay at Bay City, so this community not only had sawmills but was also a Great Lakes port. Lumber was shipped from Bay City to Detroit, Cleveland, Toledo, and Buffalo. Although the sawmills are no longer standing, their remains occur along the riverfront at Bay City. As Michigan historian Willis Dunbar notes, "Beginning in the 1850's and continuing for a generation, lumber was the lifeblood of Saginaw."

The lumber industry took advantage of many other rivers in Michigan, so that by 1860 logs were floated down the Grand River to mills in **Grand Rapids.** Lumber produced by the mills in Grand Rapids was then shipped by river boat to the mouth of the Grand River. The town of **Muskegon** at the mouth of the Muskegon River became the largest producer on the west side of the state, but there were also mills at the mouths of rivers farther north, including the Pere Marquette, Manistee, and Boardman Rivers. The town of Ludington on the mouth of the Pere Marquette River was associated with the lumber industry, as was Manistee at the mouth of the river of the same name. During the 1880s, lumber companies in the Upper Peninsula floated their logs down the Tahquamenon and Ontonagon Rivers to Lake Superior, and down the Menominee River to Lake Michigan. There were sawmills at Escanaba and Menominee by 1860.

During the first decades of the lumber industry, logging took place in winter so that logs could be loaded on sleds for transport to the nearest river where the spring runoff of melted snow would provide enough water. Because logs belonging to several companies might be floated downriver when the ice melted, they were marked or "branded" on both ends to identify the owners. Obstacles in the river were bypassed by the construction of sluiceways, and dams were built to back up water so there would be enough to carry the logs. The process of running logs downstream was a dangerous task known as **booming.**

Two inventions of the 1870s allowed lumbering companies to expand their operations to forests away from the rivers and to log all year long. **"Big Wheels"** drawn by a team of horses were an alternative to sleds for removing logs during winters where there was little snow. **Narrow gauge railroads** provided transport from lumber camps either to the rivers or to railroad depots. These temporary rail lines could be operated at greater distances from assembly points and at all times of year. Taking the timber to a depot made it unnecessary to rely on deep and swift-flowing rivers to move the logs in the spring. Portions of narrow gauge **railroad grades** are archaeological evidence of lumbering in the north woods.

The remains of **logging camps** are also common archaeological sites in the north woods of both the Upper and Lower Peninsulas. Most of these camps were occupied for the duration of a winter. Although camps differed depending on the lumber company that owned them or when they were in operation, they generally included bunkhouses for the lumber crews and stables for horses or oxen. A cooking shanty and dining area, insulated by a surrounding earthen ridge or berm, provided meals and was the focus of social life. According to common wisdom, beans, pork, bread, molasses, and strong tea were standard fare at the camps. Archaeological evidence indicates that in some cases workers were able to negotiate with their employers to get the foods they preferred. Archaeological evidence in the form of medicine bottles and liquor bottles also shows that camp rules prohibiting the drinking of alcohol were not necessarily universally observed.

Many camps included a granary to store fodder for the animals, a blacksmith and carpentry shop, and a store where men could purchase tobacco and other items. The men who lived at these camps included young New Englanders, French Canadians, and Michiganians who had other occupations in the summer but worked at logging in the winter. Some crews were from various ethnic groups such as Irish, Swedish, Finnish, and Norwegian. One question that interests archaeologists excavating lumber camps is how to identify any artifacts that might show a particular ethnic group occupied a camp. Such identification could be used to determine how different groups might have organized their camp life differently.

Lumbering was an industry that involved cutting down vast tracts of forest and then moving on to find more timber. Stumps and branches were left in place so that the land was covered with dry debris that many times became tinder for devastating **fires.** The worst fire occurred in October 1871, a few days after the Chicago fire. The preceding summer was very dry, and there were high winds that October. The fires took everything in their path, including houses, other wooden buildings, and whole towns. Because the winds came from the southwest, towns along the Lake Michigan coast burned first, including Holland and Manistee. Then everything between towns on the west coast and Port Huron was torched by the fire. In September 1881, a second fire burned towns in the thumb counties. One of these towns that was abandoned after the fire is preserved as an archaeological site that has never been investigated. Because fires were frequent in later years as well, reforestation programs began in Michigan, particularly with the work of the Civilian Conservation Corps in the 1930s. Remains of these later fires can be seen today in the form of small bits of **charcoal** that can be found scattered below the surface in the sands of the northern Lower Peninsula.

Lake Superior region **iron ore** was discovered in 1844 near Negaunee, west of Marquette. Problems of transporting the ore from the mines to a forge were solved by building forges at the mines themselves. These forges used local hardwoods that were made into charcoal in local kilns. Archaeology at the mining town at Fayette State Park on the Garden Peninsula has provided information about this company town where many of the activities of mining were concentrated: ore could be brought from the mines, there was hardwood for charcoal, and there was a port for shipping ore. One project at Fayette included excavations at the homes of unskilled workers, showing the differences in the lives of these mining employees in comparison with the lives of skilled workers and managers.

Surface mining in the Marquette Range characterized the earliest mining operations. Ore was taken from the mines by railroad to Marquette for shipping. In the late 1850s, Marquette was developed as a Lake Superior port to move the ore to the smelters. A railroad network not only carried the ore from the mines, but a railroad line was built out along a four-hundred-foot dock at Marquette to take the ore to the waiting ships. The more westerly Menominee and Gogebic Ranges were exploited for iron ore after the Civil War. The major boom for iron mining in the Upper Peninsula was from after the Civil War (1865) to about 1910. After about 1900 however, more mining took place in Minnesota.

In 1855, the Soo Locks at Sault Ste. Marie solved the major problem of shipping raw materials from Lake Superior to the ports on Lakes Michigan and Huron and the lower lakes. The water level in Lake Superior is twenty-two feet above that of Lake Huron, to which it is connected by the St. Marys River. These different water levels and the rapids in the river were a barrier to shipping. Ore had to be taken around the rapids by tram until the locks were built. A number of locks were built over the years so that now freighters one thousand feet long and one hundred feet wide can move from one lake to the other.

About Archaeology: Recovering the Past

Avocational and professional archaeologists have been working for over a century to piece together the fascinating story of Michigan's past through careful retrieval and analysis of the remains that people left behind. Many archaeologists are members of the Michigan Archaeological Society, and many are at the state's colleges and universities or, recently, in private companies. All archaeologists in the state are painfully aware that Michigan's archaeological record is a vanishing resource. Archaeological sites are being destroyed at an increasingly rapid rate by construction to meet the needs of current Michiganians, and by looters.

These problems of site destruction are so critical that there are federal and state laws to protect Michigan's antiquities. It is illegal for people to remove artifacts from or otherwise destroy sites on federal and state lands. Furthermore, whenever a development project supported by federal funds is undertaken, archaeological survey is required before the project can be implemented. Such surveys involve a systematic search for all archaeological sites in the project area. If sites are found, the archaeologist makes recommendations as to whether they will need subsurface testing or excavation before the project can continue. In most cases final decisions about when survey or later excavation is necessary are made by professionals in the State Historic Preservation Office, which in Michigan is part of the Department of History, Arts, and Libraries. Sometimes federal agencies are involved in these decisions.

Many people wonder why there is so much concern about the archaeological record. Most archaeological remains like broken pieces of pottery, the waste material from making stone tools, and bottles or nails are, after all, just garbage. What is the harm in picking up an arrowhead or a bottle? Archaeology seeks to understand and explain human life in the past by studying the materials that people left behind. The arrowheads, the bottles, the garbage were all integrated into past lifeways, or **cultures,** and are thus vital clues to understanding the lives of earlier people. Everyone makes physical objects into **artifacts** that serve a purpose, and artifacts are used in ways that are guided by culture. For example, all cultures have artifacts for producing, preparing, and consuming food. In modern America tables, chairs, plates, cups, and silverware are found wherever food is eaten. A spoon by itself tells us very little about the context of its use. A spoon found along with knives, forks, plates, and cups is certainly associated with meals, as is the dining room or kitchen where these artifacts occur. It is this **association** of artifacts with one another and with **features,** such as the dining room, that provide vital clues about the context of past human lives.

The association of artifacts and features in human culture is very complex and varies in different places and through time. The utensils in a modern American dining room reflect much more than the activity of eating a meal. Meals may be formal with rather rigid "rules" about how the table is set and where particular people will sit. Meals may be informal and may even take place outside as picnics. People gather as families, cement friendships, and conduct business in the context of a meal. Our entire nation shares the ritual of Thanksgiving, symbolized by a meal. In each of these instances, the arrangement of the artifacts and features associated with the everyday act of eating reflects the various social behavior and symbolism involved.

The evidence of the past includes artifacts and features. Additionally, archaeologists find items such as plant seeds or animal bones that provide evidence about the environment in which people lived, the animals they hunted, or the plants they gathered. For example, a feature such as a roasting pit might contain firewood, indicating some of the trees that grew in the surrounding forest. Items such as corncobs, raspberry seeds. or fish bones are evidence of past diets.

Artifacts, features, and other preserved objects occur together at locations referred to as **sites.** Sites take many forms, but places such as camps, fishing spots, farms, or towns are sites. The methods and techniques used by archaeologists to recover the evidence found at sites require very careful recording of the location of each artifact, feature, and other cultural materials because it is the associations of the evidence that tells us most about past cultures. At the very least we want to know when a site was occupied and with which past culture or cultures it was associated.

Many Michigan sites are very near the ground surface, although some are deeply buried. Artifacts and features are often mixed up and brought to the surface by farmers plowing their fields. Plowing destroys some important associations by disturbing upper portions of a site. Artifacts and features that have been disturbed in their original or **primary context** by plowing or in other ways, for example by flooding, occur in a **secondary context.** That is, the cultural associations created by a past culture have been modified by later cultural or natural activity. Secondary contexts at sites can yield some useful information if there are artifacts that tell us when a site was occupied or that give us clues as to what people were doing there. Additionally, artifacts brought to the surface by later disturbance allow us to discover the existence of a site. If these remains were buried, we would not even know a site was there.

Cultural remains at the surface provide some information but certainly not all there is to know about a site, even if they occur in undisturbed or primary context. Some features may be close to the surface, some may have their tops removed by plowing, some may be quite deep below the surface. Sometimes there are many more artifacts below the surface than there are on top. Often a site is **multicomponent,** that is it was occupied by more than one past culture so that cultural remains at or near the surface may give no hint of possible earlier occupations. The several components at a site are often mixed together but in some cases the earlier materials are covered by the later ones. Such sites are called **stratified** sites. Sometimes there is culturally sterile soil in between components. Thus, the components may be separated by natural as well as cultural strata.

Because people have been in Michigan for a long time and repeatedly lived in the same places, one of the first questions archaeologists must ask is, "How old is it? How can we decide which archaeological culture left particular artifacts or features?" Since people have been leaving things lying around Michigan for nearly 12,000 years, this is not always an easy question to answer. There are two ways to answer this question of time. The first of these methods of dating archaeological sites and materials is to determine their placement in time in relationship to other sites and materials (assemblages). **Relative dating** is able to tell us about a sequence of events or cultures, that is which one came first but does not tell us when the sequence took place. Stratified sites are particularly useful for purposes of relative dating. Remember that in stratified sites the archaeological component on the bottom is the earliest. For example, the **Juntunen site** on Bois Blanc Island in the Straits of Mackinac had layers with early Late Woodland Mackinac ware on the bottom, with Bois Blanc ware in the layers above, and, finally, with Juntunen ware in the top layers. If Bois Blanc ware is found at a different site, the archaeologist knows by comparison with the Juntunen site that it is later than Mackinac ware, earlier than Juntunen ware, and is therefore, from the middle portions of the Late Woodland.

In the case of Bois Blanc ware, we can be more specific about when this pottery was made because the layers, or levels, of occupation at the Juntunen site have been dated by **absolute dating** techniques. Absolute dates tell us when the sequence took place on a continuum of time, that is, not just whether something is older or younger but how many years old it is. There are several methods of obtaining an absolute date on archaeological materials, but radiocarbon, or carbon 14 is the most commonly used dating method at Michigan sites, including Juntunen.

Radiocarbon dating is based on the principle that radioactive carbon (^{14}C) and stable carbon (^{12}C) are taken in by organisms during their lifetime. The proportion of ^{14}C to ^{12}C is constant until the organism dies. When death occurs, the ^{14}C present at death begins to decay at a known rate, that is, half about every 5,730 years. So it is possible to calculate the age of a plant or animal specimen by calculating the difference between the amount of ^{14}C originally present and the amount now present and then comparing that difference to the known rate of decay, or **half-life,** that is, the period within which it is *probable* that half of the unstable isotopes (^{14}C) will disintegrate to form the stable (^{12}C) isotopes. Organic remains in the archaeological layers at the Juntunen site were used to determine how many years had passed since the layer was occupied.

The only way to discover the nature of a site, the modifications it has undergone since it was occupied, and its cultural associations is to **map** the site in three dimensions and to record all observations on the map. It is this need to map and record relevant natural and cultural observations that prompts archaeologists to create a site **grid** that provides lines of "latitude and longitude" from which to measure their observations. Excavation is in square units or **quadrats** that can be located according to the grid, and the soil in each quadrat is removed in natural layers or in arbitrary levels. For example, a quadrat may be thirty meters north and ten meters east of the zero point on the site grid. Since the quadrat is excavated in units consisting of soil layers, cultural materials found within quadrat N30/E10 can be located by measuring where they are within the quadrat and how far they are below the surface of the ground. The location of a hearth feature in N30/E10 may be 0.5 meters from the south wall, 0.2 meters from the east wall and from 0.6 meters to 1.0 meters below the surface. A pottery vessel mapped in next to hearth on the same level is probably associated with the hearth (fig. 77). If the vessel is 1.5 meters below the surface in a different soil layer and next to the north wall of quadrat N30/E10, it may not be associated with the hearth at all.

Careful records consisting of site maps, unit maps, feature maps, and photographs are the most important part of excavation because the critical associations of evidence at a site are destroyed by archaeology itself. Although archaeologists keep careful excavation records, they rarely excavate a site completely. Portions of a site are often left for future investigators who may have new technology for analyzing

Fig. 77. Woman cooking over a fire. Note the association of pottery and hearth feature that would be found in an archaeological site. Charcoal from the hearth could be radiocarbon dated. (Courtesy of Michigan State University Museum.)

the evidence and new questions to ask. In the past fifteen years alone, the application of new methods and technologies at Michigan sites has enormously enhanced our understanding of the past. Michigan archaeologists now routinely use **flotation** to recover very small plant and animal remains by placing a sample of site soil in water and allowing seeds, fish bone, and other light materials to float to the top. As a result of flotation we have new information about the importance of wetland foods, the ways in which people used domesticated plants, and details of local environments. Sites buried under several meters of flood deposits have been discovered by the careful use of a backhoe to excavate deep test trenches, and new techniques in radiocarbon dating have provided more exact dating of past cultures.

Finally, in addition to sites, archaeologists study the **regions** with which past cultures are associated. Just as one artifact does not convey all there is to know about an earlier culture, a single site provides only partial evidence of the past. A site may be the remains of a temporary camp where, perhaps, a few people went to fish in the spring. Other sites in the same general area, or region, may have been used by a larger group on a more permanent basis or in a different season for other purposes. By investigating several sites in a region we can compare them to obtain a more complete view of the economic and social life of a previous people.

Human burials may occur in archaeological contexts, although this is relatively rare. In fact more human remains are accidentally found in, for example, construction projects than in archaeological sites. Most obvious burial sites such as mounds were looted long ago or were destroyed by more recent construction. For example, a mound group in Grand Rapids known as the Converse site is reported to have consisted of some twenty-nine burial mounds that were destroyed by development of the city. Other mound and burial sites have been excavated by archaeologists, including another mound group in Grand Rapids, the Norton Mounds. Such sites are no longer targeted for excavation, however. For about thirty years, it has been the policy of Michigan archaeologists to excavate burials only in situations where they are in danger of being destroyed. A Federal law has been enacted concerning human remains and other Indian materials. This law provides for scientific study and the possible repatriation of materials associated with a known tribe. In Michigan it is illegal for anyone to remove any human remains without obtaining permission from the county legal authorities.

Our roadside tour of Michigan's past will require some imagination on the part of the traveler. Most sites are simply not visible, but hopefully we can help you see them in your mind. In so doing, you may come to view Michigan and its people, past and present, in new ways.

SEVEN MICHIGAN HIGHWAY TRIPS

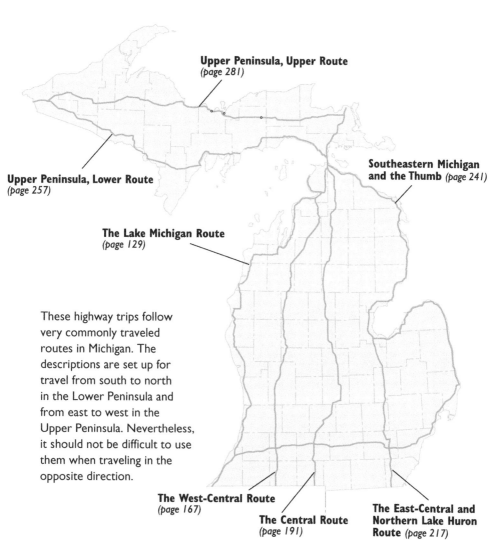

Upper Peninsula, Upper Route
(page 281)

Upper Peninsula, Lower Route
(page 257)

Southeastern Michigan and the Thumb *(page 241)*

The Lake Michigan Route
(page 129)

These highway trips follow very commonly traveled routes in Michigan. The descriptions are set up for travel from south to north in the Lower Peninsula and from east to west in the Upper Peninsula. Nevertheless, it should not be difficult to use them when traveling in the opposite direction.

The West-Central Route
(page 167)

The Central Route
(page 191)

The East-Central and Northern Lake Huron Route *(page 217)*

THE LAKE MICHIGAN ROUTE

Indiana Border to Mackinaw City (I-94 to U.S. 31)

Ludington to Mackinaw City

1. Nordhouse Dunes and Porter Creek Prehistoric District
2. Manistee and Crystal Lakes
3. Interlochen State Park
4. Greatlakian Moraine
5. Traverse City and Grand Traverse Bay
6. Traverse Corridor
7. Elk Lake and Torch Lake
8. Drumlin Country
9. Charlevoix and Little Traverse Bay
10. Beaver Island, the Bay Villages, and Petoskey
11. Petoskey State Park
12. Middle Devonian Limestones and Fossils
13. Canadian Biotic Province
14. M-119
15. Carp Lake Village and Paradise Lake

Holland to Ludington

1. Muskegs at Muskegon
2. Charles Mears State Park
3. Giant Fossil Rodent

Indiana Border to Holland

1. Archaeological Sites on the Galien River
2. Warren Woods State Park
3. Warren Dunes State Park
4. Grand Mere State Park
5. The French in Southwest Michigan
6. Van Buren State Park
7. Shipwreck
8. Michigan Maritime Museum
9. Saugatuck Dunes State Park
10. Archaeology on a "Different" River
11. Historic Holland

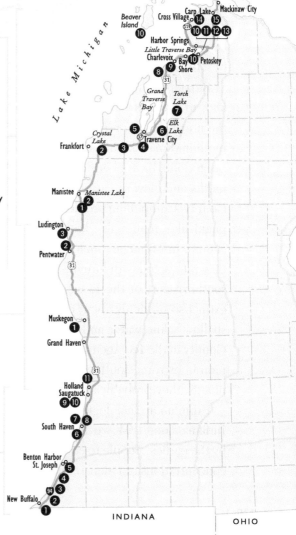

Indiana Border to Holland

This eighty-mile route, passing through the port cities of St. Joseph, Benton Harbor, and South Haven, allows ready access to the beautiful Lake Michigan shoreline as well as its magnificent dune formations, woodlands, and smaller species of vertebrate wildlife. However, one must be ready to make short diversions to several state parks, as one is lucky to get even fleeting glimpses of the big lake from the highway.

This portion of the Lake Michigan route mainly traverses an area of ancient lake plain sediments with intruding Wisconsinan end moraines (Valparaiso system) near St. Joseph and Benton Harbor and about fifteen miles south of Holland. Even when the highway is very near the lake (e.g., between Sawyer and Bridgeman in extreme southern Michigan), wooded dunes usually block the view of Lake Michigan.

Berrien County, which forms the southwestern tip of Michigan, and, to a somewhat lesser extent, adjacent Van Buren County to the north have an especially noteworthy number of Ice Age mammoth and mastodont sites (fig. 78). Eight mammoths and thirteen mastodonts have been found in Berrien County, and three mammoths and eleven mastodonts have been unearthed in Van Buren County. Compelling problems have arisen with regard to these elephant-like mammals, known as megaherbivores (giant plant-eaters), in Michigan, including (1) how they were buried, (2) how they interacted with humans, (3) why they were so abundant in the southern part of the Lower Peninsula, and (4) why they became extinct so suddenly about ten thousand years ago. The presence of shallow saline water and salt licks in the northern part of Berrien County in the Ice Age may explain why these animals were so common in extreme southwest Michigan, for like modern African elephants, they probably needed salt to survive.

From an archaeological standpoint, as we enter Michigan from Indiana along I-94, we are more or less following the way traveled by the earliest people to come here, the Paleo-Indians. The highest concentrations of Paleo-Indian projectile points reported in Michi-

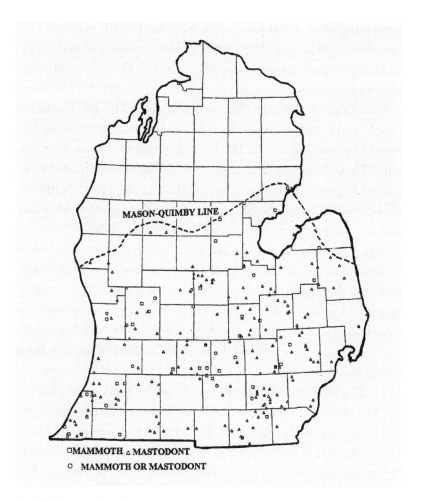

MASON-QUIMBY LINE

☐MAMMOTH △ MASTODONT
○ MAMMOTH OR MASTODONT

Fig. 78. Mammoth and mastodont distribution in Michigan. (L. Abraczinskas in *Michigan Academician*, 1993, p. 445 [courtesy of Michigan Academy of Science, Arts, and Letters].)

gan are in Berrien, Cass, and St. Joseph Counties (see fig. 68). The points represent the entire Paleo-Indian interval in Michigan and include the earliest fluted points (see figs. 18 and 67) as well as later "unfluted" fluted points (see fig. 67). The high frequency of Paleo-Indian material here is not surprising, as this area was one of the first to be deglaciated and is thought to be one of the first to be colonized by plants and animals after the glacier retreated. Could the large number of fluted points (the type used to kill mammoths in the southwest) be correlated with the large number of mammoths and mastodonts available in the area, as well as the salt source available for both the extinct giant mammals and humans?

Sometime during the last century B.C., Middle Woodland people and customs came into the Lower Peninsula from the Illinois River valley by way of the Kankakee and St. Joseph river systems. These "Hopewellian" people in Michigan were related to an archaeological culture known as the "Havana Hopewell" in Illinois. Groups settled near the St. Joseph River in southwest Michigan and along other rivers in the western part of the state.

Again, at times during the last nine hundred years, there were incursions of people known as Mississippian and Upper Mississippian into the region. We do not know what happened to the Late Woodland groups living in the area as the Upper Mississippians moved in. The two groups may have lived side by side for a time, one group may have displaced the other, or there may have been hostile confrontations.

Finally, the Lower Peninsula was virtually empty of people during the mid-seventeenth-century wars between the Iroquois and the Huron and their Algonquin allies. Resident tribes in southwest Michigan such as the Miami and the Potawatomi fled to a refuge in the neighborhood of what is now Green Bay, Wisconsin. The Potawatomi returned to their southwest Michigan homeland late in the seventeenth century by moving around Lake Michigan from the west. Again, southwest Michigan was an important entrance to the peninsula. The Pokagon Band of Potawatomi Indians lives and works near Dowagiac today.

The varied environments along the river systems of southwest Michigan were used differently by prehistoric people. For example, the oak-hickory forests of the St. Joseph River drainage provided abundant resources for Late Archaic groups who camped by lakes and small streams in the area. At these camps they worked with wood, as evidenced by ground stone axes and adzes in local collections. Stone manos, tools for grinding plants resting on an anvil (metate), show that people gathered and prepared nuts and other plant foods. Camp life also included making stone tools (see fig. 70) and probably hunting and fishing. Some material for the stone tools was picked up in glacial debris around the camps. Other artifacts were made of chert from distant locations, for example Indiana hornstone from the southern part of that state.

Farther north in the Kalamazoo River drainage basin, there was a sharp contrast with Late Archaic campsites in the St. Joseph River drainage basin. The lower Kalamazoo River seems to have been used for seasonal hunting trips, perhaps by people who had their base camps along the St. Joseph. Late Archaic artifacts along the Kalamazoo River are mainly projectile points for spears, there is very little chert from places like southern Indiana, and there are not many woodworking tools.

In the last centuries before Indian contact with Europeans, people living along the St. Joseph River may have planted corn (maize) and other crops around their relatively large settlements, as they did in historic times, and camped along the Kalamazoo River in the spring to spear sturgeon and gather tubers. This late prehistoric period in southwest Michigan was a time of considerable movement of groups, however, so potential conflict may have discouraged secure and permanent settlements with agriculture. Large village sites have been difficult to locate, and there are only three archaeological sites on the St. Joseph River with clear evidence of maize.

FEATURES

1. Archaeological Sites on the Galien River. The first river encountered along the I-94 route is the Galien, which is a short stream that empties into Lake Michigan at New Buffalo. Several small seasonal encampments were excavated on the bluff overlooking extensive wetlands along the Galien River at New Buffalo. These Upper Mississippian sites were used in the spring for gathering American lotus tubers that were roasted in deep pits, for gathering raspberries in the summer, and for hunting deer in the autumn. A charred kernel of maize was also found at one of these sites, although there was no evidence of farming. One reason why maize was such a useful crop is that it could be dried, stored, and carried along when people moved. Thus, maize might be expected at a site where it was not cultivated. These Upper Mississippian sites on the Galien River are radiocarbon dated to about A.D. 1640.

2. Warren Woods State Park (a diversion). Not only a state park, but also a National Natural Landmark, Warren Woods is an important virgin stand of various hardwood trees including several species that are typical of more southern areas in the Carolinian Biotic Province (see fig. 42) such as the shagbark hickory (fig. 79) as well as a few giant red pines. To reach this park take I-94 at the Union Pier exit (exit 6) and go 2.8 miles east on Elm Valley Road. This tract of land was purchased in the 1870s by local businessman E. K. Warren, who wished to save the site for posterity. About two miles of paths allow the visitor to walk among the virgin trees and tree-falls and to observe the interesting bird life of the park. Pileated woodpeckers occur in the woods and during the spring warbler migrations, bird-watchers assemble to see species that are rare or absent from other parts of Michigan. There still may be an eastern box turtle or two (see fig. 36) left plodding along in the woods here, so be on the lookout!

Did you ever wonder how one can tell whether one is in a regionally stable (**climax**) woodland or not? Well, look at the tiny trees coming up on the woodland floor. If these trees are different than the mature trees that form the canopy, the woods is probably still undergoing **succession** (changes leading to the climax condition). What do the tiny trees on the floor of Warren Woods look like?

3. Warren Dunes State Park (a short diversion). To reach this state park take exit 16 (about twelve miles south of St. Joseph) and follow the Department of Natural Resources (DNR) signs to the park entrance. This park allows lovely views of Lake Michigan from towering dunes as well as trails through wooded dune country. Tower Hill, a large dune (fig. 80) just west of the parking lot, is a blowout dune resulting from the reactivation of an older dune.

Fig. 79. Shagbark hickory tree near Warren Woods on Elm Valley Road, Berrien County, southwestern Lower Peninsula

Early in this section we mentioned moraines as part of the topography of southwestern Michigan. Moraines are features that formed as the result of ancient glacially deposited sediments (see figs. 15 and 16). Now that we are looking at dunes, it is probably a good time to talk about a common misconception in Michigan, that is, that prominent inland moraines are "old dunes." Actually, all high dunes are formed by wind-blown sand and are located only on or very near the coast of the Great Lakes that surround Michigan, mainly on the west side of the state. Low dunes that are so flattened that most people barely notice them do occur in some inland situations. But these are ancient dunes, some about ten thousand years old that occur in a relatively few inland areas, for example, near Saginaw Bay in the eastern part of the Lower Peninsula. These dunes formed on shorelines of ancient glacial lakes and they will be discussed later.

Fig. 80. Tower Hill Dune, just west of the parking lot, Warren Dunes State Park. For scale, note the people climbing about one-third way up the dune.

4. Grand Mere State Park (a short diversion). Up the highway to the Stevensville exit (exit 17) one goes west a few hundred feet on Grand Mere Road to Thornton Road. Turn left on Thornton and travel about one-half mile to the park entrance. This state park allows the traveler to see the ecological succession that occurs from sandy beach (fig. 81) to mature woodlands (fig. 82). You might see a box turtle (see fig. 36) in the woods if you are lucky. This is one of the finest bird-watching areas in the state with a list of over 250 species. Interesting birds that may be seen in the park include mockingbirds, various migrating warblers, and vireos. The inter-dunal lakes (North, Middle, and South) are homes to loons, cormorants, and ducks during the summer, and migrating hawks may be observed in the spring and fall. The shallow, weedy, interdunal lakes are good for turtle watching.

5. The French in Southwest Michigan. As we approach the mouth of the St. Joseph River at the city of St. Joseph, we are near the first European site in southwest Michigan. Father Rene-Robert Cavelier de La Salle founded Fort Miami in 1679 (see fig. 76). This outpost also included a mission to the Miami Indians who lived there at the time. Fort Miami was established under authority given to La Salle by the French government in Paris. The French desired to protect their interests in the fur trade by maintaining a presence at strategic points along the shores of the Great Lakes and the Mississippi River. The mouth of the St. Joseph River was such a strategic location because it overlooked any traffic along the lakeshore and along the river itself.

A second post, Fort St. Joseph, was established by the French upriver near Niles. British forces took command of this fort in 1761. The fort was taken by Potawatomi allies of Pontiac during the Indian war against the British in 1763. British troops did not return after the war, and the post was used mainly by local French traders.

Fig. 81. Typical sandy Lake Michigan beach (western Lower Peninsula)

Fig. 82. Fairly mature second-growth deciduous woodland beyond entrance to Grand Mere State Park, Berrien County, southwestern Lower Peninsula

For many years, it was assumed that Fort St. Joseph was entirely destroyed by dams built along the river there. Archaeologists from Western Michigan University are investigating remains that may represent a portion of Fort St. Joseph.

6. Van Buren State Park (a diversion). Traveling twenty-one miles north on U.S. 31, we take the Blue Star Highway south of South Haven to Ruggles Road, where we turn right and go about a mile to the park entrance. This is yet another lakeshore park, and it is bordered by wooded, stabilized sand dunes (fig. 83) along its western edge. The beach is both sandy and pebbly, and the dunes are posted to guard against the erosion of the fragile dune community caused by too many hikers.

7. Shipwreck. In November 1891, a schooner called the *Rockaway* was carrying lumber from Ludington to Benton Harbor when it was lost in the Lake Michigan waters off South Haven. The schooner was only found in 1983. Archaeologists from the Michigan Maritime Museum spent five seasons carefully excavating the *Rockaway* with help from a crew of volunteers. Because underwater excavations require the same documentation as an excavation on dry land, the wreck site was mapped according to a grid system. A great deal of time and care was taken to conserve the artifacts found underwater, as they rapidly deteriorated when exposed to the air, so that excavation of the *Rockaway* was only the first step. A conservation laboratory at the museum was established where the artifacts were stabilized against any future deterioration.

8. Michigan Maritime Museum (a short diversion). Exhibits and activities relating to the maritime history of Michigan from Indian canoes to Great Lakes freighters can be seen at the Michigan Maritime Museum in South Haven. Take exit 20 (Phoenix Road) from I-196 and go west toward Broadway. At Broadway turn right and go around the corner to the Black River bridge. Cross the bridge and find the museum on the left side of the street.

Fig. 83. Mature, wooded stabilized dune at Van Buren State Park, Van Buren County (southwestern Lower Peninsula)

9. Saugatuck Dunes State Park (a short diversion). Take exit 41 from I-96 and go west less than one-half mile to 64th Street. Then turn right to the north on 64th and go one mile to 138th Avenue. Next turn left to the west again onto 138th and go one mile to the entrance. The fact that there is a difficult one-mile hike to the beach from the parking lot over wooded dunes cuts down on the crowds at this mainly "underdeveloped" woodland area. While you are walking to the beach keep on the lookout for Fowler's toad (see fig. 34), which is found only in the western part of the Lower Peninsula of Michigan. This toad may be distinguished from the more common eastern American toad (see fig. 22) in that Fowler's toad has at least three warts in each large spot on the back (the American toad usually has only two). If you are really lucky, you might come upon an eastern hog-nosed snake (see fig. 38) sunning in or near the trail. Hog-nosed snakes use their upturned snout to root out toads resting in the sand, and perhaps they use the elongated teeth in the back of the mouth to puncture and deflate the toads, which inflate themselves to resist being swallowed whole.

10. Archaeology on a "Different" River. The Kalamazoo River empties into Lake Michigan at Douglas and Saugatuck a few miles south of Holland. This river is unusual in comparison to the other west Michigan rivers, the St. Joseph, the Grand, and the Muskegon. The Kalamazoo River, for most of its length, lacks the mature floodplains found along the other rivers, where each spring the waters overflow their banks, then recede so that a broad expanse of dry land is left where seed plants can grow. On the other hand, there are many broad and permanently wet swamps and marshes along the Kalamazoo.

The difference between the Kalamazoo River and other rivers is reflected in the ways people lived along the Kalamazoo drainage. During much of prehistory and the Historic period, various groups seemed to have used this river on a seasonal basis. For example, the Ottawa/Odawa of northern Michigan would leave their villages to hunt along the Kalamazoo in the winter. At other times of the year, this same river was used by the Potawatomi, whose villages were on the St. Joseph River.

Several Upper Mississippian sites from around A.D. 1450–1550 in the lower Kalamazoo basin show this seasonal use of the Kalamazoo River, as evidenced by deep roasting pits at the Schwerdt site that contained American lotus tubers and abundant remains of lake sturgeon. The sturgeon spawn in late May and early June, and lotus is available at the same time. Animal remains at Schwerdt included turtles, mussels, beavers, raccoons, deer, bears, and turkeys. These animals were less common than the sturgeon but, like the sturgeon and tubers, were available around the nearby wetlands in the spring. Similar roasting pits with tubers and sturgeon were found in the Upper Mississippian portions of the multicomponent Elam site. Clearly, Upper Mississippian peoples were using the Kalamazoo River for particular purposes in the spring. Their more permanent residential sites were probably to the south on the St. Joseph River.

In contrast to other groups who used the river for specific purposes, Late Woodland people moved seasonally along the Kalamazoo River all year long. This is evidenced by Late Woodland Allegan tradition pots that have been found at sites occupied at various times of the year. These Late Woodland groups regarded the Kalamazoo as their home territory (see fig. 73).

11. Historic Holland. This town is one of the centers of Dutch culture in southwestern Michigan, which has a large population of Dutch immigrants. Holland State Park is mainly a basking, swimming, boating, and fishing area. On the park's southern border, a breakwater that marks the mouth of Lake Macatawa provides a site for pier fisherman to catch salmon, trout, and perch.

Holland to Ludington

A distance of about ninety miles separates Holland and the northern port of Ludington. Among other coastal cities, U.S. 31 bypasses

Grand Haven, Muskegon, and Pentwater without views of Lake Michigan unless one exits. From a geological perspective, U.S. 31 passes through a flat region consisting mainly of glacial lake sediments from Holland to Grand Haven, where the region rather abruptly changes to a complex pattern of alternating glacial end moraines and lake sediments. This continues through Pentwater until lake sediments again dominate in the Ludington area.

Botanically, this is mainly a somewhat broad transitional zone (see fig. 42) between the deciduous woodlands to the south (Carolinian Biotic Province) and the mixed deciduous and coniferous woodlands to the north (Canadian Biotic Province). In the more inland areas, and especially on the east coast of Michigan, this transition is much more abrupt, as we shall see on other routes in this book. The transition zone offers unusual biological diversity because it has plants and animals characteristic of the oak-hickory forests to the south as well as plants and animals characteristic of the beech-maple forests to the north. The area encompasses many more square miles here on the west coast, where temperatures are more moderate than on the east coast. The west coast is protected from extreme temperatures because the prevailing west winds blow across Lake Michigan, bringing air cooled by the lake water in summer and warmed by the lake water in the colder months. Thus, summer temperatures are cooler and winter temperatures are warmer.

The biological diversity of the transition zone was used by prehistoric residents in their food quest. For example, the transition zone has virtually all the varieties of berries gathered in the summer and nuts gathered in the fall. The Carolinian Biotic Province has fewer varieties of berries, while in the Canadian Biotic Province nuts are less abundant. Thus, the transition zone offers a variety of food in a variety of natural habitats located along the several river systems draining the region, including the Grand River, the Muskegon River, the White River, the Pentwater River, the Pere Marquette River, and the Big Sable River. Most of our knowledge of how people lived in the area comes from historic records and from sites located along the Muskegon River. A site located on a small stream in the lower Muskegon River drainage was long thought to represent a warm season agricultural village. The bones and shells from this site represented large amounts of deer (and antlers), beavers, muskrats, bear, and raccoons along with other mammals, some fish, mussels, and reptiles. Most of the animals were probably the focus of fall and winter hunting. It is very possible that warm season sites also occur near the mouth of the Muskegon River and it is likely that most winter sites occur farther upstream.

The archaeological findings are very consistent with the reports of Andrew Blackbird, an Ottawa, whose 1887 history of his people describes the Indians moving south from the Little Traverse Bay region to hunt along these rivers in the fall and winter. Lake Michigan served as a highway during these seasonal travels. Blackbird says, "In navigating Lake Michigan they used long bark canoes in which they carried their whole families and enough provisions to last them all winter. These canoes were made very light, out of white birch bark, and with a fair wind they could skip very lightly on the waters, going very fast, and could stand a very heavy sea. In one day they could sail quite a long distance along the coast of Lake Michigan. When night overtook them they would land and make wigwams with light poles of cedar which they always carried in their canoes. These wigwams were covered with mats made for that purpose out of prepared marsh reeds or flags sewed together, which made very good shelter from rain and wind, and were very warm after making fires inside of them. They had another kind of mat to spread on the ground to sit and sleep on. These mats are quite beautifully made out of different colors, and closely woven, of well prepared bull-rushes. After breakfast in the morning they are off again in the big canoes" (p. 33).

FEATURES

1. Muskegs at Muskegon. A truly "northern exposure" greets the traveler about two miles north of the junction of M-46 and U.S. 31 near the city of Muskegon. On the right side of the highway, the grassy bogs laced with small streams are remnants of the once widespread Muskegs that were dominant when the area was home for Indian peoples. This bog land was a rich source of game for these native Americans.

2. Charles Mears State Park at Pentwater (a short diversion). You might wish to take a short diversion at the Pentwater exit to enjoy another look at Lake Michigan from the very nice beach at Charles Mears State Park. This beach is located four blocks west of the town of Pentwater on Lowell Street.

3. A Giant Fossil Rodent from the Beach at Ludington. The Mason-Quimby line (see fig. 18) slopes sharply down in Lake County to the junction of the borders of Oceana and Muskegon Counties at Lake Michigan. But the Mason-Quimby line should now probably be moved north to Ludington because of the recent discovery of a very important fossil mammal on the beach there.

Walking the beaches of the Great Lakes in Michigan is wonderful and relaxing recreation, and if one is at all interested in natural history, a treasure trove of natural objects are to be found during beach-combing activities. Beautiful naturally bleached fish bones and bird bones are especially interesting and decorative objects to be found on Michigan beaches, as are pieces of driftwood and other objects too numerous to mention. Moreover, in the northern parts of the Lower Peninsula, Paleozoic fossil invertebrates, especially corals, may be found.

Many folks like to walk on the beach early in the spring to avoid the summer tourists, and it was on May 6, 1989, that a young couple from Leslie (near Lansing) were walking on the beach just north of Ludington. One of them noticed what seemed to be a large bone near some other material washed up on the beach by a recent storm. It was a jaw that they realized was about the size of that of a bear, but the teeth did not resemble a bear at all. These folks brought the bone into the Zoology Department at Michigan State University, who in turn called us at the MSU Museum to see if someone there could identify the find. One zoologist said that it looked like the jaw of a mouse the size of a bear! What I (JAH) had hoped for was indeed true. It was the right jaw of a giant beaver, and it was actually larger than the jaw of an adult black bear! There are only nine other Michigan records of this animal, the largest rodent of all time, and none of them were from so far north as the Ludington jaw. The next day, a small field trip was mounted to the exact spot where the jaw was found and persons from the MSU Department of Geological Sciences made a guess that the bone arrived among solidified Lake Michigan sediments washed up on the beach in large blocks during a recent storm. In fact, we found some of these blocks nearby, and they look like they had formed in a marsh or swamp at some time when the lake level was lower during the end of the Ice Age. Unfortunately, no other Ice Age fossils were found in the blocks.

The northern limit of the Mason-Quimby line in the west now has to be reconsidered (see fig. 18), for no authentic large extinct vertebrates have ever been found north of the existing line. This is certainly an example of a true scientific treasure that was found by a beach-combing couple. Unfortunately, they declined to donate the fossil to the MSU Museum; thus the only evidence that exists is a photograph and a drawing.

Ludington to Mackinaw City

The trip from Ludington to Traverse City is a long jaunt of about 194 miles that can be driven in about four hours, but could easily be extended to a leisurely day trip if one wanted to take time to relax in the countryside and along the lakeshores. As we move northward (with a couple of bends in the highway) toward the narrow straits that divide the Lower Peninsula of Michigan from the Upper Peninsula, we will find that much of this trip is inland. Nevertheless, some of Lake Michigan's large satellite lakes can be seen from the car, as well as some nice views of Grand Traverse Bay and Little Traverse Bay. North of Little Traverse Bay we enter the Canadian Biotic Province for the first time.

Geologically, this is a trip through varied surface formations that mainly reflect the Ice Age history of the area. Moraines and glacial till plains as well as both glacial outwash plains and glacial lake plains are traversed, and several drumlin fields are available for the sharp-eyed traveler to observe. Moraine topography dominates the landscape until the Frankfort–Crystal Lake area, where the highway makes a hard right turn for twenty-six miles through mainly glacial outwash plain topography. At this point, the road swings sharply north to Traverse City, where one is soon confronted by the impressive Greatlakian Moraine, a long sloping hill that occurs before one descends into the bay country. Proceeding from Traverse City around Grand Traverse Bay to the beautiful city of Charlevoix, and then along the south edge of Little Traverse Bay to the equally beautiful city of Petoskey, we are mainly on till plain and glacial lake plain topography. Finally, turning north again to Mackinaw City and the Straits, we are mainly on glacial lake plain (with some till plain topography mixed in) all the way to the Straits.

Botanically, we remain in the transition zone between the Carolinian and Canadian Biotic Provinces (see fig. 42) all the way from Ludington until just north of Petoskey and Little Traverse Bay, where we enter the Canadian Biotic Province for the first time. From this point to Mackinaw City we see true examples of mixed coniferous and deciduous vegetation that are typical of this province.

Turning now to archaeological matters, we note that perhaps the most famous visitor to the northwestern Michigan area was Father Jacques Marquette, who with Louis Jolliet had undertaken an expedition to find and explore the Mississippi River. During the year following this expedition, Marquette went back to Illinois Country to preach to the Indians there. In 1675, Marquette, who was very ill, followed Lake Michigan's eastern shore on the trip home to the mission in St. Ignace at the Straits of Mackinac. The missionary died on this journey, either at Ludington, which is located at the mouth of the Pere Marquette River, or at Frankfort, which is at the mouth of the Betsie River. Marquette's companions buried him where he died, but two years later his bones were unearthed and taken back to St. Ignace by his Indian friends.

FEATURES

I. The Nordhouse Dunes and the Porter Creek Prehistoric District (a diversion). U.S. 31 turns north at Scottville about seven miles east of Ludington. Ten miles north of Scottville, or about eleven miles south of Manistee, there is a sign on the west side of the road directing you to the Lake Michigan Recreation Area in the Manistee National Forest. You will soon see the entrance. Follow Forest Road 5972 about eight miles to Lake Michigan. On the observation deck overlooking the lake (fig. 84) there will be interpretive signs about the prehistoric occupation of Porter Creek.

Late Woodland Indians living here in the transition zone between the biotic provinces systematically used the variety of plants and animals characteristic of this ecological setting. Such a life required not only an extensive knowledge of where foods and

Fig. 84. Scenic overlook of Lake Michigan at the Manistee National Forest Recreation Area

other supplies could be found in the various seasons but also included the use of food storage. By storing food the people could insure a supply at times when not much could be found. An example of this use of varied food stuffs and storage can be seen at the Porter Creek South campsite on the bluffs overlooking Lake Michigan and a site about one-half mile inland that consists of over one hundred deep storage or cache pits. Together, these sites are on the National Register of Historic Sites as a prehistoric district.

The site at Porter Creek was used by local extended families as a temporary camp where they organized their domestic activities around the campfire, or hearth. Pots, of a local style, were set near the fire. One of these pots was a miniature vessel that may have been made or used by a child. A few stone tools of local chert (flint) were made and sharpened in the same limited space. Someone smoked a pipe near the fire as well, and plant seeds found in a nearby feature included smoking materials.

Wood charcoal from the fires at Porter Creek indicates that the forest during the Late Woodland was composed mainly of white pine, but oak, beech, and maple trees grew there as well. A variety of fruits were eaten at the site including cherries, huckleberries, bearberries, blackberries, and chokeberries. These fruits could have been picked near the site, as they ripened in the late summer and autumn months. Burned bones from the site included beavers, turtles, and small fish. Turtles and fish, like the plants, would have been obtained during the warmer periods of the year.

Great Lakes Indians routinely stored food by placing it in woven net bags or bark boxes and then burying it in pits either in bark cylinders or lined with hay and then covered with bark, hay, wood, and earth. Virtually all kinds of plant and animal foods were stored in every season. Archaeologists believe that the pits at Porter Creek were used by Late Woodland people who camped at the site near the lakeshore, hunted and gathered plants in the surrounding forest, and placed this food in the pits. Since this activity took place in the summer and early fall, the people would have then moved on to their winter campgrounds and returned to retrieve the food in the spring on the way back to their summer sites.

Because Late Woodland pottery similar to that from the camp-site was found near the cache pits, it appears that the pits, too, date to the Late Woodland. These pits were probably dug by people who stopped at the camp on their seasonal travels and stored food in the pits to be retrieved when they returned. Cache pits such as those at Porter Creek have been excavated from time to time at several sites. Such pits are normally empty because people used the materials stored in them. They have been filled in and appear today as circular depressions.

Andrew J. Blackbird writes in 1887 of similar travels by Indians in the region. "All the Indians of Arbor Croche [on Little Traverse Bay] used only to stay there during the summer time, to plant their corn, potatoes, and other vegetables. As soon as their crops were put away in the ground, they would start all together towards the south, going to different points, some going as far as Chicago expressly to trap the muskrats, beavers, and many other kinds of furs, and others to the St. Joe River, Black River, Grand River, or Muskegon River, there to trap and hunt all winter, and make sugar in the spring. After sugar making they would come back again to Waw-gaw-naw-ke-zee, or Arbor Croche, to spend the summer and to raise their crops again as before" (p. 32).

Porter Creek is situated at the northern end of the Nordhouse barrier dunes that parallel Lake Michigan northward from Big Sable Point. These dunes, which formed during the Lake Nipissing stage about forty-five hundred years ago, contain an unusually high variety of plant habitats within a relatively small area. This variety is due largely to the high relief of the dune system. When Late Woodland people camped here in the Nordhouse dunes, there was open sand, wooded dunes forested in pines with an oak understory, moist uplands with mixed conifer forests, and tamarack-cedar forests in the moist lowlands. This variety of habitats offered varied foods and other raw materials for people of the region.

After much of the forest was felled by lumberjacks and then

burned in forest fires, the vegetation changed. Today the upland dunes are forested in oak with a pine understory, that is, the reverse of the prelumbering era. Remains of an old lumbering camp also exist along Porter Creek.

2. Manistee and Crystal Lakes, Satellites of Lake Michigan. Manistee Lake at Manistee, and the larger Crystal Lake at Benzonia near Frankfort, were cut off from the big lake by the growth of sand bars and dunes that closed off the mouths of these former small bays. Crystal Lake (fig. 85) occupies the low land between two high, tree-covered moraines, both of which are oriented in an east-west direction.

3. Interlochen State Park (a short diversion). Passing north of Crystal Lake, U.S. 31 makes a sharp turn west where one quickly passes the biblically named village of Beulah. After about a twenty-mile cross-country jaunt, we reach the Interlochen exit, which takes us south between two lovely inland lakes, Green Lake to the west and Duck Lake to the east. Duck Lake, incidentally, is one of the most northern localities for the common map turtle (fig. 86). In map turtles, the females are quite large, having very big heads with broad crushing surfaces on their jaws that enable them to crunch up shelled animals such as clams, mussels, and snails. Male map turtles are smaller, have proportionally smaller heads, and lack the jaw modifications of the females.

Nestled in the wooded Interlochen area is the world-renowned Interlochen Center for the Arts, which includes the National Music Camp and a year-round arts academy. The public campgrounds at Interlochen opened in 1917 as the first in the Michigan State Park system. This campground is located on the west shore of Duck Lake and has a truly Chautauqua-like atmosphere, as classical music wafts through stands of beautiful old trees. Cottages on the two lakes tend to be tasteful, small, and built in the woods, so that the occupants walk to the lakeshores along equally modest forested paths. A natural shoreline, free of cement barriers to beach erosion, is a joy to behold.

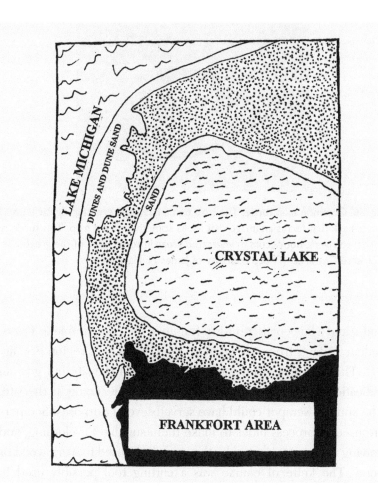

Fig. 85. Simplified map of the western part of Crystal Lake and surrounding area (Benzie County, northwestern Lower Peninsula). Stippled areas indicate modern woodlands that separate present Crystal Lake from the dunes and dune sands of Lake Michigan. Crystal Lake was a former bay of Lake Michigan, but an ancient sand bar and dunes that grew on top of that closed off Crystal Lake from the big lake. Now, Crystal Lake, an independent entity, has developed its own sandy shoreline.

A very interesting archaeological collection from the Green Lake site at Interlochen shows that this area was used by people on a regular basis for a long time. The site was first occupied late in the Paleo-Indian period, about 10,300 years ago. Although fluted projectile points have not been found, a spurred scraper, an ovate

Fig. 86. Common map turtle. The map turtle has a pattern of irregular lines on its back that forms an image that looks something like a map. This turtle is partial to rivers, but occurs in vegetated areas in some lakes of the greater Traverse City area. (Photo courtesy of James H. Harding.)

knife, and a lanceolate preform fragment are comparable to Paleo-Indian artifacts from elsewhere in the Great Lakes region (see fig. 67). These artifacts show not only the age of the site but give an indication of what the late Paleo-Indians were doing at the site. The spurred scraper could have served several purposes. Scrapers are used to process hides to make them suitable for clothing, and graving tools, represented by the spur, were used to work wood or bone. The knife of course was a cutting tool possibly used in butchering game. The lanceolate preform was a nearly finished artifact stone tool that could be completed into a final form as needed. Such preforms or blanks were a very useful way to use raw material without having to carry large pieces of suitable stone as people moved. The preform at Green Lake was made of Bayport chert, which is found around Saginaw Bay. It would have been very cumbersome to carry pieces of Bayport chert all the way from Saginaw to Green Lake.

Other artifacts at this site were from nearly all prehistoric periods. Thus, we know that this site was occupied sometime between about 10,000 and 8,000 years ago (Early Archaic), between 4,500 and 2,800 years ago (Late Archaic), between about 2,800 and 1,400 years ago (Early Woodland and Middle Woodland), and between about 1,400 and 500 years ago (Late Woodland). As was the case with the late Paleo-Indian artifacts, those from later periods indicated that a variety of activities took place here.

One of the most interesting questions about this site is why people came here during such a long period of time when the environment was changing dramatically. The Green Lake area when Paleo-Indians were here was quite different from that seen by later occupants of the site. Although the glacier had retreated and did not return, water levels in the Great Lakes dropped, rose higher than we see today, and then dropped again to current levels. The area was covered by closed spruce-fir forests with some deciduous trees when the late Paleo-Indians were here. Today the forest consists mainly of mixed beeches, maples, and conifers. The question of why people continued to come here for so long is particularly important because those who lived here were seeking wild plant and animal foods.

It is likely that the attraction of this location is related to the diversity of habitats to be found here through time. Paleo-Indian, Archaic, and Woodland peoples throughout the northern Great Lakes area consistently occupied locations surrounded by diverse habitats in every season. Such variety was important because it created the opportunity to find many foods in the different habitats nearby, and when food was scarce it was more likely that something could be found. Since there were always diverse habitats around Green Lake, it was a prime location throughout prehistory.

The site at Green Lake was discovered in 1956 by two young boys who spent their childhood summers with their families at the Interlochen Center for the Arts. Their summer adventures included collecting a number of prehistoric artifacts along the paths and other exposed surfaces near their cottages. One who is a naturalist himself, recognized the importance of these childhood treasures for increasing our understanding of Michigan's past. He contacted archaeologists at the MSU Museum about the site, had the artifacts identified, and donated his own collection to the museum. We recorded the site in the state site file maintained by the Michigan Historical Center, and it was given the number

20GT89. This number is based on a national system whereby 20 refers to the state of Michigan, GT refers to Grand Traverse County, and 89 means this is the eighty-ninth site recorded in the county. Because there is no other site in the United States with this number, any reference to 20GT89 is to this site at Green Lake. With one collector's active involvement we were able to study his collection as well as artifacts found by others who loaned them to the MSU Museum for this purpose. He also recorded the locations of each find on a map and researched environmental settings around the site.

4. The Greatlakian Moraine. A few miles past the Interlochen exit, U.S. 31 makes a turn to the north at a busy intersection where it joins U.S. 37 for the short seven miles or so to Traverse City. Very soon after the turn we ascend a very large sloping hill that is a part of the prominent Greatlakian (formerly called Valders) Moraine. The Greatlakian Moraine is the terminal moraine of the last advance of the ice in the Pleistocene (Ice Age). When we reach the flattened top of this scenic moraine, we get our first fleeting glimpse of Grand Traverse Bay. Heading down the north side of the moraine, we descend into Traverse City and Grand Traverse Bay country.

5. Traverse City and Grand Traverse Bay. After taking U.S. 31 through Traverse City and a few stoplights we come to a busy intersection at the edge of the West Arm of Grand Traverse Bay. Here we turn sharply right to continue on U.S. 31, where we soon find Traverse City State Park adjacent to the highway. The park is at the opposite end of the spectrum from places like the Warren Woods or Interlochen State Parks, as it occurs near restaurants, motels, shopping areas, condos, miniature golf courses, and fake waterfalls. But at least one can camp in a bustling area and experience views of the picturesque East Arm of Grand Traverse Bay.

Usually there are somewhat ugly clumps of inch-long white and black clamlike shells piled up on the beaches of Traverse City, as well as numerous dead shells of these creatures at high-water mark. These are the notorious Zebra mussels (fig. 87) that have literally taken over the Great Lakes. They have recently come from western Europe attached to the hulls of ships and been carried to the Great Lakes. These animals filter tiny organisms and bits of organic matter from the lake water for their food, and actually have caused some murky portions of the Great Lakes (e.g., Lake Erie) to become clear. But, as the great Great Lakes area poet Carl Sandburg once wrote about human prejudices, "Big fish eat little fish, little fish eat shrimp, and shrimp eat mud." How will the loss of the tiny organisms at the bottom of the food chain affect the other plants and animals in the lakes?

Actually, the Great Lakes are ripe for such invasions because these lakes form a relatively new system of "inland seas" that is quite vulnerable for exploitation by aquatic "weed species" of all kinds. Not too many years back the coasts of southern Lake Michigan were periodically piled high with the rotting bodies of alewives, small, silvery fishes that invaded the Great Lakes from the ocean. Commercial fishing and sea lampreys (unwanted invaders from the ocean) had all but eliminated the native, predatory lake trout from Lake Michigan by 1960, and thus the alewives, with no natural predators, multiplied into the billions until salmon, also nonnative, were introduced in the mid-1960s to eat them.

6. The Traverse Corridor. Extending roughly from the south end of Traverse Bay to just north of Little Traverse Bay is a marked

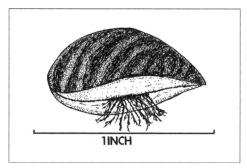

Fig. 87. Zebra mussel. One of the troublesome species introduced into the Great Lakes from Europe, the zebra mussel has become so abundant that it has clogged up drainage pipes and other man-made structures and has filtered tons of important tiny plants and animals out of the lakes for its food.

1 INCH

extension of the transition zone between the Carolinian and the Canadian Biotic Provinces. The Traverse corridor has a milder, more equable climate than other parts of Michigan at similar latitudes (see fig. 42) because of the lake effect (Lake Michigan tends to retain a warmer temperature than the air during the colder months, and prevailing southwesterly winds blow cooling air off the lake in the summer months). Check the weather map from time to time and you will find that Traverse City is usually a few degrees warmer than Grayling or Houghton Lake. Needless to say, some species of plants and animals have extended their ranges northward of other populations of the same species in the state along the transition zone. From the practical standpoint, the relatively mild Traverse Corridor is well known for producing the tasty sweet cherries and other fruits that are so popular in the Traverse City area.

The term *Traverse Corridor* indicates that this northernmost extension of the transition zone between the Carolinian and Canadian Biotic Provinces served as a continuous avenue, or corridor, of interaction between northern and southern prehistoric peoples. That evidence for such interaction is seen in the presence of both northern and southern pottery styles at sites in the area.

During the Middle Woodland, the Traverse area was used by peoples with differing subsistence practices. These differences are reflected in the fact that southern Middle Woodland Havana-related pottery is found at sites situated on small lakes where a variety of habitats such as open marshes, and mixed lowland and upland forests supported a variety of foods in the immediate vicinity. In contrast, sites with northern Laurel materials were small seasonal fishing camps oriented toward the Lake Michigan coast at the northern end of the transition zone in the Traverse Corridor. Some sites have both Havana-related and Laurel pottery, indicating the potential for a meeting between the two groups, although the nature of any interaction is uncertain (see fig. 72). Laurel peoples were most likely in the area during the spring fishing season, and Havana-related peoples may have arrived later in the warm season, so they did not necessarily meet.

North-south interaction during earlier parts of the Late Woodland, like that of Middle Woodland times, involved people who lived in different environmental zones and moved seasonally through different areas. During the Late Woodland, however, the Traverse Corridor seems to have been seasonally shared by groups who lived next to one another and had reason to be good neighbors. Conflict with these neighbors would have made it difficult to live in the Traverse Corridor, and the neighbors were also an important source of emergency aid and information.

The northerners were people of the Mackinac phase (ca. A.D. 750 to 1000) whose regular territory was mainly the Canadian Biotic Province and whose focus of subsistence was the product of the inland shore fishery of the northern Great Lakes. The fall-spawning whitefish and lake trout were important to them because the fish could be dried and carried to winter camps in the forests of the interior. Mackinac phase groups lived along the west coast during the warm season. Their immediately adjacent neighbors were Skegemog phase groups who regularly moved through the transition zone but like Mackinac phase people probably lived in the Traverse Corridor during the warm season. Both groups freely used local chert that they obtained from the Pi-wan-go-ning quarry on the northeast side of Grand Traverse Bay.

7. Elk Lake and Torch Lake. Passing northward from Traverse City toward the end of the East Arm of Grand Traverse Bay, we view Elk Lake to the right, and about thirteen miles farther north we view the north end of the very long and narrow Torch Lake. Both Elk Lake and Torch Lakes are satellite lakes of Grand Traverse Bay that were cut off from the bay about four thousand years ago when the lake level receded.

8. Drumlin Country. Drumlins (fig. 88) are the rather cigar-shaped, streamlined hills that are mainly composed of glacial till. In some places in Michigan they may be a mile long. These hills were formed by overriding Pleistocene ice and are arranged in the direction of the ice flow. Large numbers of drumlins may occur in so-

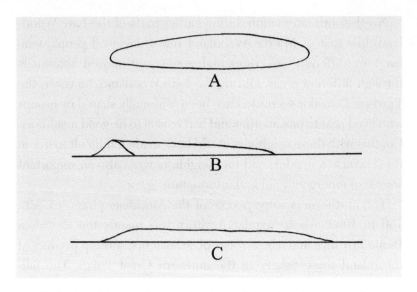

Fig. 88. Outline drawings showing the shape of drumlins. A, top view; B, angled front view; C, side view.

called drumlin fields. A large drumlin field lies between the end of Torch Lake and Charlevoix to the north. These drumlins are left over from the Greatlakian Moraine and trend in a northwest to southeast direction.

9. Charlevoix and Little Traverse Bay. Passing through the drumlin fields north of Torch Lake, we reach the beautiful old resort city of Charlevoix after about seventeen miles of inland driving. Lake Charlevoix, another satellite of Lake Michigan, and representing another closed in bay, may be seen on the right as one goes through the city.

During the early part of the twentieth century, people from St. Louis and Chicago would come to spend their summers in this resort town. Many of them stayed at the old Beach Hotel that stood on the north side of the Pine River Channel from 1899 until 1967, when the building burned. Condominiums were built on the property about five years later. Although there were reports of an archaeological site here, no work was done until 1970, when the site was rediscovered by a survey crew from the MSU Museum. Archaeologist Charles Cleland arranged for the site to be excavated before it was destroyed by the construction of the condominiums. The excavations to save the site were made possible by contributions from the citizens of Charlevoix, by assistance from city officials in removing hotel rubble, by publicity in the *Charlevoix Courier,* and by permission from the property owner.

Chert from the Pi-wan-go-ning quarry on Grand Traverse Bay was found in abundance at the Pine River Channel site near U.S. 31 in Charlevoix. The chert at this site was in the form of cores (large prepared pieces of stone) from which flakes, or pieces, were removed to make chipped stone tools (see fig. 70). Additionally, there were partially finished tools and an abundance of **debitage** (waste flakes), from making tools. Stone hammers found at the Pine River Channel site were used in making tools.

Tools made at Pine River Channel included projectile points for hunting, and scrapers for working hides. A copper awl might have been used to pierce holes in hides in the process of sewing clothing. A variety of other forms such as chipped stone drills and graving tools along with groundstone axes and adzes show that people fabricated artifacts of wood and bone. Additionally, chipped stone knives could have served a number of cutting purposes.

The remains of moose, possibly woodland caribou, white-tailed deer, beavers, and smaller mammals plus mallard ducks, Canada geese, and turkeys indicate these animals were hunted and trapped by the inhabitants of the site. All of these animals could have been found in various habitats around the site.

Charred seeds show that berries, lambsquarter, hawthorn, and elder were gathered in August and September. Other seeds might have been collected at the same time but were available as early as May. Dock and indigo bush seed were found as well. The plants, like the animals, could have been found near the site. Groundstone pestles would have been used for grinding plant foods.

Fish bones at the Pine River Channel site show that spring spawning walleyes, white suckers, and possibly redhorse suckers were caught there. The walleyes would have been found in the clear lake waters nearby, while the suckers would have been caught in the Pine River Channel when they came upstream to spawn in April. Fishing equipment at the Pine River Channel site included copper fish hooks and a stone netsinker.

U.S. 31, as it passes the Little Traverse Bay area around Petoskey and Bay View, is near the prehistoric portage between the bay and the Inland Waterway system of lakes and streams that leads to the Straits of Mackinac at Cheboygan. Continuous use of this portage connecting lake and straits is evidenced by a site that was occupied at times from the Middle Woodland through the early Late Woodland Mackinac phase. People would camp in the shelter of the dunes.

The earliest inhabited land surface at the Portage site was covered by sterile windblown sand before another occupation took place. Such a stratified site is very useful for understanding different time periods. The artifacts and other materials in one stratum are certainly associated because they are isolated from those of earlier and later occupations (fig. 89). Passing through Charlevoix and gradually angling westward, we enter Little Traverse Bay.

10. Beaver Island, the Bay Villages, and Petoskey. About a mile and a half west of the first of the bay villages, Bay Shore, there is a fine view to the northwest of Beaver Island, which lies way out in Lake Michigan. About four miles from Bay Shore we have a fine view of Little Traverse Bay at Bay Harbor (second bay village). Petoskey, another old and beautiful resort city, lies about a mile along the highway from Bay Harbor, and the final of the three bay villages, Bay View, is a little more than a mile down the road.

11. Petoskey State Park (a diversion). To reach this fine state park, drive north from Petoskey on U.S. 31 for about three miles and turn left (north) on M-119. From this point it is about a mile and a half to the park entrance. Here one can beach-comb over a long expanse of fine white sand or climb on wooded dunes behind the beaches. The views of Little Traverse Bay are stunning.

Mackinac Ware ca. A.D. 750 to A.D. 1000.
Slab manufacture.
Smoothed-over cordmarked or cordmarked exterior surface. Retains motifs of rim decoration found on Pine River ware, but new emphasis on lip and interior decoration along with changes in lip shape and profile, and rim profile that make both lip and interior highly visible.

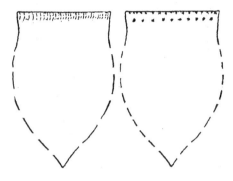

Pine River Ware ca. A.D. 650 to A.D. 750.
Coil or slab manufacture.
Plain or smoothed-over cord-marked exterior surface. Simplified decoration consists of band only, both borders only, or one border only.

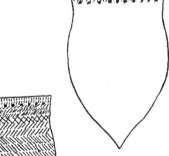

Late Laurel ca. A.D. 450 to A.D. 650.
Coil manufacture.
Plain exterior surface.
Dentate or linear stamp decorative band on rim with border at lip and at bottom of band.

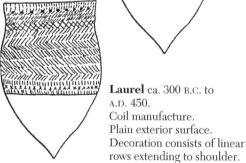

Laurel ca. 300 B.C. to A.D. 450.
Coil manufacture.
Plain exterior surface.
Decoration consists of linear rows extending to shoulder.

Fig. 89. Pottery sequence from Middle Woodland through early Late Woodland in northern lower Michigan. This pottery was found in a stratified context at the Portage site.

12. Middle Devonian Limestones and Fossils at Charlevoix and Petoskey. In the Middle Devonian (see fig. 6) the Michigan Basin (see fig. 8) was covered by a saltwater sea. Two limestone formations in the so-called Traverse Group, the Charlevoix Limestone in the Charlevoix area and the Petoskey Limestone in the Petoskey area, are the results of processes that went on in this Middle Devonian sea in what is now northwestern Michigan. Invertebrate fossils preserved in these limestones have been found in limestone quarries in both the Charlevoix and Petoskey areas, and sometimes remains of these fossils may be found on the beaches in the region.

Reef-forming stromatoporoids and corals are very common in the Traverse Group. Moreover, the reef-building coral *Hexagonaria* is the so-called Petoskey stone, which is the state "stone" of Michigan. *Hexagonaria* fossils represent the walls produced by soft-bodied, colonial animals called polyps. Do not let any Floridian tell you that there have never been any coral reefs in Michigan, although these Michigan ones existed countless millions of years ago. Bits of reef-building corals are probably the most common fossils found on northwestern Lake Michigan beaches and the shores of the larger lakes in the area. Moreover, bits and pieces of these corals that were carried by Pleistocene ice sometimes are found in fields in southern Michigan, or they might turn up in your driveway or even your backyard if commercial rocks or rock products have been unloaded on your property at one time or another.

Other rather common Middle Devonian fossils of the Traverse Group in northwestern Michigan include the shelled brachiopods and the stalked crinoids. Brachiopods are still represented in the world by the "living fossil" *Lingula*, and crinoids are animals known today as sea lilies. Sea lilies are actually related to starfishes and sea urchins. If you are lucky you might find circular bits of crinoid stems on lake beaches in northwestern Lower Michigan. The much-sought-after trilobites are not uncommon in rock quarries but are rarely found, at least in complete form, by beach-combing. Remember, one must get specific written permission and wear a hard hat to collect in rock quarries.

13. The Canadian Biotic Province, the "Emmet Island," and Giant Toads. At about the level of Harbor Springs on the north shore of Little Traverse Bay we finally leave the transition zone and enter the Canadian Biotic Province. We are now in the true "north woods." Emmet County is the most northwestern county in the Lower Peninsula of Michigan and comprises at once the northernmost and most prominent of the series of western bulges of the mainland into Lake Michigan. But Emmet County was cut off from the mainland by a wide channel in the Pleistocene Ice Age and was cut off again, probably for the last time, about four thousand years ago during the so-called Nipissing postglacial lake stage. By the Algoma postglacial lake stage about three thousand years ago, much of Emmet County was rejoined to the mainland.

As a boy before and shortly after World War II I (JAH) spent several summers on the north shore of Carp Lake (now renamed Paradise Lake) in that part of the shoreline that lies in Emmet County. There I observed the largest eastern American toads that I had ever seen at the time. Some toads were over four inches long, and one old male that hung out around the wood pile at the back of the cabin was as big as some of the giant "marine" toads that I was to see later in Mexico. Several journal articles have been written about the giant toads that live on various recent Lake Michigan Islands, both on the Wisconsin and on the Michigan side of the lake. One naturalist even suggested that the large island toads be given a separate scientific name that designated them a formal subspecies of the eastern American toad. Other scientists suggest, however, that since all toads have indeterminate growth (they grow as long as they live), that the "island effect" with its lower predation rates lead to greater longevity, and therefore to greater size. The presence of "giant toads" in Emmet County, Michigan, however, might indicate that actual genetic changes occurred in the toads of the former "Emmet Island."

14. A Long Regional Diversion, but It's Worth It! To view blue Lake Michigan from the high ground there is nothing like the M-

119 route around the western border of Emmet County through Harbor Springs, Good Hart, and Cross Village. I (JAH) have taken some of my European colleagues on this route and they have remarked that it has some of the most beautiful scenery in the world.

M-119 between Harbor Springs and the Straits of Mackinac is home to the Little Traverse Bay bands of Odawa. These Odawa (Ottawa) were important participants in the fur trade as allies of the French in the seventeenth and eighteenth centuries. Odawa corn and goods were traded to the northern Ojibwa (Chippewa) for furs that were then carried to Montreal to supply the demand for furs in Europe (see fig. 76). The Odawa moved to this area from their settlement around Fort Michilimackinac in 1742. The largest Odawa village in the region, Waw-gaw-naw-ke-zee (Good Hart or Middle Village), gave its name to the entire area. Waw-gaw-naw-ke-zee means "It is bent." Here, the name referred to a pine tree with a crooked top that was visible to anyone then navigating the Lake Michigan shore. This tree marked the location of the town. The French name L'Arbre Croche (Crooked Tree) was used by

Fig. 90. White sucker *(right)* and white sucker pharyngeal arch *(left).* The white sucker is not what most people consider a pretty fish, but has been and is an important warm-water food fish in Michigan that is especially tasty when it is smoked. The sucker pharyngeal arch (a tooth-bearing bone in its throat region) is used to grind up the food matter that is sucked up off the bottom by this fish. Sucker pharyngeal arches are often common on beaches and are interesting items to collect. (Drawings by Teresa Peterson.)

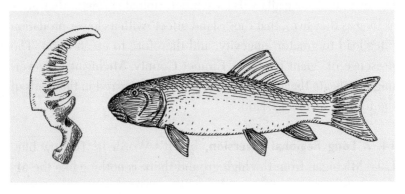

Fig. 91. Northern fishing. (Courtesy of Michigan State University Museum.)

both the French and the British to mean the entire west coast from Little Traverse Bay to the Straits of Mackinac, which encompassed other Odawa villages as well. During the eighteenth century, Waw-gaw-naw-ke-zee grew to about three thousand people. Gardens were planted and harvested at the village, but many families spent much of the year traveling to visit one another during the summer and to hunt during the fall and winter. Week-wi-ton-sing ("Small Bay Place," or Harbor Springs) and Cross Village grew around Catholic missions.

15. Carp Lake Village and Paradise Lake. Wending our way northwestward from Bay View (the last of the bay villages), we pass Crooked Lake on the right after about five miles and then turn due north again at the village of Oden. From this point to the Straits, U.S. 31 skirts the eastern end of what was at one time "Emmet Island." In proceeding from the village of Oden to the Straits we go through the villages of Alanson, Brutus, Pellston (with its small airport that traditionally brought well-to-do people from Detroit and

Chicago to the heart of the North Country), Levering, and finally the village of Carp Lake, which is about eight miles from Mackinaw City. From Carp Lake Village, large, shallow Paradise Lake can be seen from the road.

Paradise Lake was originally named Carp Lake by the Native Americans who equated the word *carp* with the word *sucker*, which is a native Michigan fish (fig. 90). Long ago, large white suckers were harvested during their spring runs by the native peoples of northwest Michigan and dried for consumption at a later time (fig. 91). Modern Michiganians often disdain the true carp, which is a European import, hence Carp Lake was changed to the name Paradise Lake after World War II. The villagers of Carp Lake, however, held on to the original name.

THE WEST-CENTRAL ROUTE

Indiana Border to Petoskey (U.S. 131)

Kalkaska to Petoskey

1. Young Lake State Park and Lake Charlevoix
2. Walloon Lake

Reed City to Kalkaska

1. Cadillac and Mitchell State Park
2. Manistee River
3. U.S. 131 Sites
4. Fife Lake
5. Kalkaska
6. Lake Skegemog

Grand Rapids to Reed City

1. Newaygo State Park
2. The Mason-Quimby Line

Indiana Border to Grand Rapids

1. The Lakes
2. The Prairies
3. Schoolcraft Area Mastodont
4. Plainwell Area Mastodont
5. Prehistoric Grand Rapids

Indiana Border to Grand Rapids

U.S. 131 runs almost straight north from the Indiana border to Grand Rapids, Michigan's second largest city, a distance of about eighty-five miles. In doing so it passes through Kalamazoo, home of Western Michigan University. The area features more lakes and woodlands than any other portion of the southern part of the Lower Peninsula.

In this traverse U.S. 131 passes directly through the heartland of southwestern Michigan. Much of southwestern Michigan is rolling country that is replete with lakes and ponds and has features ranging from marshy lowlands to wooded hillsides of beech-maple and oak-hickory climax forests. The woodlands are often associated with Wisconsinan end moraines (see fig. 15). Marshy lowlands where frogs are abundant occur in the valleys among the hills, and agricultural areas occur in the flat glacial lake plain areas in between.

The hills and valleys of southwestern Michigan contain reptile species that are uncommon or absent in other parts of the state. The eastern box turtle (see fig. 36) and the black rat snake occur in the wooded hillsides of the area, and the massasauga rattlesnake (see fig. 39) occurs in low, marshy areas. The box turtle is a wonderful example of the importance of diversity in nature. Box turtles regularly eat the fruits of may apples (fig. 92). The turtles digest the outer seed coats of the may apple fruits, but the seeds themselves pass through the box turtles' digestive tract and are spread out on the woodland floor by the wandering turtles. This makes the box turtle a true "Johnny Appleseed" of the woodland community.

The black rat snake is an often tree-dwelling snake that mainly eats small warm-blooded animals such as mice, which it kills by constriction. In Michigan it occurs only in the southwestern part of the Lower Peninsula. The massasauga rattlesnake can be rather abundant in some marshy areas in southwestern Michigan where it is probably more common than it is anywhere else in the state (it does not occur in the Upper Peninsula). As warm weather

Fig. 92. May apple. The May apple is a plant of the deciduous woodland floor. Its seeds are spread around in the feces of the eastern box turtle that can digest the seed coats but not the seeds of the plant.

approaches, this snake moves out of the lowlands into more upland areas, where it feeds on mice and voles.

Mammoths and mastodonts have been excavated from several Late Pleistocene sites in southwestern Michigan, especially from Berrien and Van Buren Counties (see fig. 78). These giant Ice Age animals are typically found in former glacial kettle holes that are presently filled with the black, mucky soil that represents what is left of the vegetational mats found in ancient quaking bogs. Mammoths and mastodonts are usually found when they are accidentally excavated by farmers who are plowing or laying drainage tiles in low places in fields, or by persons digging farm ponds or canals.

The midsections of the St. Joseph and Kalamazoo Rivers were surrounded by oak-hickory forests and scattered prairies. These forests and prairies were rich in plants and animals that supported prehistoric peoples and were sought out by early American settlers as well. The area had timber along with good soils for establishing farms. Additionally, the St. Joseph and Kalamazoo Rivers were sources of water and were transportation routes for shipping supplies. Constantine, a few miles north of the Indiana border, was a shipping point on the St. Joseph River.

The same factors of forests, prairies, water, and transportation were attractive to people long before 1818 when the U.S. Government Land Office opened in Detroit. The plentiful game, fish, and wild plants sustained hunting and gathering peoples in the past. At times people supplemented wild foods with domesticated plants. In the 1670s, Potawatomi and Miami planted gardens with maize, beans, and squash near their summer villages in this area.

The first east-west roads built by the American government were added reasons why this area was settled relatively early in the history of Michigan Territory. It is not surprising that these routes corresponded closely with important Indian trails used before American settlement took place. U.S. 12 generally follows the route of the Chicago Military Road that connected Fort Shelby at Detroit with Fort Dearborn at Chicago. The Chicago Military Road in turn is generally the same as the Old Sauk Trail used by the Indians to travel between the same places. U.S. 131 crosses U.S. 12 just west of White Pigeon, where a local land office was established in the 1830s. U.S. 131 itself takes the approximate path of a north-south Indian trail from near White Pigeon to north of Kalamazoo. A second east-west road farther north also eased western movement for settlers. This second road, which is roughly equivalent to the route of I-94, is a branch of the Chicago Military Road, and it too was in part an Indian trail.

FEATURES

1. Finding the Lakes (diversions). U.S. 131 passes mainly through a rather lakeless low ancient lake plain topography from the Indiana border for about thirty miles until it reaches the higher Kalamazoo moraine upland area near the city. But one can find the lake country within a few miles of the highway. First take U.S. 12 west about three miles north of the Indiana border and take county roads north after passing the M-40 junction. If one has a longer time for a lake diversion, one can take M-40 north to Paw Paw and I-94.

2. People and Prairies. The question of how prehistoric peoples used the small **prairies** crossed by U.S. 131 in St. Joseph and Kalamazoo Counties is intriguing. These prairies are small remnants of an extension of the "prairie peninsula" that was an expansion of the vast prairies of Illinois across northwest Indiana and into southwest Michigan during the warm period known as the hypsithermal (around fifty-six hundred years ago). As we have noted, the prairies were desired as agricultural land by American settlers in the region. The Potawatomi who lived in the area when the settlers arrived had villages and gardens oriented toward the prairies. That fact that the prairies were so important to Indians and settlers in the nineteenth century suggests that they may have been important in prehistoric times as well.

It has long been recognized that Middle Woodland mounds and sites in Michigan are strongly related to Illinois Havana-Hopewell. Because Havana-Hopewell sites in northwestern Indiana are located around upland prairies and the extensive Kankakee Marsh of that region, it is apparent that Middle Woodland peoples there were situating themselves to use the resources of both the prairie and the marsh. The Strobel site in St. Joseph County near U.S. 131 is a small Havana-Hopewell occupation site positioned so that the occupants, like those in Indiana, could use the nearby prairie and marshes along the St. Joseph River.

The Strobel site yielded ceramics that were very similar to Havana pottery from northwestern Indiana. Additionally, there was a chipped stone knife of a style like those found in Illinois. This knife along with small waste flakes from stone working were of white chert from Illinois.

The specific similarity in artifacts at the Strobel site with those from northwest Indiana Havana-Hopewell sites coupled with a similar potential for using prairie and marsh environments is a clear indication of a close relationship between the two areas. The Strobel site is easily reached by river from Havana-Hopewell sites in northwestern Indiana and from the centers of Havana-Hopewell in the central Illinois River valley. This river route runs from the Illinois River via the upper Illinois River and its tributary the Kankakee River to the St. Joseph River with a portage between the Kankakee River and the St. Joseph River at South Bend, Indiana.

While some Havana-Hopewellian peoples moved north along the Lake Michigan coast, Garland raises the possibility that sites like the Strobel site may indicate there was an interior route for Havana-Hopewell into Michigan. The south-to-north distribution of the prairies offered relatively easy passage in an area otherwise characterized by dense forests. Moreover, streams would be easier to cross in the interior, where they are not so wide as they are near the coast.

Large Indian villages were noted in the prairies of Kalamazoo County in the nineteenth century. Archaeological surveys found that the prairies themselves yielded very little evidence of prehistoric activity and no evidence of the historically recorded villages. Larger and more intensively occupied sites were found in bur oak openings around the prairies. It is likely that both prehistoric and nineteenth-century Indians made as much use of the open oak woodlands and nearby marshes as they did of the prairies.

In the last centuries before Indian contact with Europeans, people living along the St. Joseph River may have planted maize and other crops around their relatively large settlements, as they did in historic times, and used the Kalamazoo River in the spring to spear lake sturgeon and gather spring tubers. This late prehistoric period in southwest Michigan was a time of considerable movement of groups, however, so potential conflict may have discouraged secure and permanent, agriculturally based settlements. In fact, there are only three archaeological sites on the St. Joseph with clear evidence of corn cultivation.

Indirect evidence of prehistoric horticulture in the area occurred in the form of geometric-shaped ridged fields known as **garden beds.** These features consisted of earthen ridges about one and a half feet high and were reported to have been laid out in various formal shapes such as wheels and triangles, with spokes and patterned squares with the ridges facing first one way and then the other (fig. 93). Large garden beds associated with the prairies were observed by early settlers in St. Joseph County, and more of them were noted in Kalamazoo County than anywhere else in the state. As these features were not in use by local Indians, who planted their corn in hills, they were apparently prehistoric in age. All of them are now destroyed. Despite an active search for any remnants by archaeologists at Western Michigan University, there was no trace of the garden bed remnants in locations where they were historically known.

The function of the garden beds does not reflect their name, which is derived from their formal layout like that of a European garden. Rather, experiments with garden beds constructed by researchers at the University of Illinois showed that temperature differences between the top and bottom of the ridges would protect plants such as maize from an unpredictable early frost. The distribution of garden beds in Michigan and Wisconsin rather than more southerly states in the Midwest suggests that in fact they

Fig. 93. Garden beds, ridged fields. (Modified from Hinsdale 1931.)

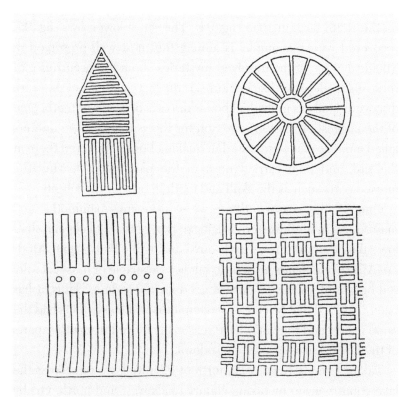

were used for gardening in areas where there was a distinct possibility of an early frost. Ridged field gardening occurs in other parts of the world for similar reasons. Excavations of garden beds (ridged fields) in Wisconsin support the idea that they were used for horticulture.

3. Schoolcraft Area Mastodont. About thirteen miles south of the I-94 and U.S. 131 junction, one comes to the town of Schoolcraft, where, nearby, a mastodont find occurred in 1995. The bones were found when a local family was digging a canal that extended from their farm pond. Muck and marl were turned over and several parts of a mastodont were found, including a splendid molar tooth.

4. Plainwell Area Mastodont. About eleven miles north of Kalamazoo we pass the M-89 junction to Plainwell. Near Plainwell, in Gunplain Township, one of the more complete Pleistocene mastodonts discovered in Michigan was unearthed in a ditch dug on the Keith farm in 1945 (fig. 94). The set of lower jaws (fig. 95) recovered with this animal is among the most well preserved in Michigan. One of the unsolved mysteries about the occurrence of these giant, elephant-like creatures is the fact that most of them are discovered only as individual bones or parts of bones or teeth. One of the suggestions as to the reason for this is that Ice Age hunters killed animals that were mired in quaking bogs, butchered them at the site, and then carried most of the parts away, leaving the unused parts such as the skull and teeth in or near the kill site.

One of the reasons there were so many mammoths and mastodonts in southwestern Michigan is because salt licks and shallow saline water occurred in the area during the Pleistocene. Modern African elephants must have salt licks available or must eat salty soil because they have a critical need for the sodium. Thus, it has been reasoned that Michigan's mammoths and mastodonts had the same needs, and they may have seasonally moved from other parts of the Great Lakes to store up sodium.

Taking County Road A-25 north of Plainwell, we can access the lake country again by taking county roads west and north. Or, by

Fig. 94. The Keith Farm mastodont skeleton near Plainwell (Allegan County, southwestern Lower Peninsula) resting on the surface after excavation. This skeleton was purchased by Michigan State University in 1940. It is one of the most complete of the many mastodont skeletons found in the state. (Courtesy of Michigan State University Museum.)

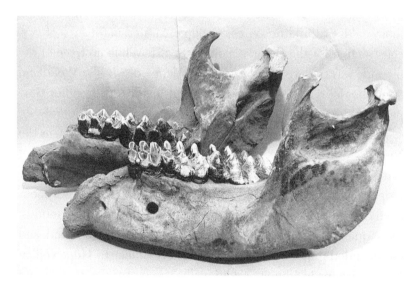

Fig. 95. The stabilized and prepared set of lower jaws of the Keith Farm mastodont, in the Michigan State University Museum. (Courtesy of Michigan State University Museum.)

continuing on M-89 about sixteen miles east of Plainwell, we can view Gull Lake, a long, deep, glacially gouged out lake. Gull Lake is the headquarters of the Michigan State University Biological Research Station. Gull Lake is one of the few inland lakes in southern Michigan that is deep enough to be temperature-stratified; thus it is an excellent place to conduct aquatic research.

5. Prehistoric Grand Rapids. When nineteenth-century settlers arrived in what is now Grand Rapids, they looked upon a large village of Ottawa (Odawa) Indians, who referred to the area as **Bow-a-ting,** meaning "rapids" of the Grand. Groups of Ottawa resided in various places along the Grand River, and many still live here. Nearly two thousand years ago, Hopewellian Middle Woodland people buried their dead in the same place where the Ottawa had their wigwams and later Americans built their city. Nearly twenty-nine Hopewell burial mounds, known as the Converse Mounds, were in present-day downtown Grand Rapids. They were destroyed by the construction of the city. Recently, archaeologists from Commonwealth Cultural Resources Group excavated in the area of new construction for the S curve along U.S. 131. While no trace of the mounds was uncovered, there was evidence of Middle Woodland domestic debris along with artifacts and features from other time periods, indicating people camped in the area near the mounds.

A group of seventeen burial mounds near U.S. 131 known as the Norton Mounds were excavated in 1964 by the University of Michigan. These mounds were important for showing that Hopewellian peoples in the Grand Rapids region were closely connected to those in Illinois. At Norton, the structures of the mounds, the sequences in which they were built, treatment of the dead, and the included grave goods were specifically similar to Hopewellian mound groups in Illinois. Additionally, some of the pottery found in the mounds was brought from Illinois, and some was clearly copied. The Illinois connection in southwest and west Michigan prehistory is very important and is also evident today. As one Michigan archaeologist expresses this, just look at the distribution of the *Chicago Tribune* in Michigan. This connection will be most obvious if you look at the number of Illinois license plates on cars along this highway.

Hopewellian peoples did not come to the Grand River area simply to bury their dead. In fact, they came here to live and chose particular locations for their sites. Middle Woodland sites along the Grand River are often at the confluence with a stream or on well-drained sandy loam soils near poorly drained marshy floodplain settings. Such settings allowed people to have a base camp in close proximity to a variety of environmental zones from which they could obtain food throughout the year. The spring floods created backwater lakes where trapped fish could be readily taken. In spring and fall, migrating waterfowl could be found on the river and, at least in spring, on the lakes. When the spring floods receded, the muck soils left behind supported an abundance of seed plants that could be harvested in the summer. The extent to which people in the area harvested these plants is a question that is currently under investigation by archaeologists at Grand Valley State University. The oak-hickory forests in the uplands adjacent to the river provided nuts and acorns in the fall and were home to deer throughout the year. The resources in these environmental zones were so plentiful that it may not have been necessary to move frequently. Ceremonial sites such as the Norton Mounds, on the other hand, were located on higher ground and were often relatively near the base camps, as was the case at the Converse site.

Grand Rapids to Reed City

Running in a rather straight course from Grand Rapids, a distance of about sixty-seven miles, we find alternating Wisconsinan end moraines and outwash plains. Numerous lakes may be found just northwest of Grand Rapids and may be approached from M-55 to the north, but in general, in the highway area between Grand Rapids and Reed City, lakes are less common than in the southwestern part of the state. We cross the Little Muskegon River near Morley, about thirty-six miles north of Grand Rapids. This area is just east of a series of small lakes formed by dams on the river. An Early Woodland site was located at the confluence of the Little Muskegon River with the Muskegon River. Here also several Hopewellian mound groups and a village site were found and excavated by archaeologists from the University of Michigan. As was the case with the Norton Mounds in Grand Rapids, there were clear indications of affiliation of the people in this area with the Hopewellians of Illinois. Additionally, pottery similar to the Middle Woodland Tittabawassee ware found in the Saginaw Valley, and projectile points similar in style to the ones found in Saginaw are indications of relationships between the Middle Woodland residents of the Muskegon drainage basin and those of the Saginaw Valley. Traffic back and forth between these two regions may have made use of a portage between the headwaters of the Little Muskegon River and the headwaters of the Chippewa River. This portage, located a few miles east of Big Rapids (exit 139), allowed people to follow the Little Muskegon River to the Chippewa River at the head of a water route leading to the Tittabawassee River and Green Point in Saginaw.

FEATURES

1. Newaygo State Park (a diversion). This state park, about forty-three miles north of Grand Rapids, may be reached by taking the Morley exit and going west on Jefferson Road to Beech Road. Turning right on Beech Road, we reach the park entrance in about one-half mile. The park is associated with a body of water six miles long and about a mile wide called Hardy Dam Pond that was created by impounding the Muskegon River. Nice transition zone (see fig. 42) vegetation may be seen from the road in the park (fig. 96) and woodlands of oak, white pine, and aspen may be found near the impoundment, which contains walleyes, northern pike, bass, and panfish.

2. The Mason-Quimby Line. From the Morley exit to Reed City, a distance of about twenty-nine miles (in between we pass through

Fig. 96. Transition zone vegetation beyond the entrance of the Newaygo State Park

Big Rapids, home of Ferris State University), we are mainly in a transition zone between the deciduous forest of southwestern Michigan (Carolinian Biotic Province) to the mixed deciduous/coniferous forests of the north (Canadian Biotic Province). Reed City lies at just about the latitude of the imaginary Mason-Quimby line (see fig. 18). No mammoths, mastodonts, or other extinct Pleistocene vertebrates, common in southwestern Michigan, have been recorded north of the Mason-Quimby line in Michigan, although there have been some false reports.

Reed City to Kalkaska

Over a distance of about fifty-seven miles, angling somewhat eastward through Cadillac and Manton and then bending more sharply eastward to Kalkaska for the last fourteen miles from the Fife Lake exit at M-186, U.S. 131 traverses an area of low outwash plains and alternating high Wisconsinan end moraines, mostly trending in a southwesterly direction. Deciduous forest stands with a few conifers are to be found in the highlands, while the lower, recently cut-over areas typically have successional forests of aspen, white pine, red pine, pin oak, and maple. Coniferous swamps and leatherleaf bogs (fig. 97) are common in the many lowlands.

As we move north through the forests toward the Manistee River, there are few prehistoric archaeological sites. Important clues as to why there are so few sites come from the experiences of an extended family of eight Chippewa who hunted in the general area during the winter of 1763–64. The family who wintered here included Wawatam, the head of the household, and Wawatam's adopted brother, the English trader Alexander Henry. In 1763, Henry was taken prisoner by the Chippewa when they captured

Fig. 97. Leatherleaf bog in southeast Grand Traverse County (northwestern Lower Peninsula). Leatherleaf cover lies over sphagnum in low areas such as this. Stunted white pines, such as the ones seen springing up from within the bog in this photo, are rather typical in the area.

Fort Michilimackinac but was released to Wawatam's custody because he was kin to Wawatam. Henry's journal of his travels with his Chippewa family is an invaluable source for information about Indian life in the mid–eighteenth century, including a year's seasonal moves to obtain food to eat and furs to trade.

During the winter, Wawatam's family of eight traveled to their interior hunting grounds in this area presently crossed by U.S. 131. They hunted here because there were habitats supporting beavers, bears, and most importantly, deer. These habitats provided deer with evergreens such as white cedar for food and shelter from winter wind. Sloping landforms in the area also offered deer shelter from the wind.

At other times of the year Wawatam's family camped alongside other related households, but winter was a time when they hunted alone. Although their relatives were in the same general region, households normally dispersed across the landscape in the winter, when there was not enough food in one area to support large numbers of people. Thus, any archaeological remains from their camps would be less dense than if many people camped in the same location.

The family remained at their winter camp for about two months. This camp would have a conical wigwam, hearths, domestic equipment, and food remains. Because the ground was frozen during this period, there would be no archaeological evidence of stains, or postmolds, aligned in a circular pattern as would be expected from the wigwam. The remains of hearths should be found along with a few lost artifacts and bones from animals eaten. Since winter storage was often on scaffolds rather than in pits dug into the frozen ground, there would be little evidence of storage at a winter site.

Henry's experience shows why there is near absence of prehistoric sites here even though it is an area where winter food would likely have been found. If prehistoric people used the area in the same way for winter hunting, the combination of scattered households, short-term camps, and frozen ground would leave little in the way of archaeological evidence. The likelihood that this area was a winter hunting ground, particularly in the Late Woodland, explains the near absence of prehistoric sites here.

There are indications that Henry's description of a seasonal round in northern Michigan is quite accurate with regard to Late Woodland times. The distribution and nature of northern Late Woodland sites is comparable to what might be expected from Henry's account of an economic year. Thus, the archaeological record seems to show a great deal of continuity in subsistence and settlement from the Late Woodland into the Historic period, and Henry's journal has proved very useful in projecting a way of life backward in time.

Unlike Indian winter hunting camps, there should be abundant archaeological evidence for late-nineteenth- and early-twentieth-century homesteads in the area. These homesteads are apparent on county atlases from the period and are recognizable archaeologically by trees such as cottonwoods and apples or lilac bushes that were planted by families settling here. Sometimes there are openings in pine plantations where a homestead stood.

The lumbering era in the region ended at about the turn of the last century. Railroads and local communities that had served the lumber industry were faced by the need to revive the economy. Farmers were offered the opportunity to purchase land at low prices in the hopes that agriculture would become the new economic base. Unfortunately, where land was available, the soils were poor for farming, as was the variable weather. Many of these farms failed, and the farmers moved on to other regions.

The archaeological record of homesteads provides an excellent opportunity to understand **homesteading** as a way of life. As agriculture alone could not sustain farm families, there should be archaeological evidence that the farmers here combined agriculture with work as wage laborers in the remaining lumber camps and mills, plus hunting and picking wild blueberries.

FEATURES

1. Cadillac and Mitchell State Park. About twenty-seven miles north of Reed City, the prosperous city of Cadillac is blessed with two excellent fishing and recreational lakes, Lake Mitchell and Lake Cadillac. Lake Mitchell is a large lake slightly to the west of the city, and Lake Cadillac is a smaller body of water adjacent to and somewhat surrounded by the city. To reach Mitchell State Park, take M-115 to the west to the park entrance. Much of the park occurs as an isthmus that lies between the two lakes. Walleyes, bass, northern pike, and panfish occur in both lakes, but Cadillac is known for its walleyes and Mitchell for its bass. Trails pass through areas where waterfowl and other bird-life may be observed.

2. Manistee River. About 18 miles north of Cadillac (about 6.5 miles north of the village of Manton), after crossing an upland moraine, we come to the famous Manistee River (fig. 98). The Manistee originates northwest of Kalkaska and winds its way in a southeasterly direction to Lake Michigan at the town of Manistee. The river is home to a variety of fishes ranging from walleyes to brown trout, as well as mink, beavers, and other wildlife. It is one

Fig. 98. Manistee River in northwestern Missaukee County, northwestern Lower Peninsula

of the rivers in the state that supports a small population of wood turtles, presently very uncommon in most of the United States. Wood turtles nest on sandy banks near the river. During the warm months of the year wood turtles wander through the woodlands eating a variety of plant and animal food. This species is protected by law in Michigan.

3. Sites along U.S. 131. The results of an archaeological survey conducted by archaeologists from Michigan State University along U.S. 131, from Cadillac to just north of the Manistee River, indicate that in this area in the interior high plains of Michigan, Indians hunted in winter, logging dominated the last decades of the nineteenth century, and homesteading the cut-over land met with only limited success. The high plains were forested in white pines and hardwoods such as oak, maple, and yellow birch. The area is quite high, as the steep and rolling moraines here reach elevations between 1,000 and 1,500 feet above sea level.

Only one prehistoric artifact was found on this survey which covered fifty-six miles of proposed right-of-way. This artifact was a small waste flake from stone tool working. These results are to be expected from an area devoted to winter hunting by small groups of people.

A variety of logging-related sites was found, however, including small camps, railroad grades, and a train "connecting" area. These lumbering sites are associated with the era from about 1871 to about 1900 when logging of the white pine forests was the main industry. Both Cadillac (1871) and Manton (1872) grew after the Grand Rapids and Indiana Railroad line provided transportation to and from the area. Direct connections via the railroad were critical to the lumber industry, as was the invention of the narrow gauge railroad in the 1870s. The narrow gauge railroads allowed companies independence from using waterways to transport their logs. Instead they could carry logs by rail to mills in Cadillac and Manton.

The railroad grades found as archaeological sites were concentrated near Cadillac and Manton. Railroad lines were probably not so common near the Manistee River, where logs could be floated downstream to the mills. There were also a few relatively small logging camps, as evidenced by depressions in the ground where structures stood. All of these camps were associated with railroad grades.

Cadillac continued to grow after 1887 when a second railroad, the Toledo, Ann Arbor and Northern Michigan line, came to the town. About 1900, when the white pine was virtually gone and lumber companies were moving elsewhere, Cadillac began to expand its economy to include industries related to the hardwood timber still available. For example, hardwood flooring, hardwood veneer, wooden handles, and wood alcohol were products made in Cadillac. In addition, locals hoped that agriculture would replace lumbering in the economy.

Plenty of cut-over land was available at low prices for homesteaders to build farms. Lumber companies were anxious to get rid of land no longer useful to them. Unfortunately for the homesteaders, most of the land consisted of excessively drained sandy soils that were unsuitable for farming. It is not surprising that the archaeological survey of U.S. 131 in this area found the remains of fourteen homesteads that were abandoned in the earlier decades of the twentieth century.

4. Fife Lake. North of Manton we enter an upland area that represents a very extended Wisconsin moraine of the Port Huron system that trends in a generally southwestward direction, from Gaylord to the northeast, to Manistee at Lake Michigan to the southwest. This moraine may be encountered in the form of an elongated ridge east of U.S. 131 from Fife Lake to Kalkaska, but it cannot be seen from the highway. Fife Lake itself (fig. 99) is a small, round, moderately deep lake that is known for its walleye fishing. It is rather typical of many of the smaller lakes in the northern part of the Lower Peninsula. It can be viewed about a mile from U.S. 131 by making a right turn at the junction of M-186 and U.S. 131. Loons are common and nest on or near Fife Lake. Their nesting area on the lake is protected by the MDNR. Bald eagles may sometimes be seen soaring over the lake looking for fish that are swimming near the surface of

Fig. 99. Fife Lake in southeastern Grand Traverse County (northwestern Lower Peninsula) has been greatly improved by a sewer system that replaced the septic tanks that previously allowed seepage and over-enrichment in the lake.

the water. Beaver lodges and ponds (see figs. 51 and 52) are common in the vicinity of Fife Lake. Beavers modify local environments by building dams that impound water. Trees are killed by drowning (see figs. 51 and 52), large ponds are formed in previously pondless areas, and existing plant associations are modified. Fig. 100, taken near Fife Lake, shows a leather-leaf bog association (in background) that is changing to a bunch grass–dominated community laced with canals due to the activity of beavers.

Late Woodland mounds and a campsite have been found near Fife Lake. These mounds were characteristic of the early Late Woodland period, and the pottery found here was similar to pottery found in the Saginaw Valley and elsewhere in southern lower Michigan. It is probable that Late Woodland people followed the river routes and trails to camp here in the winter, and here too, they buried their dead.

5. Kalkaska. From Fife Lake to Kalkaska, a distance of about fourteen miles, U.S. 131 angles northeast, and we find ourselves in a low outwash plain between two extensive morainic systems. Here the vegetation is mainly aspen, birch, and small jack pine. Many naked birch trees attest to an outbreak of gypsy moths in the mid-1990s. Kalkaska is of interest because it is mainly a typical small northern town without the usual tourist trappings. It is presently a local shopping center and was founded as a trading center during the lumbering days. Some original, mainly unrestored buildings may be seen near the railroad tracks. On the right side of the road near the center of town (in front of the Kalkaska Historical Museum) stands a famous Michigan landmark, a very large and brightly painted statue of a brook trout (Michigan's state fish) leaping into the air.

Fig. 100. Flooding caused by beaver activity in a former leatherleaf bog. This is a reversal of the ecological succession that was taking place in the absence of beavers.

6. Lake Skegemog (a diversion). Taking M-72 west from the north part of Kalkaska for a distance of about 7.5 miles, we may view the taiga-like vegetation that surrounds the south edge of Lake Skegemog from an observation point from near the top of the Greatlakian Moraine (formerly called the Valders Moraine); continue down M-72 and drive out on Skegemog point, a Paleo-Indian and Woodland Indian area, and see Lake Skegemog close at hand. The observation point is on the left side of the road (going west) and is near the crest of the Greatlakian Wisconsinan end moraine. This moraine represents an ice advance that took place 11,700 years ago. An informational sign discusses the vegetation and physical features of the area. Continuing west for about a mile, turn right on Skegemog Point Road to wind down to the lake itself. The late Paleo-Indian Samels Field site (see figs. 67 and 68) was located on the high ridge overlooking Lake Skegemog. Late Woodland peoples occupied the ridge below that from about A.D. 600 to 1500. A boat-launching area on this road allows one to approach the lake directly. A lush vegetation of ferns, horsetails, and other primitive plants lines the edge of the parking place for boat trailers. We have seen eastern garter snakes (see fig. 33) and brown snakes in this area.

Kalkaska to Petoskey

The route from Kalkaska to Petoskey, a distance of about forty-nine miles, passes through glacial outwash plains for a few miles before traversing the hilly morainal country south of Petoskey. Limestone quarries at Petoskey have yielded nice invertebrate fossils (see preceding route).

FEATURES

1. Young Lake State Park and Lake Charlevoix (a diversion). From the Boyne Falls exit about 15 miles south of Petoskey take M-75 northwest to Boyne City and go 2.5 miles northwest to Boyne

City on Boyne City Road to the park entrance. After a long drive through the park woodlands we finally come to beautiful Lake Charlevoix and its extensive sandy beach. This huge lake is home to cold-water fishes such as rainbow, brown, and lake trout as well as smallmouth bass and yellow perch.

2. Walloon Lake. Another large, beautiful lake, hook-shaped Walloon Lake, may be accessed quickly by taking M-75 south from U.S. 131 about eight miles south of Petoskey. One Late Woodland site on Walloon Lake was situated in a habitat uniquely suited for maple sugaring.

THE CENTRAL ROUTE

Indiana Border to Mackinaw City
(I-69 to U.S. 27 to I-75)

Clare to Mackinaw City

1. The Mason-Quimby Line
2. "Disappearing Hills"
3. Wilson State Park
4. Houghton Lake Basin Lowlands and Houghton Lake
5. South Higgins Lake State Park
6. North Higgins Lake State Park
7. Grayling and the Au Sable River
8. Hartwick Pines
9. Otsego Lake State Park
10. Wolverine and the Sturgeon River
11. Burt Lake State Park
12. Paradise Lake
13. Wilderness State Park
14. The Straits of Mackinac

Lansing to Clare

1. Roadside Ponds
2. Sleepy Hollow State Park
3. Ancient Occupation
4. Ancient River Bed
5. Maple River Wildlife Flooding Area
6. Oil and Gas
7. Transition Zone

Indiana Border to Lansing

1. Late Woodland Earthwork
2. Hunting Camp
3. Wetlands
4. Nineteenth-Century Settlement
5. Plank Roads

Indiana Border to Lansing

I-69 angles northeast from the Indiana border to Lansing, the capital city of Michigan, where it joins U.S. 27 north of the city, a distance of about eighty-seven miles. This stretch of road passes through or near Coldwater, Marshall, Olivet, Charlotte, and Potterville. This part of the central route traverses a somewhat varied topography of rather low moraines and outwash plains interspersed with some very narrow bands of flat glacial lake plain sediments. Nice second-growth deciduous woodlands are common along this pleasant route, especially from the Michigan border to Olivet, and numerous small lakes occur from just north of the Indiana border to about the level of Coldwater.

One sees the first of these just across the Indiana-Michigan border, where two small natural lakes may be viewed from the car window The dominant lakes from the Michigan border to Coldwater are a chain of lakes beginning with Coldwater Lake, the largest, and continuing north-northeast to about the level of Coldwater. None of these may be viewed from the highway, but they may be reached by a very short diversion. Take the first exit right from the interstate onto Copeland Road, then the first left off Copeland (Quimby Road), and a left on Miller Road just past a road to the left to Canada Shores.

This route near the center of the state is where east and west meet in Michigan. Here, near the Indiana border, we are at the upstream end of the St. Joseph River. There is evidence that this area saw some incursion of prehistoric peoples (with pottery styles normally found in southeast Michigan) who occupied defensible locations about A.D. 1200. One site suggestive of this movement from the east not only had an abundance of eastern-style pottery but also was set in an area that was enclosed, surrounded on three sides by wetlands, and had a horseshoe-shaped ditch. Earthwork enclosures, often with palisades and ditches, are rare in southern Michigan, although they do occur in parts of the northern Lower Peninsula and in the "thumb."

FEATURES

1. Late Woodland Earthwork. About three miles north of the Indiana border and about seven miles to the west another horseshoe-shaped earthen enclosure was built about one thousand years ago. This earthwork was on a low bluff overlooking water. A palisade of wood topped this earthwork in the upper reaches of the St. Joseph River. Although not much is known about this site, its location near a potential east-west boundary is interesting. Perhaps the earthwork was created for defense, for trade and exchange, or for ceremonial purposes. All of these suggestions have been made about the function of earthworks in Late Woodland society, but it would not be surprising to find that exchange or ceremony took place in a border area between two groups.

2. Hunting Camp. A site on the Grand River south of Lansing seems to have been used as a winter hunting camp, as many of the stone artifacts were projectile points, and 89 percent of the abundant animal bones here were from deer and other mammals. Some fish remains suggest the site was used in the early spring as well. Most of the pottery shows that this winter camp was mainly visited by early Late Woodland peoples who spent much of the rest of the year in the Saginaw Valley.

At this site there were also ceramics of a style usually associated with the Straits of Mackinac region and, in addition, ceramics like those found along the Kalamazoo River. Since the site on the headwaters of the Grand River is also near the headwaters of the Shiawassee and Kalamazoo Rivers, it is very possible the mixture of ceramic styles was left not only by the winter residents but by people who were passing through while traveling from one side of the state to the other. Additionally, as this headwaters region was shared by Ottawa and Ojibwa hunters in historic times, it may also have been shared twelve hundred years ago during the early Late Woodland. The northern Straits pottery in particular may have been left by people hunting outside their usual range.

3. Wetlands around Greater Lansing. Lansing was built in a basically flat area supporting lots of marshes, bogs, and boggy ponds. Glacially related uplands are not common in the vicinity of the capital city. On the other hand, the wetlands of the area are of much interest. Low woodlands (fig. 101) that become flooded in the spring are excellent places for salamanders and wood frogs (see fig. 20) of the woodland floor to breed. Moreover, small, permanent bog lakes and ponds in the area (fig. 102) are good habitats for green frogs (see fig. 24), Blanding's turtles (see fig. 29), painted turtles (see fig. 27), and snapping turtles (see fig. 26). North of the East Lansing area lies what is left of a very large feature that was once Chandler Marsh. This huge marsh provided habitats for many kinds of animals, including a large population of massasaugas, but it is now an area mainly taken up by large sod farms. Remains of large ancient vertebrates have been discovered in or near various marshy or boggy settings in the area.

An ancient bog a few miles northeast of East Lansing, near Shaftsburg, was so extensive that it was utilized as a commercial peat-producing venture for many years. Not only did it produce peat in abundance, but a very interesting vertebrate fauna (assemblage of animals) that lived in the area about fifty-eight hundred years ago was found beneath the mined peat layer in muck and marl. Here a Michigan State University Museum group, with the help of the MSU Museum Junior Explorers Club, excavated the remains of numerous elk (wapiti; see fig. 61) as well as fishes, musk turtles (see fig. 40), Blanding's turtles (see fig. 29), spotted turtles (now rare in the area, see fig. 35), and a duck. It was the first glimpse of animal life of this time period in central Lower Michigan. These animals lived during the mid-Holocene (see fig. 6) warm period called a hypsithermal.

Extinct Ice Age mammoths and mastodonts in the Lansing area have been found near the edges of small bog ponds (fig. 103) in places where sedge grasses and small willows are presently growing. Moreover, the remains of a giant beaver were found when workers were digging a golf course pond near Michigan State University. Remains of another giant beaver as well as a mastodont and

Fig. 101. Flooded woodland near Lansing, an excellent place for wood frogs to breed in the very early spring. (Photo courtesy of James H. Harding.)

Fig. 102. Rose Lake near Lansing. This well-vegetated pond provides a good habitat for frogs and turtles. (Photo courtesy of James H. Harding.)

a very small type of deer were found when I-69 west of Lansing was being constructed.

Paleontologists often attempt to find the remains of previously reported Ice Age animals by poking around in the muck and marl with long metal probes in small ponds (fig. 104). One soon learns to recognize the bones of ancient animals from pieces of wood and rocks. Rocks make a "chink" sound when touched by the pointed end of a probe; wood makes a "thunk"; bones make a sound somewhere in between. Do not try this in your backyard!

4. Nineteenth-Century Settlement. A centennial farm (occupied by the same family for over one hundred years) near Lansing gave Michigan State University archaeologists an opportunity to study the material record of settlement in this area. Several buildings at this farm were moved in 1961 when the property was crossed by the I-69 right-of-way. When a second construction of the right-of-way was proposed for 1980, land and buildings were again affected.

Fig. 103. A pond that is in the process of filling in. The area in the foreground of this pond is typical of where mammoth or mastodont remains might be recovered in this part of the state (Ingham County, central Lower Peninsula).

Fig. 104. Individuals from the Michigan State University Museum probing a small pond near Lansing for mastodont remains

Test excavations were conducted at the farm before construction took place. The archaeological work coupled with written records of the farm and remembrances (oral history) by the family and their neighbors created a picture of a century of life on a mid-Michigan farm.

Structures and foundations for structures at the farm supported other information that this family practiced mixed farming. They raised cows, sheep, hogs, and chickens. Wheat, corn, oats, and hay were planted. In addition to this combination of farm products, the family emphasized particular animals or crops at different times depending on economic conditions, including local and perhaps national demand. For example, in the first decade of the twentieth century, huckleberries that grew in the marsh on the farm property were sold locally. Later, apple and peach orchards became a main-stay. After World War II, when roads to the Lansing area markets were expanded, dairying and hog raising were most important.

The primary farm products provided cash income for the family. In addition to these products, the other plants grown and animals raised made the farm family self-sufficient. A woodlot located on the farm contributed to this income and self-sufficiency by providing lumber for building the hip roof barn and maple trees that were tapped in the spring to make syrup for sale and for the family's use. Clearly, the practice of agriculture here was successful for over one hundred years because the farm family raised a variety of foods, made use of the marsh and woodlot on their property, and were flexible enough to respond to changing economic conditions and expansion of markets with the advent of better transportation.

5. Plank Roads. An indication of the difficulties of transportation during the early years of Michigan's statehood came to light when road construction workers in East Lansing unearthed portions of a plank road that had been covered by several episodes of paving. Plank roads were popular in the middle of the nineteenth century. These roads were made of local lumber and were operated by private companies who were responsible for obtaining the planks and building a road in return for the opportunity to profit by charging a toll to users of the road. It is no accident that the plank road in East Lansing was under Grand River Avenue, which has long been a major east-west thoroughfare.

Lansing to Clare

The distance from Lansing to Clare along U.S. 27 is about eighty miles. The new I-69 bypass turns due north at East Lansing, missing the congestion around DeWitt and St. Johns, and eventually passes near the larger cities of Alma and Mount Pleasant before coming to Clare, "The Gateway to the North." During the entire Lansing to Clare route we pass mainly through flat, lake plain country. The natural vegetation from Lansing to Clare is mainly composed of typical Carolinian second-growth deciduous hardwood forest, but our view of this vegetation is mainly confined to glimpses of woodlots, as this stretch contains one of the major farming areas of Michigan. A few miles south of Clare we encounter a very narrow vegetational transition zone between the Carolinian and the Canadian Biotic Provinces.

FEATURES

1. Roadside Ponds on U.S. 27 between Lansing and St. Johns. The highway between Lansing and St. Johns is a joy to take because the Michigan Department of Natural Resources has constructed some very nice roadside ponds that have markedly increased the biological diversity along this stretch of about twelve miles. Not only does one miss the congestion of the rapidly growing area north of Lansing, but one can see ducks, geese, and other waterfowl in the ponds. Moreover, red-tailed hawks and kestrels may be seen near the highway, and deer and large snapping turtles (see fig. 26) often cross the highway, frequently with disastrous results.

2. Sleepy Hollow State Park (a diversion). About seven miles north of DeWitt take the first intersection right (a DNR state park sign is there) and drive about five miles east to Sleepy Hollow State Park. This park is built around Ovid Lake (fig. 105), an artificial body of water that was produced by damming the Little Maple River. Shallow ponds near the lake are breeding sites for frogs in early spring, and from early spring through early summer painted turtles may be seen sunning on emergent objects (see fig. 50) in the shallow flooded area south of the spillway on the south shore of the lake. Sometimes painted turtles may be observed nesting very near the road shoulder (see fig. 27). Waterfowl may be abundant on this lake during fall migration time.

3. Ancient Occupation. U.S. 27 crosses the Looking Glass River, a tributary of the Grand River, near DeWitt. This river not only flows into the Grand River but is also not far west of the headwaters of

Fig. 105. Ovid Lake. Sleepy Hollow State Park (Clinton County, central Lower Peninsula) is built around Ovid Lake, whose bays and islands provide good habitats for various warm-water fish species.

the Shiawassee River, which is a route northeast to the Saginaw area. The Looking Glass River is thus a route toward the northeast as well as to the west in this central part of the state.

Artifacts from Paleo-Indian times through the Late Woodland have been found here. It appears that the Looking Glass River area was used mainly by people who spent much of the year near Saginaw, as the majority of artifacts are made of Bayport chert, which is found around Saginaw Bay. Sites along the Looking Glass River are not very large. In fact, many of these sites and others found in the moraines and till plains north of the river may more properly be termed "findspots." Thus, it is not uncommon to find isolated projectile points or a few waste flakes from resharpening tools with no other evidence of a site. Since projectiles are the most commonly found finished tools from all time periods and they are of Bayport chert, it seems clear that people from the Saginaw area came here fairly regularly to hunt and that these hunters came well prepared. For example, some years ago, near Round Lake some four to five miles to the east of the highway, a cache of Paleo-Indian artifacts was found. This cache consisted of several unfinished pieces (blanks or preforms), of Bayport chert. With only a little work the objects could have been shaped into fluted points so characteristic of spear points used nearly eleven thousand years ago (see fig. 67). These artifacts were apparently a ready supply for use as needed.

The kinds of locations chosen over eleven thousand or so years had very consistent characteristics. Virtually all sites and findspots near the Looking Glass and northward in Clinton County were on well-drained high ground, near permanent water, and normally near wetlands or marshes. It has been suggested that these upland marshes were very important to prehistoric hunters from the Saginaw Valley because the marshes were a stable source of game. Although there were extensive wetlands in the Saginaw Valley that were very important to the people living there, they could not always be counted upon as productive sources of food. The upland marshes near and north of the Looking Glass River remained relatively unchanged for several thousand years, whereas those in Saginaw altered through time. These predictable upland sources of food would have been particularly important in the winter when other foods were scarce.

As you drive through the mid-Michigan area between the Looking Glass River and the Maple River north of St. Johns, you will continue traveling through this ancient Indian hunting ground. Prehistoric people were careful hunters even as early as about 10,500 years ago when Paleo-Indians stopped on a knoll above a confluence of two streams. The mixed spruce, oak, and basswood forest setting was an optimal location for taking a variety of game such as caribou, and the extinct woodland musk ox. The streams and wetlands below the knoll may have harbored other late Pleistocene animals such as the extinct giant beaver. Finally, the stream confluence provided an avenue to move in several directions and, thus, gave more choices about where to go for a successful hunt.

This was Indian hunting territory through the early decades of the last century. The Ottawa who had their villages on the Grand River and its tributary the Maple came here to hunt, as did the Chippewa whose villages were along the Shiawassee River and in other parts of the Saginaw area. These two groups, one living to the west and the other to the east, used this headwaters region without conflict.

4. Ancient River Bed. Notice the relatively wide and flat terrain around the Maple River. In addition to the current floodplain, this flat land was formed when the Maple River was part of the **glacial Grand River** that connected glacial Lake Chicago and glacial Lake Saginaw between about 13,800 and 12,500 years ago, much as the Straits of Mackinac link Lakes Michigan and Huron today. Thirteen thousand years ago, however, glacial ice to the north covered the Straits of Mackinac and the northern part of Lake Huron. Lake Saginaw was formed by the meltwater from the retreating glacier, and drainage was to the west into Lake Chicago through this central Michigan waterway.

5. Maple River Wildlife Flooding Area. Shortly after leaving the St. Johns area, the new stretch of limited-access interstate highway narrows to enter U.S. 27 (which has a fifty-five-mile-an-hour speed limit for about seventeen miles until just north of North Star). Here we drive through low areas of muck soils (fig. 106) where windbreak trees bend sharply to the northeast, reflecting the prevailing southwest winds of the area. Look to the right just north of the Bannister Road exit, where we cross a bridge over an extensive wetland. This area is the Maple River Wildlife Flooding area, managed by the Michigan DNR as a habitat for waterfowl. The water of this wetland is maintained at different levels to promote optimum conditions for the birds. When open water is present, one can see the numerous moundlike masses of vegetation made by muskrats.

These are commonly called muskrat houses (see fig. 53). Great blue herons and other wading birds may be seen standing near the shore waiting for fish, and various species of ducks, coots, and grebes may be seen in season. Sometimes sandhill cranes fly overhead. On the west side of the bridge, a grove of tall trees to the northwest forms the background of the wetlands and is used by herons as a communal nesting site or rookery. From time to time one sees great egrets (fig. 107) standing at the water's edge in the alert "fishing position." This is a real treat for northern midwesterners. In late spring and early summer, wetland turtles often leave the water to search for nesting sites on land. Unfortunately, many painted turtles and some snapping turtles annually wander onto the highway over the Maple River Wildlife Flooding area, and dozens of their crushed shells may litter the highway.

Fig. 106. The flat country on U.S. 27 in northern Clinton County (central Lower Peninsula). Previous wetlands have produced muckland soils for agriculture. The windbreak trees in this photo are bent in response to the prevailing southwest winds of the area.

Fig. 107. The great egret. This large, white wading bird is associated with southern marshes and shallow lakes by most people. But this bird can often be seen from the car on U.S. 127 as it passes over the Maple River in the summer months. (Photo courtesy of Richard D. Bartlett.)

6. Oil and Gas in Central Michigan. From about Alma to Mount Pleasant, and then again south of Clare, oil-drilling rigs and oil pumps as well as oil and gas storage tanks may be seen at several places near the highway. Oil and natural gas accumulated in Michigan Basin rocks (see fig. 8) in the shallow seas of the Silurian and Devonian. Oil fields in Michigan (which is seventeenth in oil production in the United States) are often associated with fossil reef formations. The Porter Oil field is northeast of Alma, and the Mount Pleasant field is near that central Michigan city.

Oil originated by the decomposition of trillions of tiny organisms (plankton) that floated in ancient seas and other tiny organisms that lived in the sediments on the bottom. For oil or gas to accumulate for commercial use, three conditions must be met. There must be a permeable rock layer called a **reservoir** that not only holds the oil but allows it to flow freely, an impermeable **roof rock** such as shale that keeps the oil from escaping upward, and a **trap rock** system that keeps the oil from flowing sideways.

7. A Transition Zone. About five miles south of Clare we enter a transition zone between the Carolinian deciduous forest biota (biological assemblage) we have been viewing in the southern part of

Michigan and the Canadian mixed deciduous/coniferous forest biota that is typical of the northern part of the Lower Peninsula and the Upper Peninsula (see fig. 42). One begins to notice stands of birch in low areas and the increasing frequency of conifers. The soil becomes sandier and even the roadside and meadowland plants are composed of species different from those we see to the south. An abundance of road-killed porcupines begins at about this level in the state. Porcupine roadkills look like blackish, spiny lumps.

Clare to Mackinaw City

From Clare U.S. 27 runs almost straight north to I-75 (exit 244) just north of Higgins Lake. I-75 continues almost straight north to Mackinaw City, a distance of about eighty-five miles. Major towns passed are Harrison, Grayling, and Gaylord. The true north woods begins just north of Clare and extends throughout the rest of Michigan. We have left the Carolinian Biotic Province and narrow transition zone behind and are now in the Canadian Biotic Province, where the land is higher, the soil is sandy, and the weather is colder, not to mention the fact that conifer trees are much more abundant.

FEATURES

1. The Mason-Quimby Line. About four miles north of Clare we see a distinct rise in the landscape representing the high glacial moraines that characterize much of the northern Lower Peninsula. This particular feature represents a part of the Port Huron morainic system that resulted from an ice advance about thirteen thousand years ago. Here we also cross the hypothetical Mason-Quimby line (see fig. 18). No evidence of Ice Age vertebrate fossils and very little evidence of Ice Age Indian people have been found north of this line (see fig. 68). The vegetation north of the Mason-Quimby line consists of mixed deciduous hardwood and conifer forests and local derivations thereof. As we proceed north of Clare toward the Houghton Lake area we see stands of deciduous forest on high areas, stands of aspens and small white pines in disturbed areas, and birch, cedar, and tamarack in low areas and wetlands. This area is in the interior high plains of the lower peninsula. Few prehistoric sites are found here because the pine forests did not offer forage for deer and other animals sought by hunters. The region may have been used by winter hunters when deer were more likely to congregate, or yard, in sheltered locations where there were conifers to browse upon.

2. "Disappearing Hills." One of the best places in Michigan to appreciate the structure of Michigan moraines is a few miles north of Clare, where the first of many moraines to come suddenly looms ahead of us. But as we ascend this hill, what first appeared to be the crest of the hill suddenly becomes level land, as if there had been no hill there at all! This situation will happen again and again as we ascend and descend the moraines of northern Michigan. In fact, farther north some of the crests of the moraines ahead will seem more like mountain range ridges than mere moraines, but they will also "disappear" during the ascension process. This phenomenon occurs because of the overall lack of steepness that one finds in moraines compared to the true hills and mountains that one finds in such places as the Appalachian or Rocky Mountains regions, where the uplands were formed by massive uplifts of the earth or by volcanic eruptions.

3. Wilson State Park (a diversion). Take Business Route 27 one-half mile north of Harrison to Wilson State Park. This small state park is built around Budd Lake, one of the first natural lakes of the north woods. Budd Lake has the reputation for being a good fishing lake and is stocked with tiger muskies, a hybrid between northern pike and true muskies.

4. Houghton Lake Basin Lowlands and Houghton Lake. Eighteen miles north of Harrison and continuing north to the M-55 junction, we see intermittent wetlands that represent the Houghton Lake basin. The shallow wetlands around the lake form excellent early spring spawning areas for northern pike. To view Houghton Lake, turn right on M-55 at the Houghton Lake exit, and this natural body of water will soon be viewed on the left. Houghton Lake is a very large, shallow body of water especially known for its ice fishing shanty town called "Tip-Up-Town." A tip-up is a fishing apparatus baited with a large minnow or small sucker (see fig. 90) that dangles through a hole in the ice. A small flag "tips up" when the bait is seized by a northern pike, walleye, or other large fish. Dog sledding and snowmobiling are other popular winter sports on the lake.

Houghton Lake and Higgins Lake are situated at the headwaters of two west-flowing rivers, the Muskegon River and the Manistee River, and one east-flowing river, the Au Sable. These rivers were important to lumbermen for floating logs downstream in the spring. Prehistoric peoples also found this meeting of headwaters to be important for moving between the east and west sides of the northern Lower Peninsula. There was an opportunity to move in several different directions along these river transportation routes, and the variety of habitats in the vicinity of the lakes could be used for hunting, fishing, and gathering, so that people could camp here en route. Several sites have been reported in the area, including a number of Late Woodland earthworks. It is interesting that these earthworks, like some others in Michigan, were located in a setting where people from different groups could meet. Research by archaeologists from the University of Michigan suggests that one function of the earthworks was to provide a place for groups to trade with one another.

5. South Higgins Lake State Park (a diversion). About six miles north of the M-55 exit to Houghton Lake, the exit to the first of two state parks associated with clear, deep Higgins Lake occurs. To find South Higgins Lake Park go six miles east of U.S. 27 on Higgins Lake Road. Both the south shore of Higgins Lake proper and the small satellite Marl Lake are available to the visitor. This part of the larger lake has a very gently sloping bottom. Marl Lake is a good place for frog and turtle watchers.

6. North Higgins Lake State Park (a diversion). About 6.5 miles north of the South Higgins Lake State Park diversion, and shortly before the junction of U.S. 27 with I-75, one takes County Road 200 one-half mile east. There, beautiful Higgins Lake with its blue-green waters is surrounded by fine woodlands with literally miles of hiking trails.

The Civilian Conservation Corps Museum is located at North Higgins Lake State Park. This museum honors the thousands of young men who worked on a variety of public projects starting during the depression in 1933 and during part of World War II. It is appropriate that the museum was established here where the land was once covered by dense forests that were devastated by logging and the fires that followed. The pine forests of the region were of course, attractive to the nineteenth-century lumber companies. Millions of board feet of lumber were cut in these forests until there was little pine left and the companies moved on to other pine lands in the Upper Peninsula, Wisconsin, and Minnesota. The CCC "rescued" Michigan's forests by planting millions of trees in a massive reforestation project.

7. Grayling and the Au Sable River. Three miles north of the diversion we took to North Higgins Lake State Park, U.S. 27 merges with I-75 (exit 249). One bypasses Grayling on I-75, but about 7.5 miles north of the merger between U.S. 27 and I-75, one passes over the Middle Branch of the fabled Au Sable River. The Au Sable ultimately flows into Lake Huron near Oscoda. The Au Sable River was once the home of the **grayling,** a game fish known by its sail-like dorsal fin. The grayling, a relative of whitefish, trout, and salmon, is now extinct in the river. The Au Sable is a famous present-day trout stream, and the Au Sable River long boat is unique to the area. These long, narrow boats, guided by a punt pole, are specialized for trout fishing and have been produced by local boat-builders for years. The Au Sable is easily approached by means of several smaller roads to the east of Grayling. Scrubby jack pine forests are common in the area.

8. Hartwick Pines (a diversion). About 10.5 miles north of the I-75 Grayling exit, take exit 259 and drive east 2.5 miles on M-93 to the entrance of Hartwick Pines State Park. Here you will get an idea of the splendor of the pinelands that greeted the first explorers of the area. Both virgin white pine, red pine, and jack pine forests are available in this 9,672-acre tract of land. Both dense forest (fig. 108) and open woodlands (fig. 109) are available for viewing. The park features a 49-acre tract of virgin white pine and a nearby reconstructed logging camp that one may reach by taking the "Virgin Pines Foot Trail." Another footpath makes two crossings of the Au Sable River discussed in the section above. A variety of forest types may be observed in the rolling country traversed by this "Au Sable Trail." Grouse, woodcock, rabbits, deer, and bears occur in the park, and small designated trout lakes are available for fishing. Mushroom and berry patches are also available in season.

The Hartwick Pines Logging Museum is a central feature of this park where you can see at first hand a virgin stand of the white pines that were so prized by lumbermen in the nineteenth century. The museum has interpretive exhibits and logging camp buildings to show what life was like during the lumbering era.

9. Otsego Lake State Park (a diversion). Nine miles north of the I-75 Grayling exit we take exit 270 to Waters. We then go west a little over one-quarter mile and turn right on Old U.S. 27. A drive of about five miles takes us to Otsego Lake State Park. Otsego Lake is a long, glacially excavated lake with perch, pike, and tiger muskies, and is especially known as a good smallmouth bass lake. The shoreline is nicely wooded, but there are no formal paths or trails.

10. Wolverine and the Sturgeon River. About nineteen miles north of Gaylord, which is a couple of miles north of the north end of Otsego Lake, we come to the village of Wolverine (take exit 301 west off I-75). The name is a picturesque one, as Michigan is called the Wolverine State and University of Michigan athletic teams are the Wolverines (although wolverines are rather aggressive carrion

Fig. 108. A dense forest habitat at Hartwick Pines State Park

Fig. 109. A relatively open woodland at Hartwick Pines State Park

eaters that have been described by mammalogist Allen Kurta [1995] as looking like a cross between a large weasel and a small bear!). Wolverines have a powerful set of jaws and can feed on frozen carcasses as well as attack mammals larger than themselves, especially in the winter when their large feet enable them to lumber over the snow at a faster rate than their prey. Wolverines, however, vanished from Michigan over one hundred years ago.

The village of Wolverine is particularly known for another famous trout stream, the Sturgeon River, which is very swift in places. To find this picturesque northern river, go west off I-75 at exit 301, and you will cross the river before you get to the village.

11. Burt Lake State Park (a short diversion). Our favorite way to go to Burt Lake State Park is to take Old U.S. 27 north along the Sturgeon River about eleven miles to the state park entrance. Or one can take Indian River exit 310 west to M-68 and follow directions to the park from there. Burt Lake is Michigan's fourth-largest lake and is one of the chain of lakes that winds forty miles across the northern tip of the Lower Peninsula. This inland waterway (fig. 110) extends from Lake Huron inland through Mullet, Burt, and Crooked Lakes and local rivers to only three miles from Lake Michigan.

It seems that during ancient times when lake levels were high, this inland waterway cut the upper tip of the Lower Peninsula off from the rest of the state, creating an island mainly composed of what is now Emmet County. In the present "Emmet Island" we find some lower vertebrate species (some snakes and toads) either with different color patterns or of larger size than the same species in the southern part of the peninsula, possibly reflecting genetic changes that occurred when these animals were living in isolation.

The town of Indian River is located where Burt Lake and Mullett Lake are connected by a short stream, the Indian River. A number of sites have been found in this area, which was systematically surveyed and excavated by archaeologists from Michigan State University. Their research was directed toward understanding how prehistoric people used and moved through the Inland

Fig. 110. Burt Lake seen from a turnout on the crest of a portion of the Greatlakian morainic system (M-75, Cheboygan County, approaching the northern tip of the Lower Peninsula). The system of lakes in the area, including Burt Lake, formed an inland waterway from Lake Michigan to Lake Huron.

Waterway between Cheboygan at the Straits of Mackinac and Lake Michigan at Little Traverse Bay. Their work on ceramic styles in the Traverse Corridor, the northern extension of the transition zone between the Carolinian and Canadian Biotic Provinces, indicated that Late Woodland people there came from the south along the Lake Michigan coast, from the north along the coast, and probably from the northeast via the Inland Waterway.

The Johnson site on Mullett Lake provides an example of how people lived in this region and used the Inland Waterway in their seasonal round of fishing, gathering, and hunting. The Johnson site was occupied periodically by northerners for a long time. Laurel Middle Woodland ceramics were found there, as were ceramics from the entire Late Woodland, including Mackinac ware (A.D. 750 to 1000), Bois Blanc ware (A.D. 1000 to 1200), and Juntunen ware (A.D. 1200 to 1700).

A variety of habitats around the site would have offered subsistence in most seasons, but the site was probably most often used in the winter. In addition to the surrounding water, swamp, coniferous forest, and hardwood forest that would have been sources for food, the site was in a sheltered location. Northerners who lived in the Canadian Biotic Province usually spent the warm season along the Great Lakes coast. Their sites with warm-season indicators are found along the coast, including the Traverse Corridor. In the fall Late Woodland people in the region were also to be found at coastal sites, where they caught and preserved the fall-spawning fish that were critical to their mode of living (see fig. 91). The early spring would have been spent maple sugaring somewhere between winter and late spring locations. Thus, the Late Woodland seasonal round normally took people away from the interior in seasons other than winter, although this Mullett Lake site offered the option to be flexible in their choice of when during the year they would come to the area.

12. Paradise Lake. About eight miles south of Mackinaw City we pass a medium-sized shallow lake on the left, originally named Carp Lake by the native Michiganians and changed to the name Paradise Lake shortly after World War II. Carp Lake Village still exists on the west side of the Lake. Ironically, the native peoples equated the word *carp* with the word *sucker*, which is a native Michigan fish. Modern Michiganians disdain the true carp, which is a European import, hence the origin of the new and allegorical name.

13. Wilderness State Park (a diversion). This beautiful state park may be reached by taking Wilderness State Park Road west about a mile south of Mackinaw City. There are more than thirty miles of coastline in this park in this narrow peninsula that separates Sturgeon Bay from picturesque Cecil Bay to the north. There are miles of white sandy beaches and miles of trails to hike. Deer are plentiful and bears are occasionally seen.

14. The Straits of Mackinac Is Extraordinary (fig. 111). If you come to Mackinaw City in the summer, don't be distracted by the crowds of people wandering the streets, going in and out of the shops, and feasting on fudge. If you come here in the winter, don't be surprised at the small numbers of people living in apparent isolation. Whenever you come here, you are part of a pattern of human activity in this area that has been much the same for over one thousand years. There are differences, of course. A different language is spoken here now; goods are purchased by cash or plastic cards instead of exchange of one set of goods for another; and transportation is by automobile and motor-driven boats rather than by foot or canoe. The Straits is an east-west highway for people visiting or passing through as well as the closest north-south connection between Michigan's peninsulas (see fig. 76). Thus, the Straits is a place where people are likely to encounter one another, and these encounters are most likely to take place during warmer seasons.

Summer and fall are times of plenty when travel to visit and trade is easy. Beginning with the Late Woodland, about twelve hundred years ago, people living on both sides of the Straits settled along the coasts in the summer to fish, hunt, harvest berries and other plants, and, at times, to plant corn. These coasts at and near the Straits were the "home of the fish," and even before twelve hundred years ago, people located their sites in the best places for catching fish with nets or spears as well as with hook and line (see fig. 91). These sites could accommodate several extended family groups as well as occasional visitors. During the winter, the larger groups disbanded into smaller groups that moved away from the coast to support themselves by hunting as well as by preserved fish and other foods stored in preparation for the severe season.

This ancient pattern of living along the coast for parts of the year and dispersing inland during the cold seasons is one reason why the Jesuits decided to establish their mission at the Straits of Mackinac,

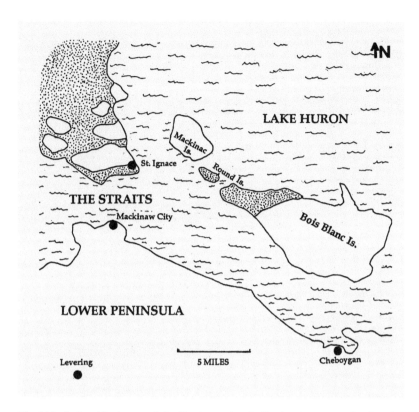

Fig. 111. A simplified map of the Straits region indicating important landmarks and islands and the bedrock geology of the area. Stippled portions represent Silurian bedrock area, and unstippled portions represent Devonian bedrock areas.

first at Mackinac Island and then on the mainland at St. Ignace. For similar reasons, the French government built fortified posts here, including Fort de Baude at St. Ignace and then in 1715, **Fort Michilimackinac** here on the south side of the Straits. Fort Michilimackinac State Park is a diversion well worth taking to experience the flavor of this place that was once the center of Great Lakes commerce and to see archaeology in action. Excavations take place at the fort every summer as part of ongoing research there by Mackinac Island State Park Commission archaeologists.

THE EAST-CENTRAL AND NORTHERN LAKE HURON ROUTE

Ohio Border to Mackinaw City (U.S. 23)

Tawas City to Mackinaw City

1. Oscoda, the Au Sable River
2. Earthwork Site
3. Harrisville State Park
4. Negwegon State Park
5. Alpena and Rogers City Quarries and Fossils
6. P. H. Hoeft State Park
7. Cheboygan State Park
8. Home of the Fish
9. Mill Creek

Saginaw to Tawas City

1. Bay City State Park
2. Bay City
3. Fossil Dunes and Dune Soils
4. Archaeology at an Environmental Edge
5. Mammoth Country
6. Tawas Point State Park

Ohio Border to Saginaw

1. Ditch Rats
2. Early Mills
3. Ancient Trail
4. Extinct Peccaries and Archaeological Site
5. Island Lake Recreation Area
6. Ancient Trail
7. Fenton Lake Fossils
8. Paleo-Indian Site
9. The River Systems

Ohio Border to Saginaw

U.S. 23 heads almost due north from the Ohio border through Ann Arbor and Flint, and then angles somewhat westward to the industrial center of Saginaw, a total distance of about 130 miles. Geologically speaking, the route from the Ohio border to Ann Arbor, a distance of about 43 miles, runs entirely over the glacial lake plains that cover most of the southeastern corner of Michigan. Thus this stretch of highway goes through one of the most intensely agricultural areas in Michigan where even small woodlots are scarce. In presettlement times, the area was wooded by oak-hickory and beech-maple climax forest of the Carolinian Biotic Province.

This route crosses the middle reaches of the River Raisin. Although there are few large archaeological sites here, people hunted the area for a very long time. It is not uncommon to find Early Archaic projectile points such as Kirk points with their distinctive serrated edges. These spear points testify to hunters being in the area at least ninety-five hundred years ago. Later points are also found to show continued use of this region.

This western part of Monroe County was settled somewhat later than other areas in the first three tiers of counties north of the Indiana and Ohio borders because the largely sand or clay soils here were less desirable for farming. Moreover, the roads built to encourage settlement were located to the north of this county.

In the vicinity of Ann Arbor the countryside becomes varied and interesting, as the drive on to Flint mainly passes alternating Wisconsin end moraines (one large enough to have been converted into a ski slope near Brighton at the junction of U.S. 23 and I-96), ice-contact stratified glacial drift deposits, ground moraines, and outwash plains. Woodlands along this portion of the trip are also more numerous with second-growth forests of mainly beech-maple visible along the roadside. Just south of Flint, I-75 and U.S. 23 become contiguous through Saginaw and the Bay City area all the way to the turnoffs to Standish near the north part of Saginaw Bay. From here U.S. 23 becomes a single route all the way to the Straits.

North of Flint the countryside becomes flat again where glacial lake plain topography is dominant until, in the Saginaw region, we cross a low section of the Port Huron Moraine. The Port Huron Moraine is the terminal moraine of the Port Huron ice advance that occurred about thirteen thousand years ago. Larger exposures of this moraine flank either side of the highway, which follows the glacial lake bed topography.

FEATURES

1. Ditch Rats. About eighteen miles north of the Ohio border, just south of Dundee, we cross the River Raisin, which is in the heart of the "ditch rat" country of southeastern Michigan. Ditch rats (called muskrats in most places), unlike beavers who like to create their own aquatic habitat, get along quite well in channelized streams and ditches in farmed land—and there are plenty of these in the area. In these types of habitats, ditch rats build bank dens, which are underground chambers located just above the waterline. One or more entrances to these chambers are hidden below the waterline. So when you startle a ditch rat (muskrat) swimming along, that is where he disappears to. Ditch rats are trapped in the River Raisin area in southeastern Michigan for both furs and food, and ditch rat dinners are popular there, especially nearer to Lake Erie.

2. Early Mills. U.S. 23 crosses M-50 at Dundee. There is a mill race on the River Raisin in the center of this pleasant old town. Virtually every early settlement in Michigan had a flour mill used by nearby residents. Often there were sawmills to supply building material, as well as a blacksmith and a general store. These early communities were relatively isolated, so that most commerce was local. Except for a few roads, the rivers were the major means of transportation.

3. Ancient Trail. U.S. 23 crosses U.S. 12 at Ypsilanti. There was a trading post here along the old "Chicago Military Road" that was the east-west link between Fort Shelby at Detroit and Fort Dearborn at Chicago. This was an ancient "highway," as the military road generally followed the Old Sauk Trail used by Indians to travel east and west. The Chicago Military Road is also approximately the same route as U.S. 12. The trading post at Ypsilanti was in a strategic location for east-west traffic not only because of its situation on the Chicago Military Road but because it was at an intersection with a second and more northerly east-west road built between Detroit and St. Joseph. This second road follows the approximate route of I-94.

4. Extinct Peccaries and an Archaeological Site from Ann Arbor. About twenty-six miles north of Dundee ditch rat country, we reach Ann Arbor, home of the University of Michigan and the Wolverines. On the university campus is a series of museums (all in one University of Michigan Museums Building) with excellent and detailed exhibits on archaeology, geology, paleontology, and zoology. These exhibits are certainly worth the short drive into the campus to see.

Crossing the Huron River at Ann Arbor, one passes near an important fossil site just east of the city and only about a mile from the Museums Building. Here, in fine sand, two little boys found bones adjacent to and just below the till on a hill deposited by the Outer Defiance Moraine during the Ice Age. Ultimately, more bones were found, until at last, the remains of at least three flat-headed peccaries were recovered. Peccaries are relatively rare finds in Michigan, and these bones consisted of three skulls and numerous other bones. Ironically, when the first peccary bones were brought to the Museums Building on campus to be identified, it was thought that they were those of domestic pigs. But it was soon realized that they were valuable Ice Age fossil peccaries over ten thousand years old. Ah, what little boys can find.

Ann Arbor is unusual among Michigan's cities because it has a local archaeological ordinance requiring a review of possible effects of proposed development on archaeological sites. The local effort to preserve archaeological resources covers projects that are not subject to federal law, as they are not federally funded.

The first application of the Ann Arbor ordinance occurred with the discovery and test excavations at site 20WA176. This site had features and artifacts indicating that it was used as a seasonal camp by Late Woodland groups, at least once around A.D. 800 and again around A.D. 1100. Very possibly the site was used between those times as well. On at least one occasion, people paused to bury their dead. Some of the groups at 20WA176 were hunters and gatherers who moved from place to place during the year, while others may have had semipermanent horticultural settlements elsewhere in the region. This short-term site use was indicated by a limited range of stone tools, pottery, and a few remains of nuts, tubers, and berries, and bones from a white-tailed deer and a sucker. One of the numerous features at the site was used as a smudge pit for smoking either fish or meat.

5. Island Lake Recreation Area near Brighton (a short diversion). Amazingly close to the greater Detroit area, the Island Lake State Recreation Area is a jewel, providing the Huron River, lakes, ponds, hilly woods, marshes, and open fields. To reach the area, take the I-96 exit from U.S. 23 east for two and a half miles and take exit 151 on Kensington Lake Road and drive about one mile south to the entrance. Soon after you enter the park you are greeted by gently rolling glacially deposited swells and swales, and by taking the various roads through the park you can find river, lakes, and ponds. On one visit to the park we saw numerous green frogs (fig. 112) in a marshy pond (fig. 113) and observed several painted turtles basking there.

6. Ancient Trail. U.S. 23 crosses I-96 at Brighton. I-96 generally parallels the same path as the most northerly of the east-west routes built to ease settlement of Michigan Territory. This road was the Grand River Road, which branched off from the Saginaw Road at Pontiac. Until Michigan became a state, this was little more than a trail and like the other east-west routes followed an Indian trail. Grand River is still the name of this road in many Michigan towns.

Fig. 112. Two green frogs fighting for position. Green frogs are territorial. (Photo courtesy of James H. Harding.)

7. Fenton Lake Fossils. About ten miles south of the junction of U.S. 23 with the I-69 exit east to Flint, Fenton Lake lies to the east of the highway. It can be reached by taking the Fenton exit east to Fenton; then at Fenton, take Business Route 23 north to the east shore of the lake. An unusual fauna of fishes, reptiles, and birds was found in the course of dredging operations on the east side of the lake. Ancient fishes, reptiles, and birds are quite rare in Michigan, and such finds excite the curiosity of vertebrate paleontologists, who hope they date back to the Pleistocene (Ice Age). But there is no evidence the Fenton Lake fossils actually do represent Ice Age fossils, as no radiocarbon dates are available from the site and no extinct Pleistocene mammals were found there. Fish fossils from Fenton Lake include a group of species that would be more typical of one of the Great Lakes than those of modern Fenton Lake and include lake trout, whitefishes, muskellunge, white suckers, long-nose suckers, carpsuckers, and walleyes. A softshell turtle was the only reptile in the Fenton Lake fossil fauna, and a duck and a bald eagle represented the birds. A guess is that these animals could range from a few hundred to a few thousand years old.

8. Paleo-Indian Site. As U.S. 23 approaches Flint, we are near one of the rare Paleo-Indian sites in Michigan. The Gainey site is the earliest (ca. 11,000 B.P.) and best-documented Paleo-Indian site in the state (see fig. 67). It has been carefully and extensively excavated by members of the Michigan Archaeological Society in consultation with archaeologists from the University of Michigan. Diagnostic "Gainey" fluted points are normally made of Upper Mercer chert, brought from eastern Ohio around the end of Lake Erie. This chert suggests Paleo-Indians at the Gainey site moved between Ohio and Michigan (see fig. 68).

The site was on a moraine that was probably in a spruce parkland. There was considerable biological diversity in the local setting, which included not only spruce but also hardwoods. Additionally, there was a nearby swamp or bog. Although the occupants of Gainey may have been seeking large game animals, the variety of habitats provided the opportunity to hunt other animals as well, and the Paleo-Indians at Gainey could have kept their options open.

9. The River Systems of Saginaw County. I-75 runs parallel to the Flint River as the highway passes north of the city of Flint toward

Fig. 113. Marshy pond at the Island Lake Recreation Area

Saginaw. This river flows north toward its confluence with the Saginaw River in the city of Saginaw. The highway crosses the Cass River just south of exit 144. The Cass River drains to the southwest through the "thumb" and, like the Flint River, joins the Saginaw River in the city of Saginaw. Two other rivers meet in the same location, the Shiawassee flowing from the southwest, and the Tittabawassee flowing from the north. These major tributaries are part of a radiating network of streams draining the Saginaw River Valley. The Saginaw River itself is a relatively short stream that empties into Saginaw Bay at Bay City. Archaeological sites have been sought throughout this extensive drainage system for more than a century, and over one thousand sites are known. It is clear that for a long time people lived and moved along these streams that provided access to the diverse and very productive wetlands and forests of the valley. Wild plant and animal foods were very abundant here, but they were scattered in "patches." Long- and short-term variations in water levels presented the people who lived here with the problem of potential failures in their food base that could not be predicted. To counteract this possibility of being without food, people would move to the margins of the valley, where the same foods were available but not so abundant.

Saginaw to Tawas City

The route from Saginaw to Tawas City, a distance of about seventy-seven miles, is mostly inland (although it closely follows the east coast of the state) until we reach Point Lookout at the top of Saginaw Bay. From this point to Tawas City the highway is near Lake Huron. Geologically, the highway mainly follows the flatter glacial lake plain topography all the way to Tawas City. Nevertheless, moraine features can be observed in the distance west of the highway from north of the Bay City area to about the level of Pinconning. From a biological standpoint, we leave the Carolinian Biotic Province and enter the transition zone at the level of Bay City State Park and leave the transition zone and enter the Canadian Biotic

Province at the level of Tawas City. This is a very much shorter transition zone than we find on the west coast of the Lower Peninsula (see fig. 42).

FEATURES

1. Bay City State Park (a diversion). A visit to the Bay City State Park is probably the best way to get an idea of legendary Bay County. To reach the park, exit U.S. 23 (which at this point runs together with I-75) north of Bay City on Beaver Road (M-247). An eastward drive of about five miles will get you to the entrance of the state park. A beach of fine sand stretches for almost a mile, allowing the visitor to study things washed up on the beach and view the bay. The shallowness of the bay water in this area is duly demonstrated, as you will find that the water is only ankle deep well out to at least one hundred feet. Saginaw Bay has produced a thriving freshwater fishery that includes such species as channel catfish, walleyes, and perch. Fortunately or unfortunately there are plenty of carp in Saginaw Bay and the waterways that emanate from it.

Bay City State Park has a nice interpretive museum, the Jennison Nature Center, off Euclid Avenue at the north end of the park. The nature center has about twenty permanent exhibits and several rotating seasonal exhibits that illustrate the geology and natural history of the Saginaw Bay area. They usually have interesting exhibits of live animals of the area, including local fishes, amphibians, and turtles. If you are a bird-watcher, just across Euclid Avenue to the west of the nature center, one finds the Tobico Marsh State Game Area, where over two hundred species of birds have been recorded. The game area also includes mammals such as beavers, muskrats, and deer.

2. Bay City. Bay City, at the mouth of the Saginaw River where it empties into Saginaw Bay, has been occupied by people at least since Late Archaic times about five thousand years ago. It is easy to see why this location has been important for so long. Not only is the area rich in fish and mammals but the town is at the confluence of two major transportation routes, Saginaw Bay and the Saginaw River. In historic times logs were floated through the Saginaw River system to the mills in Bay City. The processed lumber was then shipped through Saginaw Bay and Lake Huron to cities on the Great Lakes. At times, shipbuilding took place along the river.

Late Woodland people lived along the river in the warm season. There is evidence of intense activity here in the form of pottery, a variety of stone tools, debris from making tools, hearths, and deep storage pits. Clearly households gathered here in large numbers, probably for a season or two. A good deal of visiting probably took place at this time of year when there was plenty to eat and it was easy to travel. There is evidence in the form of northern pottery that northern neighbors did visit from time to time.

Late Archaic and Early Woodland sites were located on the higher ridge above the river. This ridge is a "fossil beach" from a high-water stage in the Great Lakes known as Algoma. The Algoma stage dates to about thirty-two hundred years ago, when the waters of Saginaw Bay would have been at the base of the ridge.

3. Fossil Dunes and Dune Soils. Fossil dunes and the sandy soils derived from them originated about ten thousand years ago during a time of high lake levels. These dunes are low compared to ones we have seen on the Lake Michigan shoreline in the western Lower Peninsula. Fossil dunes are especially abundant in the counties around Saginaw Bay, including Midland, Arenac (a few), Bay, Saginaw, and Tuscola. The stretch of highway where U.S. 23 and I-75 run together from just west of Bay City to the junction near Standish, where U.S. 23 becomes a single route again, passes over an area of fossil dunes, fossil dune remnants, and soil derived from them. Actually, the soils produced by these fossil dunes are very uniform from place to place and are both acidic and slightly salty in nature.

The distribution of many kinds of plants and animals is spotty in Michigan, and it is popular to attribute this pattern to the elimination and fragmentation of habitats by humans. This is all well and good, but one must remember that plant and animal habitats were quite recently (in the geological sense) obliterated by Pleistocene ice masses and then reoccupied in a rather helter-skelter way by plants and animals as the ice withdrew and finally melted away. Thus we still have at least two processes going on aside from those caused by human agencies: (1) some plants and animals are still continuing to reoccupy new habitats (some species more than others), and (2) other species have been left in relict habitats left over from the long warm spell (hypsithermal) that occurred about fifty-six hundred years ago. The fossil dune areas around Saginaw Bay may be such a relict habitat, particularly insofar as amphibians and reptiles are concerned.

For instance, mole salamanders are burrowing species that do not occur in the Saginaw Bay area fossil dune field (contrary to the generalized maps in popular field guides), although at least three species occur in surrounding areas. Burrowing amphibians with moist, permeable skins that tend to absorb all kinds of substances would presumably be intolerant to the acidic and salty sand in which they would have to burrow if they lived in the area. On the other hand, the six-lined racerunner lizard, found in a single population in Tuscola County, does not occur anywhere else in Michigan. The six-lined racerunner lizard is partial to dry, sandy soils, and the nearest population occurs on the sandy shores of Lake Michigan in northwest Indiana.

4. Archaeology at an Environmental Edge. As the highway heads north around Saginaw Bay near Pinconning, it passes near an interesting site in the rather narrow transition zone between the Carolinian and Canadian Biotic Provinces. This site, known as the Butterfield site, was occupied during the winter in the Late Archaic and Late Woodland periods. The Late Woodland component has nearly equal numbers of early Late Woodland Wayne ware vessels and early Late Woodland Mackinac ware vessels. Since Wayne ware was made by people who regularly lived in the Saginaw Valley and Mackinac ware was made by northerners who usually lived near the Straits of Mackinac, it is clear that two groups used this area near an environmental boundary (see fig. 73). Apparently this joint use was without conflict, although it is not known whether both groups were at the Butterfield site during the same winter season.

5. Mammoth Country. Sites in Arenac and Iosco Counties have provided interesting fossil mammoth discoveries near Saginaw Bay. Moreover, the Iosco mammoth is, by far, the northernmost record of a Pleistocene mammoth in Michigan (see fig. 78) and forms the northernmost point of the Mason-Quimby line. Ice Age mammoths found in the general Saginaw Bay area are thought to have been there principally to feed in the marshy grasses that colonized the land during the withdrawals of ancient Saginaw Bay.

The Arenac County mammoth remains were found in an excavated pond (fig. 114) near Alger, northwest of Standish. These consisted of a large molar tooth measuring 9.5 inches (as measured through the root and the crown) and a first right rib. Most mam-

Fig. 114. Excavated pond where mammoth remains were discovered in Arenac County near Standish, central-eastern Lower Peninsula. The mammoth occurred above sand that was interpreted as being an old Pleistocene beach. Based on a radiocarbon date on one of its ribs, the mammoth lived there about 11,300 years ago.

moths and mastodonts I (JAH) have seen have been found in peat and marl in ancient kettle bogs or shallow basins. But the Alger mammoth remains were found in a black organic soil above about eight feet of white sand. Below the white sand was clay and gravel of glacial origin. The sand probably represented an old beach during a time in the Pleistocene when Saginaw Bay was more extensive. The mammoth probably came there later after the withdrawal of ancient Saginaw Bay when grasses that formed the black organic soil were replacing the beach sands. A radiocarbon date on a rib from the Alger mammoth indicated it lived there 11,280 (plus or minus 70) years ago.

The Iosco County mammoth was unearthed at East Tawas near Tawas City at the top of the Saginaw Bay area. This mammoth was represented only by a third lower left molar, which was 12¼ inches long as measured through the root and the crown. Imagine that critter having a toothache! The Iosco County mammoth was buried in a more conventional setting in a mixture of peat and marl. The excavation of a drainage ditch led to the discovery of this northernmost fossil mammoth in Michigan. Recall that one crosses the transition zone between the Carolinian and Canadian Biotic Provinces into the Canadian Biotic Province north of East Tawas and Tawas City.

6. Tawas Point State Park (a short diversion). Tawas State Park is located on the hooklike point that extends out into Lake Huron, forming Tawas Bay. To reach the park turn east on East Tawas Drive just northeast of East Tawas and drive about 2.5 miles to the entrance. A special feature of this park is a remarkably well preserved historic lighthouse that is over one hundred years old. This structure joins a house where U.S. Coast guardsmen presently live. On foggy nights the atmosphere of the area is enhanced by the sound of foghorn signals on the point. There are many acres of fine white sand in this park, as well as low dunes and interdunal ponds (fig. 115) where one can look for frogs and garter snakes. Good bird-watching occurs in the park during spring migration.

Fig. 115. Interdunal pond at Tawas Point State Park

Tawas City to Mackinaw City

The drive from Tawas City to Mackinaw City, a distance of about 160 miles, is one of the most beautiful drives in the state. Here, many views of Lake Huron may be seen directly from U.S. 23. Geologically, the route runs almost entirely along an area of glacial lake sediments. From the paleontological standpoint, some interesting fossils have been found in the area. Biologically, we are now in the true "north woods" of the Canadian Biotic Province all the way to the Straits. Many excellent views of white pine, red pine, jack pine, and birch will be seen along the way. Temperatures are cooler on the east side of Michigan from Tawas City to Mackinaw City compared to areas of similar latitude on the lake on the west side of the state. This is due to the residual heat held in Lake Michigan during the winter and the warm southwesterly airflow that dissipates itself over the land before reaching the east coast.

FEATURES

1. Oscoda, the Au Sable River, and the Riddle of the Whales. About fourteen miles north of Tawas City we find the comfortable Lake Huron town of Oscoda. Here the famed Au Sable River enters Lake Huron. Moreover, one of Michigan's most controversial fossils was discovered in the vicinity. The Au Sable River begins in the central part of the Lower Peninsula with several tributaries, including the north and middle and south branches, well known by trout fishers. East of McKinley in Oscoda County, the Au Sable becomes a single stream, flowing southward through Alcona County and then turning eastward to Oscoda and Lake Huron. One of the interesting geological features of the Au Sable River is the fact that it has cut through an ancient delta west of Oscoda, leaving terraced remnants above the water level along its newly cut stream valley.

Let's turn now to whales. In 1928 during the excavation of a schoolhouse in Oscoda, the rib of a bowhead whale was found about five feet below the surface in sands supposedly of Lake Nipissing age. This high water encroached the area about four thousand years ago. In the 1970s it was suggested that the bowhead whale wandered into the St. Lawrence River from the sea and then traveled through the Trent Valley in Ontario into the Great Lakes (fig. 116). Bowhead whales get to be about sixty feet long and can weigh up to seventy tons.

But in 1988 radiocarbon dates were obtained, not only from the bowhead whale rib from Oscoda, but from bones of a fin whale and a sperm whale at two other localities in Michigan. These dates showed the sperm whale bone was less than 190 years old, the fin whale bone was about 720 years old, and the bowhead whale rib from Oscoda was about 750 years old. It was then pointed out that during this time period water levels were so low that there would have been no passageways for whales to have traveled from the sea to the Great Lakes.

The suggestion was then made that the bones were carried in by people, perhaps by way of early Native American trading routes

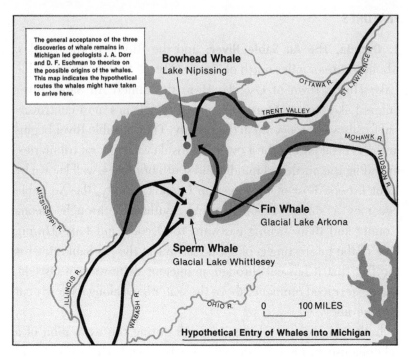

The general acceptance of the three discoveries of whale remains in Michigan led geologists J. A. Dorr and D. F. Eschman to theorize on the possible origins of the whales. This map indicates the hypothetical routes the whales might have taken to arrive here.

Bowhead Whale
Lake Nipissing

OTTAWA R.

ST. LAWRENCE R.

TRENT VALLEY

MOHAWK R.

HUDSON R.

MISSISSIPPI R.

Fin Whale
Glacial Lake Arkona

Sperm Whale
Glacial Lake Whittlesey

ILLINOIS R.

WABASH R.

OHIO R.

0   100 MILES

Hypothetical Entry of Whales Into Michigan

Fig. 116. Possible routes of ancient whales into Michigan. (From J. A. Holman, *Michigan Natural Resources Magazine,* 1991, p. 35 [courtesy of *Michigan Natural Resources Magazine*].)

from the Atlantic coast. However, because of other undated whale bones and teeth found in varying parts of Michigan, the jury still may be out on the question of the natural occurrence of whales in the Great Lake system. One find of a sperm whale tooth that had presumably washed out of a deep bank in Pine Creek near Manton in northwestern Michigan is especially enticing, as organic sediments about forty thousand years old have been found in the general area. Bowhead whales did make it as far inland as eastern Ontario (Renfrew County) about ten thousand years ago when the St. Lawrence River valley became inundated and formed the so-called Champlain Sea toward the end of the Pleistocene.

2. Earthwork Site. An earthwork north of Oscoda is one of a number of Late Woodland earthworks that were located along some of the rivers north of Saginaw Bay. Northern Juntunen ware pottery and southern Younge tradition pottery suggests this site at least may have been a center for trade. This suggestion is particularly interesting because this site and most other earthworks date between about A.D. 1400 and 1500. The dates here are at the time known as the "Little Ice Age," when temperatures were colder and winters longer. This same time saw the development of the historically known pattern of regular exchange between different groups whereby corn grown in the south was traded for meat and hides that were abundantly available in the north. Perhaps this earthwork north of Oscoda was a location where such exchanges took place.

3. Harrisville State Park. About eighteen miles up the coast from Oscoda one comes to Harrisville State Park, about one mile south of the town itself. This ninety-four-acre park is known for its abundance of northern trees, including cedar, balsam, birch, ash, and maple. The best place to observe the vegetation is along the Cedar Run nature trail, which can be walked in under an hour. A sandy beach is available for walking, swimming, and observing Lake Huron. You might wish to test the water to see if this beach, fully on Lake Huron, is as shallow near the edge as the beach was at Bay City State Park on Saginaw Bay.

4. Negwegon State Park (a diversion). If one wishes to walk a lovely sandy beach with over six miles of shoreline of small bays and coves, and with a lining of birch and fragrant cedar behind the beach, it takes a little effort to get there. The first part is simple. From Harrisville drive twelve miles north on U.S. 23 to Black River Road (well marked from the highway), where you turn east and go about a mile and a half to an unmarked two-track (Sand Hill Trail). Turn north on the two-track and drive about two and a half miles to a gravel road. Turn east again on the gravel road and go a little over a mile to the parking lot. During the warm summer months it is possible to get stuck in loose sand along the two-track (Sand Hill Trail) in a vehicle that does not have four-wheel drive.

5. Alpena and Rogers City, Rock Quarries, and Paleozoic Fossils. Continuing up the coast from the Black River Road exit, we get nice views of Lake Huron and Thunder Bay before we reach Alpena, and then a good look at the western shore of Grand Lake before we go cross country to Rogers City. Devonian age (see fig. 6) limestones and dolomite (see tables 1 and 2) for various commercial uses, including road-building materials and steel production, are mined in the Alpena and Rogers City area. Fine exposures of Devonian limestones occur along U.S. 23 near Rogers City. In fact, the world's largest limestone quarry, the Calcite Quarry, is located at Rogers City itself.

Invertebrate fossil collecting is good in these Devonian limestones in and near Alpena and Rogers City, but, of course, permission must be obtained to collect fossils on any private lands. Brachiopods, bryozoans, crinoids, and corals are common fossil types, and by the way, these fossils lived in ancient Devonian saltwater seas, not freshwater lakes. Broken pieces of colonial types of corals often occur on the beaches in the northern Lake Huron area. The "Petoskey stone," the state stone of Michigan, is actually a fossil reef-building Devonian coral called *Hexagonaria* that has been polished by wave action on the beach. These fossils get their name from the fact that they were once very abundant near the city of Petoskey on the northwest coast of the Lower Peninsula.

In and near Alpena, Devonian rocks have yielded strange, armored Devonian fishes called placoderms (see fig. 19A and B). These fishes were so bizarre that the late, great vertebrate paleontologist Alfred S. Romer of Harvard referred to them as the "funny fishes." Devonian placoderms have been collected for years by paleontologists from the University of Michigan, where collections reside in the Museum of Paleontology on the campus in Ann Arbor. The largest of the placoderms was a huge armored fish called *Dunkleosteus* with enormous traplike jaws. This predator of the Devonian inland seas probably reached a size of about forty feet long from the tip of the head to the end of the tail. Parts of this monster were found at the Alkali Quarry at Alpena and at Squaw Bay, four miles south of Alpena on U.S. 23. So do not take casually odd things you might find on the beach, or even on the roadside by limestone outcrops. Fossils continually erode out of limestone as it weathers. Another placoderm called *Protitanichthyes* (see fig. 19A and B) was found at Rockport near Alpena. Other funny fishes with astounding names, as well as fossil sharks (see fig. 19E), have also been found in the Alpena-Rockport area.

6. P. H. Hoeft State Park. Four miles northwest of Rogers City on U.S. 23 one finds P. H. Hoeft State Park, which several people have told us is the most lovely park on the Lake Huron shore. A wonderful mile-long shoreline of soft white sand is available for beachcombing and viewing the lake, and behind this are well-developed low-dune habitats. Beyond the dunes there are typical northern woodlands. For plant lovers, one of the enticements here are species of orchids and irises that are rare in other parts of the state. Animal life includes deer, snowshoe hares, squirrels, and woodcocks.

7. Cheboygan State Park. About thirty-four miles northwest of P. H. Hoeft State Park one finds the entrance to Cheboygan State Park off U.S. 23 with a combination of several scenic turnouts and roadside parks along the way. The major lake view of the park is scenic Duncan Bay (fig. 117), which takes up much of the eastern border of the park. This shallow bay is home to northern pike, smallmouth bass, and panfish. The southeast portion of the park is well known for its wetlands, which are created by the many slow channels of Little Billy Elliot's Creek. Park trails pass through low dunes, marshes, interdunal ponds, and forested areas, so that a diversity of wildlife may be observed. Again, for plant lovers, several kinds of wildflowers found in the park occur only in this area of the state. The vegetational associations are typical of the Canadian Biotic Province.

8. The Home of the Fish. The large island in the Straits of Mackinac north of Cheboygan is Bois Blanc Island (see fig. 111). A site near the western end of the island provides abundant evidence of

Fig. 117. Scenic Duncan Harbor seen from Cheboygan State Park

why Father Claude Dablon observed in 1669, "This spot is the most noted in all these regions for its abundance of fish; since, [according to the Indian saying], 'this is its native country.' Elsewhere, although they exist in large numbers, it is not properly their 'home' which is in the neighborhood of Michilimackinac" (see Thwaites 1959, vol. 55).

The site on Bois Blanc Island was occupied throughout the Late Woodland from the earliest Mackinac phase (A.D. 750 to 1000), through the Bois Blanc phase (A.D. 1000 to 1200) and through portions of the latest Juntunen phase (A.D. 1200 to 1450). All of these Late Woodland peoples were at the site during the warm season, when they hunted, fished, and gathered plant foods, but most importantly people were there in the autumn. Abundant fish bones and processing features are testimony to the importance of the fall-spawning whitefish and lake trout that can be found in the Straits. This inland shore fishery was critical to Late Woodland peoples because these nutritious fish were abundant at a most critical time of their year. The fish could be dried and carried along on the winter hunt (see fig. 91). These supplies of fish were an important source of winter food, particularly because hunting was not always successful.

To the northwest of Bois Blanc Island and the smaller Round Island lies Mackinac Island, described by Father Dablon in the *Jesuit Relations* of 1669:

> Michilimackinac is an island of note in these regions. It is more than a league in diameter, [and elevated in some places by such high cliffs as to be seen more than twelve leagues off]. It is situated exactly in the straits connecting [Lake Huron and Michigan], and forms the key and the door for all the peoples of the south, as does the Sault for those of the north, for in these regions there are only those two passages by water; for very many nations have to go by one or other of the two, in order to reach the French settlements.
>
> This presents a peculiarly favorable opportunity, both for instructing those who pass here, and to gain ready access to their countries. (see Thwaites 1959, vol. 55)

Some of the high cliffs described by Father Dablon at Mackinac Island rise some 750 feet above sea level. The cliffs, appearing like steps, were at one time beaches and wave-cut cliffs/terraces formed as the Wisconsinan glaciers melted. The highest cliff on the island resulted when the first melting of the ice created Lake Algonquin about 11,000 years ago. Lake Algonquin encompassed both present-day lakes, Michigan and Huron. The steplike configuration of the cliffs on the island represents a succession of beaches from the Lake Algonquin high down to a series of beaches, known as the Upper Group, formed as Lake Algonquin receded beginning about 10,300 years ago. The last of the "steps" at 650 feet represents the beach left by Lake Nipissing about 5,500 years ago.

The waters of Lake Algonquin were at a level of 620 feet above sea level. How can it be that the beach cliffs at Mackinac Island are as much as 130 feet above the level of the former lakes? How can all the water-created cliffs be above the level of the lakes that made them? This interesting phenomenon is the result of another geological process related to the melting of the great ice sheets. The ice was very thick (one to two miles) and very heavy. The glacier pressed the land down, and when the glacier was gone, the land bounced back up. The effect of rebound was much more dramatic when the weight of the glacier was first removed, but rebound at the Straits continues today at a rate of about eight inches every one hundred years.

9. Mill Creek (a diversion). About four miles east of Mackinaw City on the south side of U.S. 23 lies the Mill Creek site. This late-eighteenth-century/early-nineteenth-century mill and farm complex was restored by the Mackinac Island State Park Commission. Ongoing archaeological excavations can be observed when the site is open during the summer months. A book about archaeological investigations of the site is available for those who wish to know more about how archaeology and historic documents can be used together to create a more complete picture of this former industrial and domestic location.

When archaeologists arrived at Mill Creek for the first full season of excavation in 1973, there were slight indications on the ground surface that it was the site of a saw and grist mill, farm, and homestead nearly two centuries before. Old documents such as maps, deeds, records, and the like showed that Mill Creek was the location of a mill that supplied lumber to the British and later, the American fort on Mackinac Island. Beef and hay as well as lumber and flour were products of this 640-acre tract of land. In 1973, the site could be reached by climbing a steep wooded slope on the west side of the creek. Crossing to the east side was via railroad tracks. Cribbing from a dam was observed in the cliff banks along the creek, but there was no evidence of a mill. The area to be excavated was covered with scrub vegetation. On the east side of the creek, a grass-covered mound of earth next to a relatively deep depression showed that a building had stood there. The track of the Old Mackinaw Road was visible on the south end of the site. Fish bones and hooks on the surface were obviously left by recent fishermen.

The steep banks of Mill Creek consist of Devonian age Bois Blanc limestone. This limestone outcrop made the location particularly suitable for building a crib dam to store the water for powering the mill. The buildings associated with the mill complex were located atop a relatively level Nipissing age wave terrace. Limestone outcrops at the site were mined and quarried early in the twentieth century.

In addition to its natural suitability for a mill, Mill Creek is situated opposite Mackinac Island, so it is on a direct route for transporting lumber, flour, and beef to supply the island fort. Indeed, the site at Mill Creek was established as an industrial complex sometime after 1781, when the British moved their fort from the mainland at Mackinaw City. The new fort and associated settlement on the island required the services of a mill as well as supplies of agricultural products.

SOUTHEASTERN MICHIGAN AND THE THUMB

Ohio Border to Bay City (I-75 to I-94 to M-25)

Ohio Border to Bay City

1. Lake Erie and Sterling State Park
2. Ribbon Farms
3. Salt
4. Early Detroit
5. Late Woodland
6. International Boundary
7. Small Arctic Mammals
8. Lakeport State Park
9. Gales of November
10. Straight Coastline
11. Fossil Beach
12. Lumber Town Site
13. Around the Tip of the Thumb
14. Albert E. Sleeper State Park
15. Sand Point
16. Productive Coastline

This is the most roundabout of the five Lower Peninsula journeys. The reason for this is that the Lower Peninsula of Michigan is shaped like a mitten with a large southeastern area sticking out between Saginaw Bay and Lake Huron like a thumb. If you ask any Lower Peninsula Michiganian to locate the town or village where he or she lives, they will automatically hold up one hand like a mitten and point to the proper area with a finger from the other. Being a Hoosier from Indiana just arrived, when I (JAH) first worked the student registration table at Michigan State University back in the late 1960s, I thought at first that the students in line introducing themselves to one another were deaf and using sign language. Okay, visitors, for starters try Detroit, Lansing, Bay City, Grand Rapids, and Traverse City. It really works, doesn't it?

This route begins at the Ohio border at Toledo, skirts Lake Erie and Detroit, continues northeast to Port Huron, and finally around the tip of the thumb to Bay City. We are at the Michigan-Canadian border at Detroit (Windsor, Ontario) and again at Port Huron (Sarnia, Ontario). Along this route one goes from I-75 to I-94 in driving through Detroit, and changes to M-25, the thumb route, just north of Port Huron.

Geologically, this Ohio route follows a path within glacial lake sediments almost all the way to Bay City, so it is mainly a flatland trip. From the standpoint of biotic associations, we are in the deciduous climax forest area of the Carolinian Biotic Province from the Ohio border to north of Lakeport. Here we enter the transition zone and stay in it all the way to Bay City. Turning to the Mason-Quimby line, however, we find that the tip of the thumb area from a little below Forestville on the Lake Huron coast diagonally across to Bay Port on the upper eastern shore of Saginaw Bay is above the Mason-Quimby line (see fig. 18).

This route along Lake Erie's western shore has been an entrance for people into the Lower Peninsula for about 11,000 years (see fig. 68). A large number of Paleo-Indian fluted points have been found in this area. The earliest of these fluted points, Gainey points, are characteristically made of Upper Mercer chert, which has its source in Ohio (see fig. 67). The Late Woodland ceramic sequence is similar from western Ontario around the west end of Lake Erie and into southeastern Michigan, and like the Paleo-Indians, early Late Woodland peoples made projectile points of Upper Mercer chert. When the federal government built roads to encourage settlement in Michigan, some of these roads were from Detroit to Maumee rapids near Toledo. New settlers from Ohio and Indiana did come into Michigan along these roads, and many other settlers from New York came by ship, and via the Erie Canal.

FEATURES

1. Lake Erie and Sterling State Park (a diversion). Lake Erie is the shallowest and warmest of all of the Great Lakes, and is also the one that makes the least contact with the state of Michigan. Lake Erie, of course, has always been a very important shipping route, but because of its shallowness and warmness, it has developed a different type of biota (assemblage of living forms) than the other Great Lakes. It has always had a warm-water fishery, including quite desirable food fishes such as yellow perch and walleyes, but also less desirable species such as carp, bullheads (fig. 118A), and freshwater drum (fig. 118B).

Recently, zebra mussels (inch-long, striped clamlike critters) (see fig. 87), accidentally imported from Europe, have made an unexpected impact on Lake Erie by clearing up the water to a remarkable degree. This is because these mussels filter out tiny organisms and organic matter from the water during their feeding processes. It remains to be seen how this will all play out, however, for many of the tiny organisms consumed by the zebra mussels are an important food item at the base of the Lake Erie food chain. There is also the chance that zebra mussel populations might peak and then fade again to "normal-sized" populations, as has happened before with some introduced species in North America.

To become familiar with nearshore habitats and the essence of eastern Lake Erie, take exit 15 off I-75 and go north on Dixie Highway less than a mile to Sterling State Park. This park is mainly used for a fishing access to Lake Erie, where king walleye is the most

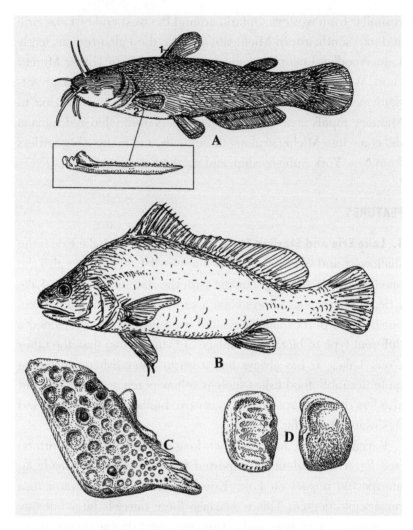

Fig. 118. Two abundant warm-water fishes of southeastern Michigan. A, yellow bullhead, 1, dorsal spine, 2, pectoral spine; B, freshwater drum; C, freshwater drum tooth plate; D, opposite sides of freshwater drum otolith ("ear stone"). Bullhead spines and other kinds of catfish spines as well as freshwater drum tooth plates and otoliths are interesting objects that often identified as Ice Age archaeological remains and are commonly found by beachcombers in Michigan. (From J. A. Holman, *Ancient Life of the Great Lakes Basin* [Ann Arbor: University of Michigan Press, 1995].)

sought after fish in the area. But near the park one also can catch yellow perch, pike, crappies, and black bass, as well as the less sought after bullheads and freshwater drum.

On the other hand, Sterling State Park offers extensive shoreline and sheltered lagoons that offer bird-watchers views of herons, egrets, gulls, and terns, and even ospreys are seen from time to time. Actually, this park was once an undesirable area of mainly stagnant water. Its restoration as a desirable area attests to the effect of tough antipollution laws.

2. Ribbon Farms. The American settlers were not the first to establish farms here. French farmers settled around Fort Pontchartrain (Detroit) in 1701 and have been living in southeastern Michigan for the last three hundred years. When the British defeated the French in their contest for control of North America in 1760, they took control of the fort in Detroit. The French farm families never sold or relinquished their land to the British, nor did they sell to the Americans. Instead, the new American government honored French land claims. A local dialect of French can still be heard spoken in Detroit and Monroe.

The original French "long lots" or "ribbon farms" are depicted on today's maps of Michigan. The long lots were laid out along a river, such as the River Raisin at Monroe. The narrow side of the lot faced the river and the long sides were measured back from the river. Such a system meant that each farm had waterfront property for sending and receiving shipments via water transport. Behind the riverfront there would be enough land for a garden, a house, an orchard, fields for planting crops, pasture, and finally, a woodlot along the narrow side at the back of the farm.

The French were not the first to plant crops here in southeastern Michigan. There is evidence of a shift in Late Woodland settlement locations when cultivation of maize and other crops became more important, after about A.D. 1000. These later peoples occupied settings close to land that was easily cultivated, usually around Lake Erie, Lake St. Clair, and in the major stream valleys. Unlike the French farmers, these Late Woodland peoples did not stay in their horticultural settlements all year long. Instead some, or all, members of a group would move in different seasons to camps while they fished, hunted, and gathered wild plants. Obtaining wild foods in season was still a very important part of the subsistence system.

3. Salt below Us. Driving now up into the greater Detroit area, just north of the Woodhaven exit, we are only a few miles west of the Detroit River and Wyandotte, the home of a huge salt-mining operation. We have seen valuable natural resources on the surface of Michigan ranging from farmland to fisheries, but far below the surface lies a wealth of mineral resources, including salt in several areas where Silurian and Devonian (see fig. 7) seas occurred millions of years ago. As of 1970, Michigan supplied 20–25 percent of the salt output of the United States. The salt at Wyandotte formed during the Silurian period when extensive seas were present in the Michigan Basin (see fig. 8). The basin then was encircled by shallow shoals and reefs that produced an evaporative environment that led to the drying up of the seas and the deposition of deep layers of salt and other valuable minerals such as gypsum (see table 2).

4. Early Detroit. The French established a settlement at Detroit in 1701 because the location was strategic for exerting control over the trade in furs (see fig. 76). This setting on the narrow strait linking Lake Erie through Lake St. Clair and the St. Clair River to Lake Huron gave command over shipments of furs from the north and west to markets in the east through Lake Erie and Lake Ontario. It also controlled shipments of trade goods from the east through the upper lakes to the north and west. In particular, the French were in a position here to prevent British traffic in furs and trade goods through the interconnected lakes. Since their Indian allies also settled here, the French were in a position to maintain their trade relationships at the expense of any British encroachments.

Fort Pontchartrain, which was located in present downtown Detroit, was more than a military outpost. Cadillac envisioned this fort as the commercial trading center for the western fur trade. In addition to a military garrison, the settlement included French settler/farmers, or *habitants.* Many of the Indian tribes who traded with and were allied with the French also settled there, including the Huron, the Ottawa, and other groups.

Except for a few isolated finds, Fort Pontchartrain is virtually unknown archaeologically. Maps of the fort, however, reflect Cadillac's vision in providing for a settlement that went beyond military purposes. The square fort was originally about two hundred feet on each side, and each corner had an "arrow-shaped" bastian. Thus, it was a defensive structure. Within the palisade there were the expected military housing and storage facilities, but there were also named streets, *habitant's* houses, the Chapel of St. Anne, and related church buildings. The settlement did become a major commercial center, and by 1749 expanded to include a large population.

With the surrender of Montreal and New France in 1760, the British occupied Fort Pontchartrain. Here they successfully withstood a siege in 1763 when Indians allied to Pontiac attacked a number of British installations. Other British forts in Michigan fell to Pontiac, including Fort Michilimackinac at the Straits of Mackinac and Fort St. Joseph in Niles.

During the American Revolution, the British constructed a new fort in Detroit. This structure, Fort Lernoult, was built in 1778 and 1779. Archaeologists from Wayne State University documented that Fort Lernoult was surrounded by a palisade placed within a dry moat. Steep earthworks were placed inside the palisade and moat. Thus, there were two defensive barriers at this fort. Americans renamed Fort Lernoult in 1805, when it became Fort Detroit. Fort Detroit became Fort Shelby in 1812.

5. The Late Woodland. A series of sites around the north end of Lake St. Clair is representative of the Late Woodland sequence in southeastern Michigan. The earliest Late Woodland occupants of this area were makers of ceramics known as Wayne ware. These vessels are relatively small or medium-sized pots with exterior surfaces that were marked with a cord-wrapped paddle. Wayne ware is quite plain, but the rim and lip areas may be variously decorated with cord-wrapped sticks, or plain tool incising. On some vessels the incising is "criss-crossed" or crosshatched. This crosshatched motif is common on earlier Middle Woodland vessels in the Great Lakes region, which suggests that Wayne ware began to be made early in the Late Woodland, ca. A.D. 600. Wayne ware continued to be made in this area for another three or four hundred years, although it lasted longer in the Saginaw region.

Oddly, the interesting thing about Wayne ware is the fact that it is plain and rather boring. The distinguishing attributes of Wayne ware, smallish, globular, cord-marked pots with some rim decoration, are characteristic of early Late Woodland pottery found throughout southern lower Michigan. Allegan ware in southwest Michigan, Spring Creek ware in west-central Michigan, and "northeastern Wayne ware" in the Saginaw Valley are all very similar to Wayne ware. In many respects these ceramics all look alike. There are differences in the pottery from each region, but these differences are not obvious, and they characterize groups of pots, not individual pots.

The reason why this early Late Woodland pottery is so similar but differs from region to region has to do with how early Late Woodland people related to one another. Late Woodland households, like hunter-gatherers elsewhere, would consistently travel through a known territory, such as a river system, where they could get food throughout the year. Households living in the same region tended to make similar pottery. There was no doubt a lot of visiting back and forth with people in other regions, however, and people in southern Michigan were kin and friends. They married one another, they aided each other in emergencies, and they exchanged information. Their pottery is so similar because the boundaries between these groups were very fluid and readily crossed (see fig. 73).

A second Late Woodland ceramic tradition here in southeastern lower Michigan, known as the Younge tradition, overlaps in time with the Wayne tradition but replaces it here at about A.D. 1000. Unlike Wayne ware, Younge tradition pottery is distinctive enough to be easily identified in comparison to other late wares in Michigan. In fact, Younge tradition ceramics are most similar to materials found around the western end of Lake Erie, including western Ontario, and differ from other wares in Michigan (see fig. 74).

Younge tradition peoples cultivated corn (maize) and other crops during part of the year and had satellite camps where they fished, hunted, and collected wild foods. They had more tightly organized communities than did Wayne tradition peoples. Their organization is reflected in one site where two longhouses were found with hearths and ash pits along the center of the houses. Similar longhouses among the Ontario Iroquois were home to a group of people who were related to one another through a common maternal ancestor. Each nuclear family had space on one side of the longhouse and shared a hearth with a similar family on the other side. The related residents in a longhouse controlled the agricultural land cultivated by the group, and associations coordinated the activities of a "village" with several longhouses.

Visible group identity in the Younge tradition is seen not only in distinctive pottery and communities with longhouses, but in the ways in which Younge tradition peoples buried their dead. Younge tradition cemeteries in Michigan are characterized by ossuaries (graves) in which a large number of individuals were buried together. These individuals were probably members of the same group, as the ritual of burial reflected group membership.

6. International Boundary. A key defensive location was Fort Gratiot at Port Huron, about sixty miles north of Detroit (see fig. 76). This fort, near the present Blue Water Bridge, was built by the Americans in 1814 to guard their border between British Canada and the United States. Port Huron is situated at the south end of Lake Huron, where it connects via the St. Clair River to Lakes Erie and Ontario. Like the forts at Detroit, this fort was at a location overlooking a route through which any commercial or naval traffic must pass. Thus, any British intentions for a naval assault on Detroit from bases around Lake Huron could be detected and thwarted at Fort Gratiot.

Fort Gratiot was not a trading post and was never intended to be a commercial center. Fort Gratiot was a defended garrison. This is in contrast to Forts Pontchartrain and Michilimackinac, where the French intent was to assemble participants in the fur trade at a single central location and thereby control commerce and out-compete British rivals in the trade. Neither of the French forts was on a political border. Fort Gratiot, on the other hand, overlooked a newly created border along a traditional Indian trade route. The other side of the border was controlled by Britain, a power with whom many of the Indian tribes were allied during the American Revolution, and with whom the new country was at war when the fort was built. The War of 1812 was in progress at the time, and tensions along this border in Michigan Territory were real.

Fort Gratiot was abandoned and reoccupied several times but was abandoned for the final time in 1879 when it was no longer needed as a defensive outpost on a territorial frontier. During Michigan's period as a territory, the garrison at Fort Gratiot provided services beyond defense to the local area. For example, roads were built and medical aid was supplied so that the area attracted settlers who in turn provided goods purchased by the soldiers based here.

7. Small Arctic Mammals in Ice Age Michigan. Making our way through the Detroit area, we pass exits to our neighbors in Windsor, Canada. Then, passing the Lake St. Clair area to the east, we travel inland for a half hour drive or so to another entry point to Canada between Port Huron, Michigan and Sarnia, Ontario. The distance from Detroit to Port Huron is roughly sixty miles. Just northwest of Port Huron at Mill Creek (see your Michigan highway map), a quite unique Ice Age fossil site was unearthed and studied by paleontologists at the Royal Ontario Museum in Canada. Most fossil vertebrates in Michigan are the bones of very large extinct mammals (e.g., mammoths, mastodonts, woodland musk oxen), but the tiny vertebrate fossils at the Mill Creek site represent bones of fish, shrews, ermine, mice, voles, and a hare or rabbit. Several of the small mammals from the site do not presently occur in Michigan but are found in Alaska and northern Canada today.

The exact age of the fossil site is not precisely known, as dating methods used showed that the animals occurred at least fifty-seven thousand years ago and possibly as many as three hundred thousand years ago. This indicates that the assemblage lived in Michigan previous to the last glacial advance over the area, but still in Late Pleistocene times. As a whole, the fossil vertebrate assemblage at Mill Creek contains animals that live in Michigan today as well as those that represent arctic species that live far north of Michigan. Species such as suckers (see fig. 90) and freshwater drum (see fig. 118B), pygmy shrews, ermine, deer mice, red-backed voles, and meadow voles are presently found in Michigan. Species such as collared lemmings, northern bog lemmings, and brown lemmings are found in Alaska and northern Canada today.

One cannot find an area today where all of these species occur in the same place. Therefore one must hypothesize two situations: (1) either the fossils of the deposit were a mixture from different time periods (a heterochronic assemblage) or (2) the climate in the area was different than it is at present. If hypothesis 2 is true, one might suggest that summers were somewhat cooler than at present, allowing for the survival of the northern species and that winters were not much colder than at present, allowing for the survival of the species living in Michigan today. This site cannot be visited by the public.

8. Lakeport State Park. About ten miles north of Port Huron on M-25 we find the entrance to Lakeport State Park. This park has a beach about a mile and a half long where one can view the lake and watch freighters heading in or out of the St. Clair River, which flows from Lake Huron at Port Huron. What kind of products would you predict they are carrying to Detroit from the north or from Detroit to the north?

Second-growth deciduous trees typical for the general area may be seen upon entering the park and in several stands of trees in the park, although extensive woodland trails are not available. On the other hand, marshy creeks bordered by tall marsh grasses typical of low areas near Lake Erie and lower Lake Huron are easy to find (fig. 119).

9. Oh, the Gales of November. In November, when the cold winds from the far north sweep into contact with the warmer air rising from the Great Lakes, great storms can and do occur. North of Lexington on M-25 about eleven miles north of the Lakeport State Park, a Michigan Historic Site Marker can be easily seen on the east side of the highway. This marker describes the great storm of November 9, 1913, which wrought particular havoc on Lake Huron. All in all, in the Great Lakes, ten ships sunk, many others were driven ashore, and more than 235 seamen drowned. On Lake Huron alone eight ships were lost, and all of the people aboard these vessels perished. The furious gales of this storm persisted for a full sixteen hours.

Fig. 119. Marshy creek bordered by tall marsh grasses, typical of low areas near Lake Erie and southern Lake Huron

10. A Straight Coastline. Few prehistoric archaeological sites are known along the Lake Huron shore between Port Huron and Pt. aux Barques. This low number of sites is not too surprising. The coast here is straight and lacks the small bays and points of land where there are varied offshore conditions that support different fish populations. Varied bottom habitats were preferred by prehistoric fishers. Additionally, there are no major rivers emptying into the lake here that people could move through during the year. Coastal sites are more common around Saginaw Bay, where fishing was better. On the other hand, sites are found in the interior of the "thumb," where there was good hunting through prehistory and on into the Historic period. The thumb was a late fall and winter hunting territory for Chippewa in the nineteenth century. The same area was a destination for "big game" hunters from Ohio, such as Oliver Hazard Perry, who published a journal of his hunting trips here. The last native elk (wapiti) was killed in the thumb in the late 1800s.

11. Fossil Beach. On the west side of M-25 north of Harbor Beach there is a sharp rise above the coastal plain traversed by the highway. This rise, which trends from southeast to northwest, is a fossil beach formed during one or both of the high-water stages in Lake Huron. The steep slope down toward the present coast is the wave terrace associated with these high lake levels. Lake Huron during the first high-water stage was part of Lake Algonquin, which was formed as the glaciers retreated about 11,800 years ago and lasted until the water began to drop about 10,300 years ago. Water levels were again high during the Nipissing stage about 5,500 years ago. During both these stages, the water was at 605 feet above sea level. Nipissing waters dropped to the current elevation of Lake Huron at 580 feet above sea level when the outlet at Port Huron through which the upper lakes drain into Lake Erie was eroded to 580 feet.

12. Lumber Town Site. About three miles north of Harbor Beach there is the site of Forest Bay, a lumbering town that burned and was abandoned when fire swept the thumb in 1881. Much of this site has been covered by later activities. M-25 cuts through the old town, which included homes, a schoolhouse, a blacksmith shop, a post office, possibly a boarding house, and a mill. Forest Bay was a good location for transporting logs because a railroad carried them from the forest to the town, from which they could be shipped by water. Lumbering in the thumb relied on railroad and lake transport as this area had no large rivers for floating logs such as were found elsewhere in the state.

13. Around the Tip of the Thumb to Port Crescent State Park. Driving up M-25 from the Lexington area, we remain in the vegetational transition zone between the Carolinian and Canadian Biotic Provinces around the tip of the thumb and down again to Bay City on Saginaw Bay, where this route ends. The distance from Lexington to Crescent State Park is about sixty-eight miles. Along the way there is a nice roadside park about ten miles north of Lexington just south of Port Sanilac and a fine scenic turnout south of Forestville and about thirteen miles from Port Sanilac. From here, around to the tip of the thumb we go to Port Crescent State Park, which is just two miles west of Port Austin, which lies just about the middle of the tip of the thumb.

Port Crescent State Park is one of the finest state parks in the thumb area. It has a full two and a half miles of sandy beach to comb and view. Moreover, behind the beach one finds low dunes replete with dune grasses and wildflowers. The Pinnebog River winds through the park and can be reached from several sites. Here perch and walleye can be fished for, as well as salmon and trout in season. More than two miles of hiking trails are available to observe the local vegetation and wildlife.

14. Albert E. Sleeper State Park. Continuing west of M-25 about eighteen miles, we come to Albert E. Sleeper State Park. Here one finds a combination of lakeshore, dunes, and forest. For people living in southeastern Michigan, this is one of the nearest state parks with a truly northern setting that contains many acres of undisturbed woodlands with over four miles of hiking trails. Those that think of the thumb as a boring agricultural area will find this park a pleasant surprise indeed.

15. Sand Point (a short diversion). About four miles down the thumb from Caseville, one finds an exit to the west out onto the needlelike Sand Point. Here one can view Wild Fowl Bay to the south. This shallow bay and protected waters of nearshore islands to the south indeed provides an excellent refuge for "wild fowl." The distance from Sand Point down the thumb to Bay City and the end of this route is about forty miles. A roadside park occurs about five miles down the west side of the thumb from Sand Point. In this area, another view of the Wild Fowl Bay islands may be seen.

16. A Productive Coastline. There are many more archaeological sites along the coast of Saginaw Bay on the west side of the thumb than there are along the Lake Huron coast. These sites are situated in varied settings that allowed people to fish, hunt, capture wild fowl, and gather plants nearby. In later times people may have added the cultivation of crops to their activities here.

Archaeological remains from one of these sites illustrate how Late Woodland people used this coastline. This site, 20HU164 is located near Caseville at Sand Point. This point of land forms the north side of Wild Fowl Bay. Evidence from 20HU164 includes a variety of artifacts concentrated around a deep roasting or cooking pit. The pit was filled in with domestic refuse after it served its first purpose. The area around the pit included pottery, pipe fragments, lumps of fired clay, stone tools, bones, shells, and fire-cracked rock. The pottery assemblage included fragments of two miniature pots that may have been made and used by children. The abundance and variety of materials in this small space indicate an undisturbed "living floor," possibly a house floor, where domestic activity took place.

Clearly people cooked food, smoked pipes, and processed food here. Foot and leg bones from deer had been split by the occupants of the site, probably to obtain the marrow. Additionally, both spring- and fall-spawning fish were found along with remains of a raccoon and a painted turtle. There were also burned butternut and acorn hulls.

Stone tools were made at this site, as evidenced by cores and waste flakes (see fig. 70). Some of this stone work took place at a distance from the domestic area. It is not surprising that most of this stone was Bayport chert. This raw material is found at various locations around Saginaw Bay.

It is likely that sometime around A.D. 1000, an extended family camped at 20HU164 for perhaps a single season. During that time they obtained a variety of foods from the surrounding area. One interesting piece of pottery has oval impressions that appear to have resulted from impressing a corn cob into the wet clay before the pottery was fired. The significance of this tiny pottery fragment is that people may have grown corn at 20HU164 or at least had access to it.

UPPER PENINSULA, LOWER ROUTE

Mackinaw City to Ironwood (U.S. 2)

Iron Mountain to Ironwood

1. Bewabic State Park
2. Simple Life near Iron River
3. The Timid Mink Site
4. The Lake Country
5. Ironwood

Manistique to Iron Mountain

1. Indian Lake State Park
2. Bays de Noc
3. Fayette Historic Townsite
4. Escanaba in Ordovician Country
5. Dairy Farms and Cambrian Rocks
6. Inland Economies
7. The Menominee Range

Mackinaw City to Manistique

1. Mackinac Breccia
2. Historic St. Ignace
3. Straits State Park
4. Silurian Bedrock Outcrops
5. Fish
6. Scenic Turnouts
7. Manistique and Manistique Group

Mackinaw City to Manistique

This segment of the route is about ninety-four miles long. Making a junction with U.S. 2 from I-75 shortly after crossing the spectacular Mackinac Bridge, we drive near cold and beautiful Lake Michigan for about forty-two miles to Naubinway and then turn inland the rest of the journey to Manistique back on the coast. From the geological standpoint, we will now find that bedrock formations (see figs. 7 and 8) are exposed on the surface in the Upper Peninsula to a much greater extent than they were in the Lower Peninsula. Bedrock formations of Devonian age (see fig. 6) outcrop on both sides of the Straits of Mackinac (see fig. 111). Then, bedrock formations of Silurian age (see fig. 6) begin to outcrop from time to time from about Gros Cap, a few miles northwest of St. Ignace all the way to Manistique and beyond. Glacial features at the surface are represented by glacial lake plains from St. Ignace to the vicinity of Epoufette, where ground moraine and outwash plain topography as well as some moraine remnants are found until we enter glacial lake topography again from about the Blaney Park exit down to Manistique.

From a vegetational standpoint we are fully into the Canadian Biotic Province throughout the Upper Peninsula, and pine, cedar, tamarack, spruce, and balsam are a striking part of the scenery. Relative to animal life that might be seen on or near the road, porcupines are likely to be the most abundant roadkills rather than raccoons, and an occasional black bear can be spotted from the car from time to time. Because bears are more road-shy than deer, we have usually spotted UP bears by looking down railway tracks from railway crossings, where we get fleeting glances at these large animals using these ready-made trails through the woods. The chance of seeing a moose in the Upper Peninsula may be the greatest in the eastern part of the area, including Mackinac and Schoolcraft Counties, which are traversed by this U.S. 2 route to Manistique. In the summer months moose are most likely to be seen in or near wetlands in coniferous marshes (cedar swamps) or alder-willow thickets bordering rivers or lakes. Dawn or dusk is the best time to see these horse-sized animals. Any place along this route where the road comes near Lake Michigan one can sometimes see osprey that have alighted on dead limbs with fish prey in their talons.

FEATURES

1. Mackinac Breccia near the Straits. The Devonian period (see fig. 6) is called the "age of fishes" by paleontologists because of the abundance of primitive types of fishes found in some Devonian beds. But the Devonian was also a time when various invertebrate animals were abundant. One of the best places to see Devonian outcrops along the highway in Michigan is on both sides of the Mackinac Bridge across the Straits of Mackinac. These Devonian rocks make up a formation called the Mackinac Breccia. The Mackinac Breccia consists mainly of masses of broken pieces of dolomite (see tables 1 and 2) jumbled together. These masses are often collapsed down into older Silurian shales.

Engineers planning the Mackinac Bridge over the Straits were worried about the strength of the bedrock composed of Mackinac Breccia and the possibility that modern collapses might occur. Thus, geological investigations had to be made prior to the construction of the piers and abutments that support the bridge you are about to cross, are now crossing, or have crossed. Aside from highway outcrops of Devonian Mackinac Breccia just across the bridge (fig. 120), a local landmark called Castle Rock that is easily seen from the road in St. Ignace is composed of Mackinac Breccia.

2. Historic St. Ignace. The town of St. Ignace takes its name from the mission established by Father Jacques Marquette in 1671. Marquette's mission was placed here at the Straits of Mackinac, where Marquette was able to bring his Christian message to many people in one place. Many Indian groups gathered in the area, particularly for the fall fishing. During other times of the year, these groups were widely spread across the landscape. Because it was at an east-west crossroads, St. Ignace was also a central place for the trading of furs between Indians and French (see fig. 76). At St.

Fig. 120. Outcrop of Mackinac Breccia just north of Mackinac Bridge, Mackinac County, eastern Upper Peninsula. Mackinac Breccia is of Devonian age and is composed mainly of masses of broken pieces of dolomite. (Photo courtesy of James H. Harding.)

Ignace Marquette's efforts were aided by the fact that the Huron and Ottawa settled here in stockaded villages north of the mission. "We have also wintered here in order to form plans for the mission of Saint Ignace, when it will be very easy to gain access to all the Missions of Lake Huron when the Nations shall have returned each to its own district." (Fr. Claude Dablon; see Thwaites 1959, vol. 55).

The Jesuit mission was established in St. Ignace to minister to these Huron, Ottawa, and other tribes in the region of the Straits of Mackinac. The Huron and Ottawa in particular, together with the Jesuits, had passed the previous years to the north and west, first at Chequamegon on Lake Superior and then at Sault Ste. Marie. By 1671, when the Iroquois wars ended, both tribes returned to the region of their old homelands in the neighborhood of Lake Huron and the Straits.

French traders and later, a garrison at Fort de Baude, completed the multiethnic population at St. Ignace in the 1680s. Fort de Baude was established in 1683 mainly to protect the interests of the French in the fur trade. The presence of the soldiers served to prevent British traders from the north who sought to establish their own trade relations with Indians.

Antoine Lamothe Cadillac, commandant of Fort de Baude from 1694 to 1697, described in his *Memoir* the French situation here. "The position of this post is most advantageous, because it is on Lake Huron, through which all the tribes from the south are obliged to pass when they go down to Montreal and in coming back, as well as the French who wish to trade in the upper country. None of them can pass without being observed, for the horizon is so clear that canoes can be seen from the fort as far as the keenest sight can reach. In short, it may be said that this place is the center of the whole of this farther colony, where one is in the midst of all the other posts and almost at an equal distance from them, and among all the tribes which have dealings with us" (1947, 4–5)

The mission was abandoned and burned in 1705 when the Ottawa and especially the Huron moved to the area of Fort Pontchartrain at Detroit, where Cadillac encouraged them to join him at this new French post. The Jesuit missionaries were not invited to Detroit by Cadillac, who was the last commander at Fort de Baude. Cadillac and the Jesuits had strong differences of opinion on the conduct of fur business, particularly over the use of brandy. Those Indians and unlicensed traders *(coureurs-de-bois)* who remained in the area were not Christians and were unlikely to be converted. Thus, maintaining a mission at St. Ignace would have had little chance of success.

When the French returned to establish a post at the Straits, they chose to build on the south side at Mackinaw City. St. Ignace was no longer a center of activity and the locations of the mission, the fort, and the Indian villages were forgotten. In September 1877, Father Edward Jacker excavated the apparent remains of a building uncovered when a person was creating a garden and thought it to be the mission church.

Professional archaeologists have been testing and excavating at the Marquette mission site for many of the last twenty-six years. The abundant seventeenth-century artifacts of French and Indian manufacture plus features including post lines, trash pits, storage pits, and hearths show how active a place St. Ignace was during Father Marquette's day and why it is difficult to identify the mission or to locate the Ottawa village and Fort de Baude.

A palisaded village thought to have been occupied by the Tionontati Huron who lived north of the mission has been located. The Tionontati occupied a village of about six acres. Evidence of three or four longhouses has been uncovered. Within these houses there were the remains of small hearths and household refuse. Huron longhouses generally were over one hundred feet long and were home to lineages, that is, families who were related to one another through the same maternal ancestors. These families would have separate living spaces on either side of the longhouse and would share cooking fires in the center between them. At the Tionontati Huron site in St. Ignace, there were deep bark-lined storage pits between the longhouses. Animal remains from the site show that people relied on catching different species of fish and hunting deer and bears. The Huron also ate corn, beans, and squash and gathered wild plants growing in the vicinity.

The Museum of Ojibwa Culture in the city of St. Ignace includes indoor exhibits about the Ojibwa (Chippewa) people in the region and about Indian contacts with the French. A park outside the museum building features a longhouse (Huron) as well as other outdoor exhibits.

3. Straits State Park. There are fine places to view the Straits of Mackinac on both sides of the bridge, and Straits State Park is one of the best places to stop and look at one of the very important historic places in North America. To reach the park we go about one-half mile right on U.S. 2 from the intersection of I-75 and U.S. 2

and turn right again on Church Street. A paved road in the park loops around to a scenic overlook of the Straits and the bridge.

This park is the setting for the Father Marquette National Memorial. Unfortunately, the Father Marquette Museum building with interpretive material about Marquette and French and Indian cultures was struck by lightning and destroyed by fire on March 9, 2000. Archaeologists from the Michigan Historical Center in Lansing conducted salvage excavations of the museum as soon as it was safe to go in.

4. Silurian Bedrock Outcrops. Silurian shales occur under the Devonian Mackinac Breccia along road cuts on both side of the "Mighty Mac" bridge and as we follow U.S. 2 westward from the bridge we shall see occasional road-cut exposures of Silurian rocks (see fig. 12). These rocks consist mainly of limestones, dolomite, and some shales. These exposures continue westward to Manistique and beyond. Invertebrate fossils, mainly corals, brachiopods, and bryozoans, have been found in some of these outcrops. These animals thrived in Silurian saltwater seas. Upper Peninsula Silurian limestones and dolomites are important commercially in the manufacture of cement, lime, road aggregate, agricultural lime, and even building stone.

5. The Importance of Fish. As we move west of St. Ignace along U.S. 2 we pass Gros Cap, the site of an historic Indian cemetery and seventeenth-century village. This settlement, like those in St. Ignace, was surrounded by a palisade. The heavy reliance on fish as seen in the animal remains from Gros Cap is a seventeenth-century example of an ancient pattern in the eastern Upper Peninsula whereby people spent the warm season on the coast and moved inland to hunt in the winter. Coastal sites were a source for fish from the spring spawning periods of fish such as lake sturgeons and suckers through October and November, when people caught the fall-spawning whitefish and lake trout. The fall fishery was a mainstay for Late Woodland peoples of the region who thus were able to secure a source of nutritious food that they could dry and carry with them for winter use (see fig. 91).

Many of these coastal sites were visited repeatedly by Middle and Late Woodland people. Settings were often along embayments with variable offshore bottom conditions where different species of fish might be found. This variation in fish habitat at a single site created an opportunity to catch fish in every season from the same location. People usually went to such sites in the spring, when fishing was important after a long winter. But they had the option of moving on, remaining only through the warm season, or staying for the critical fall fishing.

Whether or not people chose to remain at a site throughout the warm season and into the fall probably depended on variable environmental and social conditions in a given year. The important point is that they had a very flexible means of subsistence. This flexibility can be seen not only in the ability to catch a variety of fish but in the fact that people could hunt game and gather plants in the same vicinity.

A series of sites along the Lake Michigan coast west of St. Ignace illustrate how fishing was integrated into the lives of Upper Peninsula peoples who relied on fishing, hunting, and gathering for their subsistence. These sites are located on points of land including Pt. aux Chenes, Scott Point, and Seul Choix Point. All of these sites are stratified, with strata at Pt. aux Chenes and Seul Choix Point separating Middle from Late Woodland occupations and strata at Scott Point delineating the Late Woodland sequence from the Mackinac phase (A.D. 750 to 1000), the Bois Blanc phase (A.D. 1200 to 1400), and the Juntunen phase (A.D. 1400 to 1700).

6. Scenic Turnouts and Rest Stops. The drive from the junction of U.S. 2 and I-75, west on U.S. 2 to Naubinway (where the road turns inland for some distance) is one of the most beautiful ones in Michigan, and in North America for that matter. A nicely spaced and well-located series of scenic turnouts and rest areas enhances the trip. Scenic turnouts are located west of Pt. aux Chenes, between Pt. aux Chenes and Brevort, near Epoufette, and near Little Hog Island.

A roadside park is also found at Epoufette (fig. 121) and a "safety rest area and welcome center" with a teletype device for the deaf is located between Little Hog Island and Naubinway. As you continue your drive through the Upper Peninsula you will see names given by the French explorers to various streams and early settlements as well as native American names.

Along this route look for white pine and jack pine stands in the higher lands. In low, marshy areas look for vegetational associations called "cedar swamps" by the locals. These characteristic habitats include such species as tamarack, spruce, cedar, and balsam. For those of you who are not familiar with Upper Peninsula smoked fish (smoked "chubs," whitefish, salmon, and lake trout), one can find good places to purchase such savory items advertised along the route. Additionally, one can try a pasty, the "UP national dish," which was brought to the UP by miners from Cornwall, England,

Fig. 121. A view of beautiful Epoufette Bay (U.S. 2, Mackinac County, eastern Upper Peninsula). (Photo courtesy of James H. Harding.)

Fig. 122. Cattail pond east of Naubinway (U.S. 2, Mackinac County, eastern Upper Peninsula)

who ate them at mealtime in the mines. Although pasties come with a variety of fillings inside their pie crust, many connoisseurs favor the rutabaga pasty.

7. Manistique and the Manistique Group. Just east of Naubinway U.S. 2 leaves the lakeshore and takes off into the countryside for about the next forty-six miles until we reach the harbor city of Manistique. Along this stretch we get a good view of what the eastern interior of the lower part of the Upper Peninsula looks like. Aside from some farmland we can observe Canadian Biotic Province mature woodlands as well as some nice streams and marshy ponds (fig. 122) where green frogs are abundant and one might be lucky enough to see the mink frog (see fig. 25), which, in Michigan, occurs only in the Upper Peninsula.

Manistique is the type locality for the Manistique Group, which contains Middle Silurian formations of rocks. These Middle Silurian rocks angle down into the Garden Peninsula, where they form most of the bedrock of this area. In the old, abandoned White Lime Company Quarry at Manistique, Manistique Group rocks from the Cordell Dolomite and Schoolcraft Dolomite (named after Schoolcraft County, Michigan) have yielded numerous Middle Silurian fossils, including corals, brachiopods, ostracods, bryozoans, and a few mollusks.

The town of Manistique was built around the lumber industry (fig. 123). Logs were floated down the Manistique River to the sawmills in the town. Manistique also served as a port from which to ship the cut lumber.

Manistique to Iron Mountain

The route along U.S. 2 from Manistique to Iron Mountain, a distance of about 105 miles, is a varied one including bay views and an overland jaunt of about 52 miles to Iron Mountain near the north-

Fig. 123. Log storage yard, at Gulliver, Manistique County. (Photo courtesy of James H. Harding.)

eastern Wisconsin border. From a geological standpoint we journey over bedrock ranging from the Silurian to the Precambrian and representing an absolutely staggering amount of time (see fig. 6). We remain in an area of Silurian bedrock from Manistique all the way to the level of the eastern portion of the lobe (see Nahma on the state map) separating the two arms of Big Bay de Noc. From this point all the way to just west of Cunard about 10 miles east of Norway we are over Ordovician rocks. From the Cunard area and to just west of the village of Waucedah we traverse a narrow belt of Cambrian rock. West of Waucedah we enter, at the village of Vulcan, a broad Precambrian zone that spreads westward over the remainder of the Upper Peninsula. This is a clear example of the fact that older rocks succeed younger rocks as we go from the center to the periphery of the Michigan Basin (see fig. 7).

Relative to the glacial topography of this segment of the route, we are mainly in glacial lake sediment topography until we are about the level of Harris, about thirteen miles west of Escanaba, when we enter an area of ground moraines and outwash plains (fig. 124) that continues the rest of the way to Iron Mountain. In general, the vegetation can be categorized as that typical of the Canadian Biotic Province. Turning to the vertebrate animal life of the area, we have a good opportunity here to discuss the routes used by some of them to reoccupy the Upper Peninsula after the withdrawal of the last Pleistocene ice sheet.

Actually, unless they were good swimmers, only one major route was available to these animals, and this was directly from Wisconsin (fig. 125) since the Upper Peninsula is otherwise surrounded by water. It is possible, however, that some could have made it across the Straits from the Lower Peninsula. Among the reptiles, hognosed snakes (see fig. 38), brown snakes, and blue racers (see fig. 37) made it from Wisconsin only as far as Menominee County, Michigan, which dips well down into the Green Bay area. On the other hand, western fox snakes, sometimes seen dead on the road, made it as far east as the eastern borders of Schoolcraft and Alger Counties, about two-thirds the way across the UP. The northern water snake (see fig. 31) probably swam across the Straits to the

Fig. 124. Glacial outwash (U.S. 2, Dickinson County, western Upper Peninsula). (Photo courtesy of James H. Harding.)

UP, as it now occupies all of the eastern part of the peninsula westward to the western edges of Menominee, Delta, and Alger Counties, in other words, about two-thirds of the way across the UP, going the other way.

Western painted turtles entered the Upper Peninsula from Wisconsin, and midland painted turtles evidently swam across the Straits from the Lower Peninsula to the Upper; or somehow entered from Ontario. Western painted turtles exist in pure form in about the western one-third of the UP, whereas intergrades between the two subspecies occur in the eastern two-thirds of the UP. Unfortunately, painted turtles are often highway casualties when they are moving overland to dig their nests in early summer.

Turning now to mammals, several of them have obviously

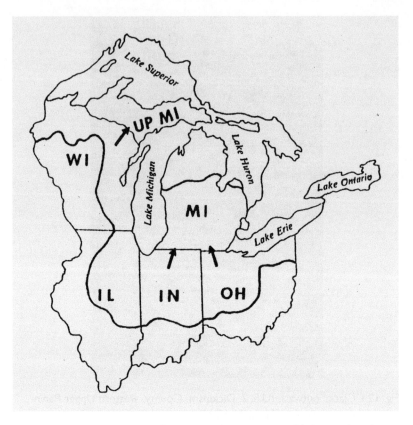

Fig. 125. Routes used by vertebrate animals to reoccupy Michigan after the withdrawal of the ice sheet

invaded the Upper Peninsula from Wisconsin. Obvious ones include the opossum (see fig. 41), a very recent invader, the eastern cottontail, and the thirteen-lined ground squirrel, all of which have advanced eastward to the same areas, namely about the middle of the lobe that separates the two arms of Big Bay de Noc from one another in Delta County. Pay sharp attention to the roadkills east of Big Bay de Noc to see if any of these animals are extending eastward. Eastern pipistrelle bats have reinvaded about the western one-fourth of the UP, and southern flying squirrels and white-footed mice have reoccupied parts of the western half of the UP near Lake Michigan.

FEATURES

1. Indian Lake State Park (a diversion). Five miles west of Manistique on County Road 442 one finds Indian Lake State Park. By the way, this short run is a place where you might watch for roadkills of opossums that moved eastward from the Big Bay de Noc area. The park makes broad contact with Indian Lake, which is the fourth largest lake in the Upper Peninsula. Indian Lake is a remarkable structure, shaped like a vast, shallow saucer, with over 90 percent of its surface less than fifteen feet deep. This makes it a fine place to fish for perch, pike, bluegills, and even walleyes if you can learn where to find them. Two marked hiking trails are available. The one-mile trail is perfect for nature lovers with varied interests. This trail starts from the picnic area and follows the shore of the lake until it turns along a creek, and finally winds through deep woods.

2. The Bays de Noc. About a half hour drive west on U.S. 2 from Manistique we come to two of the most famous bays on Lake Michigan, which lie in close proximity to one another just before the Lake Michigan shoreline curves southward down the long stretch to Menominee on Green Bay. Big Bay de Noc can be observed at the village of Garden Corners at the top of the Garden Peninsula, which forms the east arm of the big bay. Passing inland from here, we have a little more than a half hour drive inland until we see little Little Bay de Noc at Masonville at the top of the little bay and then again at Gladstone and the village of Wells down the bay. Both Gladstone and Wells are commercial harbors.

Several Woodland period fishing sites are located along the undulating coast of Big Bay de Noc. One well-known location here is the Summer Island site, located on an island of the same name just south of the Garden Peninsula. Laurel Middle Woodland people lived in structures housing extended family households. The focus of their life here was fishing, as evidenced by abundant remains of lake sturgeon as well as fishing equipment such as toggle-head harpoons, spears, and hooks. In addition to stone tools, there were tools made of copper, bone, and antler. After taking advantage of the spring spawning runs, the residents of Summer Island continued to fish but also hunted here.

3. Fayette Historic Townsite (a diversion). This historic park is located at Garden, Michigan, about sixteen miles south of U.S. 2 and Garden Corners. Follow M-183 along the east side of the Garden Peninsula to reach this town, which was once a highly successful iron-smelting center. Pig iron was produced at this locale by the Jackson Iron Company from after the Civil War to 1891. Local hardwoods provided the fuel for two blast furnaces and charcoal kilns, and local limestone was used to purify the ore. This park is a Michigan Historical Museum System facility operated by the Michigan Department of History, Arts, and Libraries and Michigan Department of Natural Resources.

Fayette has been the subject of more than two decades of archaeological investigations by archaeologists from Michigan Technological University, who have examined differences in the lives of managers, skilled laborers, and unskilled workers in this company town. Many homes belonging to managers and skilled laborers are still standing, so excavation focused on the homes of the unskilled laborers and included discerning the structures themselves, the artifacts of daily life, and animal remains as clues to diet. Additional work has been done on the company barn and hotel privy.

4. Escanaba in the Heart of Ordovician Country. Escanaba is a thriving city on the west side of Little Bay De Noc near its entrance to the Greater Green Bay area. Escanaba lies in the valley of the Escanaba River, which empties into Little Bay de Noc just north of the city at Wells. Outcrops of shales and dolomites in the Escanaba River valley in road cuts and stone quarries have produced many kinds of invertebrate fossils of Middle Ordovician age in and within a few miles of the city. These fossils include corals, gastropods, brachiopods, trilobites, mollusks, echinoderms, and graptolites. These animals lived in an offshore saltwater sea that covered much of the Michigan Basin at the time.

5. Dairy Farms and Cambrian Rocks. U.S. 2 makes a sharp turn to the west at Escanaba, where we go overland for about fifty-two miles to Iron Mountain. During this traverse we are in the northern part of Menominee County for about half the route from the village of Bark River to a couple of miles east of the village of Waucedah. This is an area of diary farms, some wooded land, and a few small rivers with English names. From Escanaba to the vicinity of Cunard we remain over Ordovician rocks, but from Cunard to just west of Waucedah we traverse a narrow belt of Cambrian (see fig. 6) rocks. These rocks represent the Late Cambrian and are mainly composed of sandstone. Trilobites found near Waucedah attest to the saltwater origin of these sands in the Late Cambrian.

6. Inland Mixed Economies. As we move west on U.S. 2, we are leaving the area where coastal fishing sites were very abundant. Here, in the western area of the Upper Peninsula, people relied on a diverse mix of resources obtained by fishing, hunting, and gathering. The numerous inland lakes and streams in the region offered a variety of resources. Fish, of course, could have been found, as well as various mammals that frequented streams and lakeshores. It has been suggested that these mammals were important in the nearby North Lakes region of Wisconsin, where Late Woodland peoples of the Lakes phase practiced a mixed economy that included systematically hunting beavers (see fig. 75). Given the occurrence of Lakes phase pottery at sites in the western Upper Peninsula, it would not be surprising to find a similar use of this region.

In addition to the availability of fish and aquatic mammals, the region's forests included hardwoods, birch, cedar, and hemlock. The various upland and lowland forest communities would have supported other potentially important animals such as deer and bears. Moose and caribou could also be found in the area until the early twentieth century.

7. The Menominee Range. West of Waucedah we enter an area of Precambrian bedrock (see fig. 6) that spreads out over the rest of the Upper Peninsula both in the north and in the south. Though the Precambrian lasted for countless millions of years, very few fossils are known from Precambrian rocks, and most of those represent exceedingly simple forms of life. Precambrian rocks produce the iron ores that are essential to the iron industry in Michigan in three main ranges called *iron ranges.* These iron ranges are the Marquette Range, the Gogebic Range, and the Menominee Range.

Iron ore in the Menominee Range is concentrated in two iron formations. One of the formations, the Vulcan Iron Formation, is on our route and occurs at Vulcan just west of Waucedah, Norway just west of Vulcan, and at the city of Iron Mountain itself. The ore in the Menominee Range was formed naturally by leaching in Precambrian rocks. Look for piles of mainly dark-colored, residual rocks left over from iron-mining operations in the area, and we promise you will see some huge ones. Iron, of course, forms the basis of the steel industry, and in turn, the steel industry is the basis for all of the great modern industries in the world. Ironically (no pun intended) in Michigan we mine the most ancient rocks in the world to run the most modern industries in the world.

Iron Mountain to Ironwood

The route from Iron Mountain to Ironwood along U.S. 2, a trip of about 128 miles, makes a short dip into Wisconsin just north of Iron Mountain, then turns north to enter Michigan again about 10 miles south of Crystal Falls. The rest of the route to Ironwood is inland, but it passes through a marvelous topography enhanced by many lakes and rivers. The entire route passes through Precambrian bedrock with areas of exposed granite near Watersmeet (fig. 126) and another more extensive area near Ironwood itself. This river and lake country is enhanced by moderate relief brought about by a glacial topography that is a mixture of moraines, ground moraines, and outwash plains. From a vegetational standpoint it is an area dominated by wetland conifers in low areas and by coniferous/deciduous mixtures typical of the Canadian Biotic Province in the higher areas. The animals that many people are interested in along this route are fish, as the larger lakes and even some of the small ones are a fisher's paradise. On the other hand, seasonal bodies of water are of great interest to the naturalist, as these kinds of wetlands are essential breeding places (fig. 127) for salamanders and frogs of the woodland floor.

It is remotely possible that one might see a gray wolf in this portion of the UP if one is lucky, especially at dawn or dusk. The wolf population is actually increasing in the Upper Peninsula of Michigan due to immigrations from Ontario and especially Wisconsin and also because of a very careful reintroduction program carried out by the Michigan Department of Natural Resources. There are probably about two hundred gray wolves now in Michigan, all in the Upper Peninsula.

Many times coyotes (common in northern Michigan) and large dogs, especially German shepherds on the loose, have been mistaken for wolves. How can you tell if you have really spotted a wolf?

Fig. 126. Granite boulders from outcrop (in background) near Watersmeet (U.S. 2, Gogebic County, eastern Upper Peninsula)

Fig. 127. Typical salamander and frog breeding pond in the western part of the Upper Peninsula (Dickinson County). (Photo courtesy of James H. Harding.)

A wolf is twice as big as a coyote and compared to a German shepherd has a narrower chest, bigger feet, and much longer legs. The fur around the mouth is generally white in a wolf, but this area is darker in most dogs. Even more than bears, wolves are shy of roads and humans. In the Great Lakes region the most common food for wolves is deer and moose, although in difficult times they will eat smaller prey, even mice and voles.

FEATURES

1. Bewabic State Park. Four miles west of Crystal Falls on U.S. 2 we come to Bewabic State Park, which has been described as being in the "middle of nowhere." It is indeed one of the most remote state parks in Michigan. What better place could there be for people with true naturalist instincts? Here glacially deposited, densely forested hills and a chain of lakes form the basis of a park that is about as far away from any big city as you can get in eastern North America. Fortune Lake, which is actually a chain of four lakes, may be traversed by canoe or by rental boats at the park. These lakes are home to perch, walleyes, pike, and bass, and a variety of trees, other plants, and wildlife may be seen on the shores.

2. Simple Life near Iron River. People are often bewildered to find out that simple living things lived on the earth as long as 1.7 billion years ago. I (JAH) for one, being a college teacher for forty years, have yet to comprehend how much a billion really is, nor have I ever tried to calculate how many wheelbarrows full of dollars it would take to make a billion-dollar deposit at a bank. But 6.5 miles north of Iron River colonies of oval organisms resembling the living bacterium *Nostoc* (formerly called a "blue-green alga") have been found in a formation called the Michigamme Slate. This slate has been scientifically determined to be 1.7 billion years old. This is one of the oldest records of life in the world. These simple forms are microscopic and were described on the basis of photomicrographs of very thin sections of the slate.

3. Timid Mink Site. This site is one of the few excavated prehistoric sites in the region. This site, located on the shore of one of the many glacial lakes, was examined by U.S. Forest Service archaeologists, who found the remains of a Middle Woodland house structure. Evidence for the house includes a midden (domestic debris) distributed in a "ringlike" pattern around the edge of the house, suggesting that there was a low earthen berm around the structure. Additionally, large rocks around the house feature may have been used as "anchors" for thin strips of bark passed over the bark roof to hold it down. Rocks were used in a similar manner by the Ojibwa, who made small domed bent-pole structures they called *wag-in-o-gan.* Postmolds (stains left when posts rotted) at the Timid Mink site were of a size expected for a wag-in-o-gan and were angled as expected if they were placed in the ground, then bent toward the center into "arches."

A hearth near the center of the house probably served as the domestic focal point for a small family household in midsummer. Warm-season occupation is indicated by raspberry and elderberry seeds found. Artifacts within and outside of the house show a variety of activities such as making stone tools, hunting, and preparing hides for later use.

4. The Lake Country. Moving along westward from Iron River we enter an area of a myriad of lakes and streams for about the next fifty miles. Although improved roads into the interior of this country are not as numerous as one would expect in more populated areas, several improved roads of gravel or stone winding northward or southward can be found if one is on the lookout for them. Being a herpetologist (person who studies amphibians and reptiles), I cannot help but point out a jewel of a herpetological species that might be seen dead on the road or under litter near the roadside.

This species is the beautiful little ring-necked snake that has been found in both Iron and Gogebic Counties, the ones that are traversed in this last segment of the lower Upper Peninsula route. This snake is so gentle and harmless that even people I know who generally loathe snakes are not disturbed by having ring-necked snakes around. Obviously, other species of wildlife such as amphibians, fishes, birds, and mammals are abundant in the lake country. If you have, by chance, spent the night at Iron Mountain, a logical place to quarter for many people, make sure to get up early enough the next day to drive through the lake country at dawn.

5. Ironwood. Almost at the very western tip of the Upper Peninsula about six miles from the Wisconsin border we find Ironwood, an historic center for iron production. As we recall, the Gogebic Range (named for Gogebic County) is one of the three so-called iron ranges of the UP. The Gogebic Range extends from the western tip of the Upper Peninsula westward into Wisconsin, where iron ore has also been produced for many years. Ironwood, however, is the principal Michigan city for iron ore from the Gogebic Range.

UPPER PENINSULA, UPPER ROUTE

St. Ignace to Wakefield (I-75 to M-28)

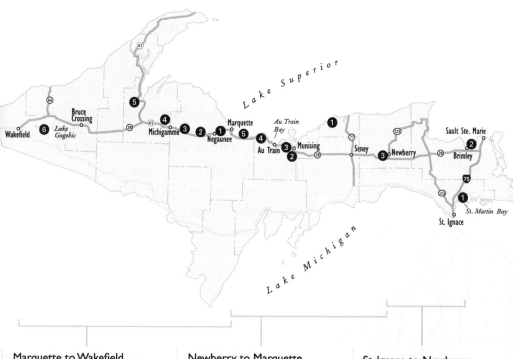

Marquette to Wakefield

1. Michigan Iron Industry Museum
2. Paleo-Indians in the UP
3. Van Riper State Park
4. Craig Lake State Park
5. A Land for Many Peoples
6. Lake Gogebic and Gogebic State Park

Newberry to Marquette

1. Pictured Rocks Area National Lakeshore
2. Wagner Falls Scenic Site
3. Three Bays of Munising
4. Logging in the UP
5. Marquette

St. Ignace to Newberry

1. St. Martin Bay
2. Brimley State Park
3. Ordovician Fossils

Note: This was the most difficult of the seven Michigan routes to define. In this book, we wanted to (1) pick generally traveled major routes in the state, and (2) have them be important from the standpoint of geology, biology, and anthropology. In the present route we have lost an area of such interest because of the distance of sites in Baraga, Houghton, and Keweenaw Counties (in the vicinity of Lake Superior and the Keweenaw Peninsula) from major east-west highways.

St. Ignace to Newberry

This segment of the Upper Peninsula, upper route, carries the traveler quickly northward up I-75 to about six miles south of Sault Ste. Marie, a distance of about forty-six miles. Here at M-28 we turn sharply west and inland for about sixty-three miles during the remainder of the trip to Newberry (which actually lies three miles north of the highway). From a geologic standpoint, the bedrock formations on the route are as follows. As we pass northward from St. Ignace on I-75 we are able to view several views of the Devonian Mackinac Breccia (see fig. 120) in various road cuts up to about the junction of I-75 and M-123 North. Continuing to travel on I-75, we are now over Silurian bedrock until at the Mackinac County–Chippewa County border we are over various Ordovician bedrock formations for the remainder of the trip.

Turning to the glacial topography of this segment of the route, we travel in glacial lake plain country from St. Ignace to north of the M-123 junction, where we encounter ground moraine and outwash plain topography for about ten miles. Then we enter lake plain topography again until just south of the west turn onto M-28. The nearly straight route west to Newberry carries us through alternating ground moraine and outwash plain topography to moraine topography, and finally to glacial lake plain topography again near Newberry. Vegetation along the route is typical of that of the Canadian Biotic Province with conifer marshes (cedar swamps) in the lowlands and mixtures of deciduous hardwoods and conifers on the higher ground. The main animals we have seen along the highway in this segment of the upper UP route have been porcupines both live and dead, but friends have seen coyotes in the road in some of the more open country along the route. Coyotes may be distinguished from foxes on the basis that they are much larger and more ruggedly built than either of the fox species in Michigan. A coyote may be told from a dog in a couple of ways. A coyote has erect ears, while a dog typically has ears that are folded back. A coyote's tail is bottle shaped and constricted at its base. A dog, however, has a more brush-shaped tail of rather constant width. Moreover, a running coyote holds its tail below the back, whereas a dog carries its tail straight out or raised. We have heard more coyotes than we have seen in Michigan.

FEATURES

1. Summer at St. Martin Bay. As the highway begins to bend to the northeast, about fourteen miles north of St. Ignace, we can see St. Martin Bay on the right. As recorded in Alexander Henry's journal, the Chippewa family of Wawatam spent the summer of 1763 at camps along the shore of the bay and on St. Martin Island. This household of eight people, including an infant, born at the camp on shore, fished and caught wild fowl. After the birth, the family moved to the island, where they fished for lake sturgeon until moving on in late August. These large fish were the mainstay for the family during the summer months.

2. Brimley State Park (a diversion). This is the first chance to view the coldest and deepest of the Great Lakes, and there will not be another chance for a long time as we stay inland for many miles until we reach the lake again at Munising. To find the park, one drives west on M-28 about seven miles from the I-75 intersection. At this point, turn north on M-221 to Brimley. Go three miles to Six Mile Road in Brimley, turn right on Six Mile, and go one mile to the park entrance. This park has the reputation of being one of the very best places in Michigan to view Lake Superior. At the park you can view historically important Whitefish Bay (remember the Edmund Fitzgerald song) to your heart's content. The Lake Superior shoreline is rocky in many places; thus the nice beach at Brimley State Park is one to take advantage of for swimming and beachcombing. A mile and a half or so of trails are available for observing trees and wildlife.

3. Ordovician Fossils near Newberry. Traveling west on M-28 we reach Newberry, which is actually three miles north of M-28 on M-123. Newberry is a thriving town of about eighteen hundred people and is the only town of any size between Sault Ste. Marie and Munising. This would be a marvelous place to take a short detour, find a local restaurant for a coffee break, and take in some of the local color in this out-of-the-way place in the north woods. Near Newberry, some fine invertebrate fossils have been found in Ordovician (see fig. 6) deposits of loose surface blocks in gravel. These animals include trilobites, graptolites, brachiopods, and a cephalopod (shellfish related to octopuses). All these animals lived in the warm Ordovician seas that invaded Michigan many many millions of years ago.

Newberry to Marquette

The distance from Newberry to Marquette is about 105 miles. About the first 62 of these miles traverse sparsely populated interior country to the harbor city of Munising, where we reach the Lake Superior coast again. Then we travel another 43 miles or so that are within sight of the lake to Marquette, a harbor city of about twenty-two thousand people. Turning to geology, we remain over various Ordovician bedrock formations all the way from Newberry to just south of Munising, where we pick up Cambrian rocks until, in about three miles, we turn sharply west, where we are in Precambrian rocks the rest of the way west, except for a brief incursion of Cambrian rocks east of Au Train Bay.

From the standpoint of glacial topography, we are in glacial lake plain topography to about the M-77 junction at Seney, where we enter an area of more relief with ground moraines and outwash plains. Near Munising we ascend the Munising Moraine as we pass the Trout Bay–Grand Island viewing area, finally entering glacial lake plain topography again from the arm that separates Trout Bay and Au Train Bay to Marquette. Vegetation along the route again consists of conifer wetland and marshes (cedar swamps) in low areas and mixtures of conifers and deciduous hardwoods in the more upland areas. Wildlife likely to be seen along this segment is similar to that likely to be seen in the first of the three segments of this route. We have seen bears on gravel roads north of the junction at M-28 and M-77 at Seney.

FEATURES

1. Pictured Rocks Area National Lakeshore (a diversion). For those that wish to take some time to see spectacular scenery that is closely related to important geological features, there is no better area in Michigan than the Pictured Rocks Area National Lakeshore. To get there from M-28 take County Road H-58 east from Munising. Features that may be observed in this National lakeshore include waterfalls, inland lakes, streams, large sand dunes, beaches, and of course the vertical cliffs on Lake Superior.

The cliffs and waterfalls will be most interesting to the geologist. The west end of this national lakeshore contains about fifteen miles of sheer cliffs that rise from about fifty to two hundred or so feet above the water. Wind and water erosion has carved these cliffs into arches, caves, pillars, and other interesting forms. Miners Castle (fig. 128) formed as two major wave-cut layers of rocks that were etched out during earlier glacial lake levels. These stacks of rocks are sandstones representing the Late Cambrian (see fig. 6). Chapel Rock (see fig. 10) was sculpted into a complex sea cave during earlier glacial lake levels. It is also composed of Late Cambrian sandstones. One must note that the wave-cut features of both Miners Castle and

Fig. 128. Miners Castle, Alger County, central Upper Peninsula, formed of Late Cambrian rocks that were etched out by the waves of earlier glacial lakes. (Photo © 2001 by Rod Watson, used with permission.)

Chapel Rock took place about 500 million years later than the Pale-ozoic Late Cambrian sea where the sandstone was originally deposited and that the Late Cambrian saltwater sea had nothing to do with modern Lake Superior. Among seven other falls in the area, Munising Falls (fig. 129), a beautiful structure indeed, is capped by dolomitic sandstone of Middle Ordovician age (see fig. 6).

2. Wagner Falls Scenic Site (a short diversion). This Michigan waterfall is near enough to be seen by a very short diversion. To visit this impressive site drive west on M-94, which intersects M-28 a mile south of Munising. After about a half mile there is a parking area on the south side of the road. A trail about eight hundred feet long rises along Wagner Creek, and soon one hears the noise of the falls rushing over Ordovician age rocks. The structure of the falls consists of several rocky ledges over which white water rushes down and over a mix of boulders and tree trunks. A nice variety of trees and shrubs may be seen down the stream valley.

3. The Three Bays of Munising. M-28 turns sharply north just west of the harbor city of Munising and ascends the small eastern lobe of the arm that separates Trout Bay from Au Train Bay. The large Grand Island is soon seen offshore in Trout Bay. Grand Island is actually a complex body of land, as it consists of a large western portion connected to a much smaller southeastern portion by a nar-row land bridge. This produces two mini bays north and south of the land bridge.

The bedrock situation on Grand Island is also complex. Both Cambrian bedrock (Munising Formation) and Precambrian bedrock (Jacobsville Sandstone) occur on the island, but they do not line up in longitudinal bands like they usually do in the main-land of the UP. Precambrian rocks occur in small areas at both the north and the south ends of the large western part of the island, and a strip of Precambrian rocks runs down the middle of the large western part of the island. Moreover, the land connection to the small eastern portion of Grand Island is also composed of Precam-brian bedrock. The rest of the island is Cambrian bedrock.

Fig. 129. Munising Falls, Alger County, central Upper Peninsula, gushing over rocks of Middle Ordovician age. (Photo © 2001 by Rod Watson, used with permission.)

Middle Woodland fishing sites have been found on Grand Island. Among the fish caught there were fall-spawning whitefish. Quartzite tools and abundant fire-cracked rock were also found.

As it nears the shore of Trout Bay, M-28 turns sharply west and crosses the main arm that separates Trout Bay and Au Train Bay, and we are able to see views of beautiful Au Train Bay and Shelter Bay. Actually there are four scenic turnouts in a row beginning at the tiny community of Au Train to the east and ending at Shelter Bay, the smallest of the three bays. Many think that the bays of Lake Superior are the most scenic ones in Michigan.

4. Logging in the UP. The forests to the south of Lake Superior are filled with hundreds of lumber industry sites. These include dams used to back up the water when floating logs down the rivers to the sawmills, railroad grades, and logging camps. The location of the camps varied depending upon the years during which they were occupied. During the early period of logging in the Upper Peninsula, camps were located near rivers to make it easier to float pine logs down river to the mills. Later, when the pine was logged off, companies turned to cutting hardwoods. With the advent of narrow gauge railroads, they no longer needed to rely on river transport to take the hardwoods to the mills. Thus, later logging camp sites are associated with railroad grades.

U.S. Forest Service archaeologists have examined logging camp debris with a view to understanding life at the camps. Using seemingly boring artifacts such as tableware and cut bone, they were able to see the ways in which different logging companies provided for their work crews and the extent to which they accommodated the preferences of the lumbermen themselves.

For example, during the 1870s when pine was being cut, preserved meat such as salt pork was fed to the loggers along with dried vegetables such as peas and beans, dried fruit, and biscuits. The only fresh meat served was wild game such as venison. Records indicate that the loggers themselves far preferred fresh domestic meat to preserved meat or wild game. Animal remains from later camp sites indicate that the larger companies were able to provide fresh beef, which sometimes was raised on company farms in the area. Butchered bones show that the beef served was not necessarily the choicest cuts but consisted of cuts suitable for making the stews and roasts needed to feed large numbers of men who ate a lot of food.

5. Marquette, the First Iron City in Michigan. For the last portion of the second segment of the Upper Peninsula, upper route, we leave the Shelter Bay area and turn inland for a few miles, then travel near the Lake Superior shore again to the harbor city of Marquette. Along the Lake Superior part of this trip we find, in order, two well-placed scenic driveouts and a rest stop, and finally a Department of Transportation welcome center just outside of Marquette. The Marquette Range was the first of the three iron ranges to actively produce iron ore in Michigan, this operation beginning in 1848. Think about the long trip in Lake Superior, then down through the Sault Ste. Marie locks and around the Straits to Lake Michigan, and finally down to Chicago. Geologists may wish to travel north of Marquette to see the wave-cut shores of Lake Superior, which are graced by several nice exposures of the Late Precambrian Jacobsville Sandstone overlying wave-cut cliffs (see fig. 9).

Marquette to Wakefield

This segment of the Upper Peninsula, upper route, consists of a relatively straight inland trek west, with the largest bodies of water to be viewed being Lake Michigamme in eastern Marquette County and Lake Gogebic, which we view in western Ontonagon County, but which extends well southward into Gogebic County. The trip to Wakefield is about 139 miles long. Precambrian bedrock is under us and outcropping around us from time to time all the way to Wakefield, and several formations are traversed. The bedrock gets very complex in the Ishpeming region about 12 miles west of Marquette. Here several named Precambrian formations as well as unnamed volcanic rock intrusions occur within a 10-mile radius of Ishpeming (fig. 130). The bedrock situation becomes less complicated as we proceed westward. As for glacial topography, almost the entire route is either in moraine or ground moraine and outwash plain country, so that the topography is mainly hilly and varied. Nevertheless, some glacial lake plain topography does occur from about the intersection of M-28 and U.S. 45 in eastern Ontonagon County to the Lake Gogebic area. Vegetation follows the Canadian Biotic Province pattern, as it has in other segments of the route, as well as the animal life that is likely to be seen on or near the road. It is usually a good plan to get up early and catch the dawn hour if one wishes to see animal life near the road.

FEATURES

1. Michigan Iron Industry Museum at Negaunee (a diversion). About eight miles west of Marquette near Negaunee there is a museum where the Jackson Iron Company operated the first iron

Fig. 130. The complex rock formations near Ishpeming, Marquette County, western Upper Peninsula. It would be hard to find another place in the world where the bedrock is more complex. These rocks all represent the Precambrian. The small amount of shading in the northeast corner of the diagram represents Lake Superior. *1*, Archaean granite and gneiss; *2*, Jacobsville Sandstone; *3*, Negaunee Iron Formation; *4*, Chocolay Group rocks; *5*, Siamo Slate and Ajibik Quartzite; *6*, Archaean volcanic and sedimentary rocks; *7*, Archaean ultramafic rocks; *8*, Michigamme Formation.

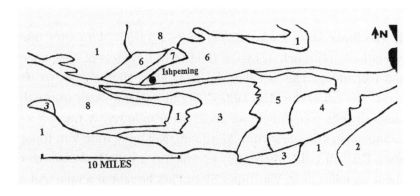

forge in the region. The high-quality iron ore deposits here were wrought into iron at the Carp River forge from 1848 to 1855. Iron ore from the Marquette Iron Range is still being mined and still provides much of the nation's supply of the metal.

2. Paleo-Indians in the UP. A series of sites were found on old shorelines of inland lakes here in the center of the Upper Peninsula west of Marquette. These sites were reported by an avocational archaeologist and investigated with archaeologists from Northern Michigan University during a brief period when the water in the lakes was drawn down. These sites that are again underwater provide evidence for early occupation of the area by late Paleo-Indian peoples. Beautifully worked projectile points of a style known as Eden-Scottsbluff show the area was occupied soon after the final glacial retreat, that is, at about 9,500 B.P. (see fig. 69). Unlike the Paleo-Indian colonization of the Lower Peninsula, where people came from the Illinois and Ohio areas, points in the Upper Peninsula show that Paleo-Indians came here from the west. Eden-Scottsbluff points are associated with late Paleo-Indian sites on the Plains and in the western Great Lakes region. Raw materials here also show a western Great Lakes relationship, as they are made of Hixton silicified sandstone that outcrops in Wisconsin. Archaeologists differ as to whether the people at these Upper Peninsula camps went to the Wisconsin quarry themselves or traded for the Hixton material. It is clear, however, that the material was specially reserved for projectile points, as other stone tools were made from locally available quartzite, quartz, and chert.

3. Van Riper State Park. Moving westward from Marquette, one can either go through or bypass the two iron centers of Negaunee and Ishpeming. The fact that the Ishpeming High School sports teams are called the "Hematites" (recall hematite is an iron-rich mineral) tells you something about local industry. A thirty-five-minute or so drive west from Marquette will bring us to Van Riper State Park on Lake Michigamme, which is a large body of water about six miles long. Van Riper State Park lies about a mile and a half west of Champion, a colorful and legendary western UP outpost where you might wish to stop for a cup of coffee.

Lake Michigamme itself lies in a beautiful setting, as it is surrounded by heavily wooded hills. Perch and walleyes are the fish most sought after in the lake, but other panfish and bass are also part of the local fauna. In the vicinity of the park and in the park itself are signs that read "Moose Crossing Areas," although few if any moose have actually been seen in the park. Abandoned mine shafts (be careful!) and four miles of hiking trails through wooded forests are available to park visitors.

4. Craig Lake State Park (a diversion). This state park is somewhat difficult to find and several miles off the main highway, but if one wants to see a real out-of-the way paradise in the western UP, this is the place to take a break. To get to the park, we start looking for Craig Lake Road to the left (north) about five miles west of Champion. When we find this road, we travel about five miles, where we take the left fork, and after about seven more miles we arrive at the park. Whereas Van Riper State Park is graced by the shore of one very big lake, Craig Lake contains seven small ones. Craig Lake itself, however, has the best fishing reputation. Bass are most frequently caught there, but walleyes and the standard delicious food fish, yellow perch, are also to be caught. Whereas moose have apparently not adapted well to Van Riper State Park, several moose have been observed at Craig Lake State Park. Passing westward again from the Craig Lake State Park Area, we travel only about eighteen miles or so before we must make a decision where U.S. 41 (which has been a part of M-28 since we left Marquette) veers off to the north to the famed Keweenaw Peninsula. The Keweenaw, in its way, is another world. Whereas we have been in iron country for many miles, the Keweenaw is the heart of the copper country, and there is not only new scenery, including Lake Superior lakeshore vistas to behold there, but people of a different cultural background.

5. A Land for Many Peoples. As the highway moves west from Michigamme toward Ironwood we are entering a region where pottery representing several Late Woodland traditions has been found (see fig. 75). For example, a site called Sand Point about twenty miles north of the junction of U.S. 41 with U.S. 141 near the base of the Keweenaw Peninsula yielded mainly Lakes phase pottery. The Lakes phase centered in the glacial lakes district of northern Wisconsin and clearly extended into the Upper Peninsula. Ceramics from other traditions were also found at Sand Point, however, including Upper Mississippian Oneota, which can be found in Wisconsin and Minnesota; Middle Mississippian Ramey incised from as far south as St. Louis; and Juntunen ware, which is associated with the eastern Upper Peninsula and other areas in the Canadian Biotic Province. Other Upper Peninsula sites, including some on Isle Royale, have northern ceramics known as Blackduck ware.

It seems likely that the western Upper Peninsula was open to households from many different areas and traditions. One attraction for people beyond fishing, hunting, and gathering in the area was probably the native copper to be found on the Keweenaw Peninsula and on Isle Royale. The importance of this copper was not confined to the Late Woodland. Rather, archaeological evidence in the form of prehistoric copper mines along with tools for extracting the metal, sites with unworked copper nuggets along with copper ornaments and tools, and the occurrence of Lake Superior copper in locations far from the Upper Peninsula attest to the fact that people came here for at least eight thousand years to obtain and work the metal into artifacts. These artifacts were traded widely at various times and were used differently by different peoples. Copper artifacts are found as tools in campsites, they are found in burials from Late Archaic, Early Woodland, Middle Woodland sites, and copper was apparently valued by Middle Mississippian peoples of the southeastern United States.

6. Lake Gogebic and Gogebic State Park (a diversion). Continuing westward on M-28 from the U.S. 41, we turn north and find a stretch of about fifty-eight miles of sparsely populated country traversed by numerous rivers, but lacking observable lakes until we reach legendary Lake Gogebic, the largest lake in the Upper Peninsula. We can observe part of the north end of Lake Gogebic from M-28, but if we wish to visit Lake Gogebic State Park, we must drive eight miles south on M-64 from its intersection with M-28.

To begin with, Lake Gogebic is the most famous walleye lake in Michigan. But I must warn the casual fisher that finding these delicious fish on such a large lake can take some time, no matter what the advertisements might say. On the other hand, walleyes are not the only fish in the lake, as pike, perch, and bass are also abundant. Still, on a large lake, these fish need some locating. A nice lakeshore and a three-mile-long nature trail that winds through a swath of undisturbed back country are in the park, and brochures explaining the trail are usually available.

BOOKS YOU MIGHT TAKE ALONG OR READ BEFORE YOU GO

These books can help you look up plants, animals, and other natural objects that you are not able to identify on your trip, or supply general information in layperson's terms.

Geology and Paleontology

Ancient Life of the Great Lakes Basin, Precambrian to Pleistocene. J. Alan Holman. Ann Arbor: University of Michigan Press, 1995. Available at the University of Michigan and Michigan State University Museum Gift Shops and some bookstores.

Atlas of Michigan. Lawrence M. Sommers, ed. East Lansing: Michigan State University Press, distributed by Wm. B. Eerdmans, 1977. This book supplies a wealth of information, but unfortunately is out of print. Real Michigan buffs should try their book dealers.

Geology of Michigan. John A Dorr Jr. and Donald F. Eschman. Ann Arbor: University of Michigan Press, 1970. Available at the University of Michigan and Michigan State University Museum Gift Shops and some bookstores. This book not only covers Michigan geology but has marvelous pictures of Michigan invertebrate fossils.

Geology of Wisconsin and Upper Michigan. Rachel K. Paull and Richard A. Paull. Dubuque, Iowa: Kendall/Hunt, 1977. Best to order from the publisher.

Michigan's Fossil Vertebrates. J. Alan Holman. East Lansing: Publications of the Museum, Michigan State University, 1975. Available at the Michigan State University Museum Gift Shop.

The Pleistocene Vertebrates of Michigan. R. L. Wilson. Publication of the Michigan Academy of Science, Arts, and Letters, vol. 52. Ann Arbor, 1967. Contact the Michigan Academy of Science, Arts, and Letters, Argus Bldg. II, 400 Fourth St., Ann Arbor, MI 48103–4816. More advanced than other books listed here.

Rocks and Minerals of Michigan. O. Poindexter. 3d ed. Publication 42 of the Michigan Geological Survey, Lansing, 1931. Best to contact the Michigan Geological Survey, Lansing.

Vegetation

Atlas of Michigan. Lawrence M. Sommers, ed. East Lansing: Michigan State University Press, 1977.

Deciduous Forests of Eastern North America. E. Lucy Braun. New York: Hafner Press, 1967. At some bookstores.

A Field Guide to Eastern Forests. J. C. Kritchner and G. Morrison. Boston: Houghton Mifflin, 1998. At many bookstores.

A Field Guide to Eastern Trees: Eastern United States and Canada, Including the Midwest. G. A. Petrides and J. Wehr. Boston: Houghton Mifflin, 1998.

Michigan Flora. E. G. Voss. Bloomfield Hills, Mich.: Cranbrook Institute of Science, 1972. At many bookstores in Michigan.

Michigan Trees: A Guide to the Trees of Michigan. Burton V. Barnes and Warren H. Wagner Jr. Rev. ed. Ann Arbor: University of Michigan Press, 1994. At many bookstores in Michigan.

National Audubon Society Field Guide to North American Trees, Eastern Region. Elbert L. Little. New York: Alfred A. Knopf, 1980. At many bookstores.

The North Woods of Michigan, Wisconsin, Minnesota. Glenda Daniel and Jerry Sullivan. San Francisco: Sierra Club Books, 1981. At many bookstores.

Shrubs of Michigan. C. Billington. Bloomfield Hills, Mich.: Cranbrook Institute of Science, 1949. Contact Cranbrook Institute.

Trees of the Eastern and Central United States. W. M. Harlow. New York: Dover, 1957. At many bookstores.

Wildflowers of Michigan. Stan Tekielo. Cambridge, Minn.: Adventure Publications, 2000. At many bookstores in the Great Lakes area.

Endangered Michigan Wildlife

A Guide to Michigan's Endangered Wildlife. David C. Evers. Ann Arbor: University of Michigan Press, 1992. At many Michigan bookstores.

Fishes, Amphibians, and Reptiles

Amphibians and Reptiles of the Great Lakes Region. James H. Harding. Ann Arbor: University of Michigan Press, 1997. At many regional bookstores.

A Field Guide to Freshwater Fishes, North America North of Mexico. Lawrence M. Page and Brooks M. Burr. Boston: Houghton Mifflin, 1991. At many bookstores.

A Field Guide to Reptiles and Amphibians, Eastern and Central North America. Roger Conant and Joseph T. Collins. 3d ed. Boston: Houghton Mifflin, 1998. At many bookstores.

Fishes of the Great Lakes Region. Carl L. Hubbs and Karl F. Lagler. Ann Arbor: University of Michigan Press, 1958. At some Michigan bookstores, or contact the University of Michigan Press.

Michigan Frogs, Toads, and Salamanders. James H. Harding and J. Alan Holman. East Lansing: Cooperative Extension Service, Michigan State University, 1992. At many Michigan bookstores, or contact Cooperative Extension Service, Michigan State University.

Michigan Snakes. J. Alan Holman, James H. Harding, Marvin M. Hensley, and Glenn R. Dudderar. East Lansing: Cooperative Extension Service, Michigan State University, 1989. At many Michigan bookstores, or contact Cooperative Extension Service, Michigan State University.

Michigan Turtles and Lizards. James H. Harding and J. Alan Holman. East Lansing: Cooperative Extension Service, Michigan State University, 1990. At many Michigan bookstores, or contact Cooperative Extension Service, Michigan State University.

Birds and Mammals

The Atlas of Breeding Birds of Michigan. Richard Brewer, Gail A. McPeek, and Raymond J. Adams Jr. East Lansing: Michigan State University Press, 1991. At some bookstores, or contact Michigan State University Press.

Birds of Detroit. Chris C. Fisher and Allen T. Chartier. Renton, WA: Lone Pine Publishing, 1997. At many Michigan bookstores.

Birds of Michigan. Stan Tekiela. Cambridge, Minn.: Adventure Publications, 1999. At many Michigan bookstores.

A Field Guide to Animal Tracks. O. J. Murie. Boston: Houghton Mifflin, 1998. At some bookstores.

A Field Guide to the Birds: A Completely New Guide to All of the Birds of Eastern and Central North America. R. T. Peterson and V. M. Peterson. Boston: Houghton Mifflin, 1998. At many bookstores.

A Field Guide to the Mammals. William H. Burt and Richard P. Grossenheider. Boston: Houghton Mifflin, 1998. At many bookstores.

Mammals of the Great Lakes Region. Allen Kurta. Ann Arbor: University of Michigan Press, 1995. Available at the University of Michigan and Michigan State University Museum Gift Shops and some bookstores.

Michigan Mammals. Rollin H. Baker. East Lansing: Michigan State University Press, 1983. At some bookstores, or contact Michigan State University Press.

National Audubon Society Field Guide to North American Birds, Eastern Region. John Bull and John Farrand Jr. Rev. ed. New York: Alfred A. Knopf, 1994. At many bookstores.

Archaeology

Excavations at Charlevoix: How an Archaeologist Works to Reconstruct Our Past. Margaret B. Holman. Educational Bulletin 4. Publications of the Museum, Michigan State University, 1977. Contact Michigan State University Museum.

Retrieving Michigan's Buried Past: The Archaeology of the Great Lakes State. John R. Halsey, ed., and Michael D. Stafford, assoc. ed. Cranbrook Institute of Science Bulletin 64. Bloomfield Hills, Mich.: Cranbrook Institute of Science, 1999. At many bookstores and museum shops.

Ethnohistory

People of the Three Fires: The Ottawa, Potawatomi, and Ojibway of Michigan. James A. Clifton, George L. Cornell, and James M. McClurken. Grand Rapids: Grand Rapids Inter-tribal Council, 1986. Available in many museum stores.

PLACE-NAMES AS PRONOUNCED IN MICHIGAN

The place-names included here come primarily from a list compiled by the Michigan Department of Natural Resources.

Ahmeek	ah MEEK
Algonac	AL ga nack
Allouez	Al o way
Amasa	AM a saw
Arenac	AIR a nack
Au Gres	aw GRAY
Au Sable	aw SAHBle
Au Train	aw TRAIN
Baraga	BARE a ga
Batavia	ba TAYV ya
Bay de Noc	bay de NOCK
Bete Grise	bay degree
Bois Blanc	Bob low (or bwa BLAHNK)
Bonifas	BONN i fuss
Brevort	bre VAWRT
Buchanan	bew CANon
Canandaigua	canon DAY qwa
Capac	Kay pack
Carlshend	CARL'S end
Charlevoix	SHAR la voy
Charlotte	shar LOT
Cheboygan	she BOY gun
Chelsea	CHEL see
Chesaning	CHESS a ning
Chicora	chi CORA
Chippewa	CHIP a wah
Chocolay	CHALK a lay
Cisco	SIS koe
Clio	KLY oh
Coloma	ka LOW ma
Copemish	COPE a mish

Covert	COVE ert
Cusino	kooz i naw
Deford	DEE ford
Detour	dee TOUR
Detroit	de TROYT
Dowagiac	do WAW jack
Eau Claire	aw clair
Engadine	ENG ga dine
Epoufette	E poe fet
Escanaba	ess ka NAH ba
Fanny Hooe	fanny ho
Frankenmuth	FRANK en mooth
Gaastra	GAS tra
Galien	ga LEEN
Ganges	gan JEEZ
Gogebic	go GEE (G as in go) bik
Goquac	GO qwack
Gourley	GURR ley
Grand Marais	grand ma RAY
Grand Portal	grand PORT al
Gratiot	grass shut
Gros Cap	grow cap
Grosse Ile	gross eel
Houghton	HOE ton
Ingham	ING um
Interlochen	INter lock en
Iosco	eye AH skoe
Ishpeming	ISH pa ming
Isle Royale	aisle royal
Kaleva	KAL a va
Kawkawlin	caw CAWL in
Kearsarge	kear sarge
Keweenaw	KEY wa naw
Kitchitikipi	kitch itty kippy
Labranche	la BRANCH
Lac La Belle	lock la bell
L'Anse	lay ahnce
Leelanau	LEE la naw

Les Cheneaux	lay shun OH
Luce	loose
Macatawa	mack a TAW wa
Mackinac County	MACK in awe county
Mackinac Island	MACK in awe island
Mackinaw City	MACK in awe city
Manistique	man iss TEEK
Manitoulin	man i TOOL in
Marenisco	mare n ESS koe
Marquette	mar KET
Mecosta	ma COST a
Medora	ma DOOR a
Menominee	men AH ma knee
Mesick	ME sick
Michigamme	mich i GAHM me
Milakokia	mill a COKE a
Milan	MILE un
Millecoquins	mill a COKE in
Missaukee	mi SAW ki
Munising	MEW ni sing
Munuscong	mun US kong
Muskalonge	MUSK a lunge
Muskegon	muss KEY gun
Nahma	NAY ma
Naomikong	nay AHM i kong
Naubinway	NAW bin way
Neebish	KNEE beesh
Negaunee	na GONE ee
Nisula	NISS oo la
Nunica	NOON ick a
Ocqeoc	AH key ock
Ogemaw	OH ga maw
Okemos	OAK em us
Onekama	oh NECK a ma
Onondaga	on an DAY ga
Ontanogon	on ton AH gun
Osceola	ah see OH la
Oscoda	ahs CODE a
Ossineke	AH sin eek
Owosso	oh WAH so

Pequaming	pe KWAHM ing
Petoskey	pe TAH ski
Pinconning	pin CON ning
Pinnebog	PIN a bog
Pt. Aux Barques	point oh barks
Pt. Aux Chenes	point oh shane
Pte. Aux Pins	point oh pan
Pte. Mouille	point moo YEA
Pokagon	poh KAY gun
Pori	POUR eye
Potaganissing	pot a GAN iss sing
Presque Isle	presk eel
Quanicassee	kwahn icka SEE
Quinnesec	KWIN ness sec
Sagola	sa GO la
St. Jacques	saint jocks
Sanilac	SAN ill lack
Saugatuck	SAW ga tuck
Sault Ste. Marie	sue saint ma ree
Sebewaing	SEE ba wing
Seney	SEE knee
Seul Choix Pt.	SISH wah point
Shiawassee	shy a WAH see
Skandia	SKAN dee a
Tahquamenon	ta KWAH men un
Tapiola	tappy OH la
Tawas	TAH wahss
Tecumseh	te COME suh
Tekonsha	te KON sha
Tittabawassee	tit a ba WAH see
Toivola	TIE voh la
Topinabee	TOP in a bee
Traunik	TRAW nik
Trenary	tren AIRY
Wacousta	wa KOOSE ta
Wahjamega	wah ja ME ga
Watervliet	water VLEET
Waugoshance	wah go SHAUNTS
Ypsilanti	ip sill ANT ee

INDIAN PLACE-NAMES ENCOUNTERED ALONG THE WAY

There are various nineteenth- and twentieth-century references to the meaning of Indian place-names in Michigan. Many of these sources are cited in "A Map of Michigan in the Indian Language" by E. F. Greenman and A. J. Jelinek, originally published in the *Michigan Archaeologist* in 1962 and reprinted in Selections from the Michigan Archaeologist volumes 1–10, *Michigan Archaeological Society Special Publication Number 1* (1969): 177–89, assembled by James E. Fitting. Several articles about Upper Peninsula place-names by Bernard C. Peters have appeared in *Michigan Academician.* Recent volumes on this topic are readily available in the Michigan section of bookstores.

The meanings of Indian words for places are not always obvious. Many of these Algonquin language words were translated by speakers of French or English, some of whom were fluent in the Indian languages, but some of whom were not. In some cases, the place-name was provided by an informant who was not local to the area. There are instances where over the years the name for a single place became used for an entire region (Waw-gaw-naw-ke-zee or L'Arbre Croche in the northwestern Lower Peninsula), and there are instances where people have debated the meaning of a place-name (Michilimackinac). Finally, some place-names arose from simple misunderstandings. The Shiawassee River received its name in 1816 when a French trader asked directions to an Indian village. The Indians who answered his question replied, "Shiawassee," which means "straight ahead." The trader thought they were pointing out the name of the river. There is no question however, that the word *Michigan* means "Great Lake."

Indian Name	Meaning	Modern Name
Ahnumawatik-o-meg	"Pray tree place"	Cross Village
Amikgokenda		Beaver Island
Bowating	Rapids	Grand Rapids and Sault Ste. Marie
Esconawba	River that drains the country, also flat rock, smooth rock	Escanaba

Indian Name	Meaning	Modern Name
Ishpiming	Spirit land in the west, or *up* as used in hymnals for heaven	Ishpeming
Keewaydin	North	
Manitominis	"Island of spirits"	Manitou Island
Michilimackinac	"Great Turtle," as with reference to profile of Mackinac Island, or Great Road to refer to the Straits	
Muskegon	Swamp or marsh	Muskegon
Muskegonsebe	Marsh river	Muskegon River
Naomikong	Sandy shoals where trout spawn	Naomikong Point
Owashinong	Far away place	Grand River
Pinconning	Place of the wild potato or ground nut	
Sagina	River mouth	Saginaw
Sebewens	Little river	Sebewaing
Shiawassee	"Straight ahead"	Shiawassee River (from misunderstanding of spoken directions)
Tittabawassee	"Rolling calmly along," "parallel stream"	Tittabawassee (river parallels shore of Saginaw Bay)
Waw-gaw-naw-ke-zee	"It is bent"	L'Arbre Croche (crooked tree), from bent pine tree that marked the boat landing at Good Hart; later referred to entire coastline north from Little Traverse Bay
Weekwitonsing	Small bay place	Harbor Springs, Wequetonsing
Weyoskodag	"Where meat was hung in the trees"	Oscoda
Wougooshance	Little fox	Waugooshance Point

BIBLIOGRAPHY

A list of field guides and books of Michigan interest is provided in a separate section of this book. Most of these can be used by the layperson. The following are more advanced guides to the material presented in this book.

General

Albert, D. A., S. R. Denton, and B. V. Barnes. 1986. *Regional Landscape Ecosystems of Michigan.* Ann Arbor: School of Natural Resources, University of Michigan.

Geology and Paleontology

Allaby, A., and M. Allaby. 1999. *A Dictionary of Earth Sciences.* 2d ed. New York: Oxford University Press.

Benn, D. I., and D. J. A. Evans. 1997. *Glaciers and Glaciation.* New York: Oxford University Press.

Benton, M. J., and D. A. T. Harper. 1997. *Basic Paleontology.* London: Longman.

Briggs, D. E. G., and P. R. Crowther. 1990. *Palaeobiology: A Synthesis.* London: Blackwell Scientific Publications.

Carroll, R. L. 1988. *Vertebrate Paleontology and Evolution.* New York: W. H. Freeman.

———. 1997. *Patterns and Processes of Vertebrate Evolution.* Cambridge: Cambridge University Press.

Cowen, R. 1990. *History of Life.* Boston: Blackwell Scientific Publications.

Crowley, T. C. 1991. *Paleoclimatology.* New York: Oxford University Press.

Eicher, D. L. 1976. *Geological Time.* Englewood Cliffs, N.J.: Prentice-Hall.

Eicher, D. L., A. L. McAlester, and M. L. Rottman. 1984. *The History of the Earth's Crust.* Englewood Cliffs, N.J.: Prentice-Hall.

Farrand, W. R., and D. F. Eschman. 1974. "Glaciation of the Southern Peninsula of Michigan: A Review." *Michigan Academician* 2:79–91.

Flint, R. F. 1971. *Glacial and Quaternary Geology.* New York: John Wiley and Sons.

Hallam, A. 1990. *Great Geological Controversies.* 2d ed. New York: Oxford University Press.

Haynes, G. 1991. *Mammoths, Mastodons, and Elephants: Biology, Behavior, and Fossil Record.* Cambridge: Cambridge University Press.

Holman, J. A. 1995. *Pleistocene Amphibians and Reptiles in North America.* New York: Oxford University Press.

———. 2001. *In Quest of Great Lakes Ice Age Vertebrates.* East Lansing: Michigan State University Press.

Holman, J. A., ed. 2002. "Michigan's Ice Age Behemoths." *Michigan Academician* 34:221–392.

Hughes, T. J. *Ice Sheets.* 1998. New York: Oxford University Press.

Kemp, T. 1999. *Fossils and Evolution.* New York: Oxford University Press.

Kenrick, P., and P. R. Crane. 1997. *The Origin and Early Diversification of Land Plants.* Washington, D.C.: Smithsonian Institution Press.

LaBerge, G. L. 1994. *Geology of the Lake Superior Region.* Tucson: Geoscience Press.

Leet, D. L., S. Judson, and M. E. Kaufman. 1978. *Physical Geology.* 5th ed. Englewood Cliffs, N.J.: Prentice-Hall.

Martin, P. S., and R. G. Klein, eds. 1984. *Quaternary Extinctions: A Prehistoric Revolution.* Tucson: University of Arizona Press.

Martini, I. P., ed. 1997. *Late Glacial and Postglacial Environmental Changes—Quaternary, Carboniferous, Permian, and Proterozoic.* New York: Oxford University Press.

Matsch, C. L. 1976. *North America and the Great Ice Age.* New York: McGraw-Hill.

McKinney, M. L. 1993. *Evolution of Life: Processes, Patterns, Prospects.* Englewood Cliffs, N.J.: Prentice-Hall.

Neese, W. D. 1999. *Introduction to Mineralogy.* New York: Oxford University Press.

Prothero, D. R., and R. M. Schoch, eds. 1994. *Major Features of Vertebrate Evolution.* Knoxville: University of Tennessee Paleontological Society.

Shrock, R. R., and W. H. Twenhofel. 1953. *Principles of Invertebrate Paleontology.* New York: McGraw-Hill.

Smith, A. B. 1994. *Systematics and the Fossil Record.* Oxford: Blackwell Scientific Publications.

Stearn, C. W., R. L. Carroll, and T. H. Clark. 1979. *Geological Evolution of North America.* New York: John Wiley and Sons.

Stokes, W. L. 1982. *Essentials of Earth History.* 4th ed. Englewood Cliffs, N.J.: Prentice-Hall.

Sutcliffe, A. J. 1985. *On the Track of Ice Age Mammals.* London: British Museum (Natural History).

Trenhaile, A. S. 1998. *Geomorphology, A Canadian Perspective.* New York: Oxford University Press.

Williams, M., D. Dunkerley, P. DeDecker, P. Kershaw, and J. Chappell. 1998. *Quaternary Environments.* 2d ed. New York: Oxford University Press.

Wilson, R. L. 1967. "The Pleistocene vertebrates of Michigan." *Papers of the Michigan Academy of Science, Arts, and Letters* 52:197–257.

Vegetation and Ecology

Benton, A. H., and W. E. Werner Jr. 1958. *Principles of Field Biology and Ecology.* New York: McGraw-Hill.

Blackburn, B. C. 1952. *Trees and Shrubs in Eastern North America.* New York: Oxford University Press.

Brewer, R. 1988. *The Science of Ecology.* Philadelphia: W. B. Saunders.

Bronmark, C., and L-A. Hansson. 1998. *The Biology of Lakes and Ponds.* New York: Oxford University Press.

Clements, F. E. 1928. *Plant Succession and Indicators.* New York: H. W. Wilson.

Daubenmire, R. F. 1947. *Plants and Environment.* New York: John Wiley and Sons.

————. 1968. *Plant Communities.* New York: Harper and Row.

Delcourt, P. A., and H. R. Delcourt. 1987. *Long-Term Forest Dynamics of the Temperate Zone: A Case Study of Late-Quaternary Forests in Eastern North America.* Springer-Verlag Ecological Studies, vol. 63. New York: Springer-Verlag.

Dice, L. R. 1952. *Natural Communities.* Ann Arbor: University of Michigan Press.

Fernald, M. L. 1970. *Gray's Manual of Botany.* 8th ed. New York: Van Nostrand.

Giller, P. S., and B. Malmqvist. 1999. *The Biology of Streams and Rivers.* New York: Oxford University Press.

Glaser, P. H. 1987. *The Ecology of Patterned Boreal Peatlands of Northern Minnesota: A Community Profile.* Washington, D.C.: U.S. Department of the Interior, Fish and Wildlife Service.

Gleason, H. A., and A. Cronquist. 1964. *The Natural Geography of Plants.* New York: Columbia University Press.

Gore, A. J. P., ed. 1983. *Mires: Swamp, Bog, Fen, and Moor.* Vol. 4A, *General Studies.* Amsterdam: Elsevier Press.

Kapp, R. O. 1999. "Michigan Late Pleistocene, Holocene, and Presettlement Vegetation and Climate." In *Retrieving Michigan's Buried Past: The Archaeology of the Great Lakes State,* ed. J. R. Halsey and M. D. Stafford, 31–58. Cranbrook Institute of Science Bulletin 64. Bloomfield Hills, Mich.: Cranbrook Institute of Science.

Lincoln, R. J., G. A. Boxshall, and P. F. Clark. 1982. *A Dictionary of Ecology, Evolution, and Systematics.* Cambridge: Cambridge University Press.

Odum, E. P. 1983. *Basic Ecology.* Philadelphia: W. B. Saunders.

Oosting, H. J. 1958. *The Study of Plant Communities.* 2d ed. San Francisco: W. H. Freeman.

Pianka, E. R. 1978. *Evolutionary Ecology.* New York: Harper and Row.

Shelford, V. E. 1963. *The Ecology of North America.* Urbana: University of Illinois Press.

Smith, R. 1966. *Ecology and Field Biology.* New York: Harper and Row.

Swift, M. J., O. W. Heal, and J. M. Anderson. 1979. *Decomposition in Ter-*

restrial Ecosystems. Berkeley and Los Angeles: University of California Press.

West, D. C., H. H. Shugart, and D. B. Botkin, eds. 1981. *Forest Succession, Concepts, and Application.* New York: Springer-Verlag.

Wiens, J. A., ed. 1971. *Ecosystem Structure and Function.* Corvallis: Oregon State University Press.

Wilson, D. S. 1980. *The Natural Selection of Populations and Communities.* Menlo Park, Calif.: Benjamin/Cummings.

Wright, H. E., ed. 1983. *Late Quaternary Environments of the United States.* Vol. 2, *The Holocene.* Minneapolis: University of Minnesota Press.

Fishes

Bond, C. E. 1979. *The Biology of Fishes.* Philadelphia: W. B. Saunders.

Eschmeyer, W. N., C. J. Farrans, Jr., and I. Hoang. 1998. *Catalog of Fishes.* San Francisco: California Academy of Science.

Helfman, G. S., B. B. Collette, and D. E. Facey. 1997. *The Diversity of Fishes.* Oxford: Blackwell Science.

Jordan, D. S., and B. W. Everman. 1969. *American Food and Game Fishes.* Rev. ed. Reprint, New York: Dover.

Lagler, K. F., J. E. Bardach, R. R. Miller, and D. R. Passino. 1977. *Ichthyology.* 2d ed. New York: John Wiley and Sons.

Love, M. S., and G. M. Cailliet, eds. 1979. *Readings in Ichthyology.* Santa Monica, Calif.: Goodyear.

Moyle, P. B. and J. J. Cech, Jr. 1998. *Fishes: An Introduction to Ichthyology.* Upper Saddle River, N.J.: Prentice-Hall.

Nelson, J. S. 1994. *Fishes of the World.* 3d ed. New York: John Wiley and Sons.

Paxton, J. R., and W. N. Eschmeyer, eds. 1998. *Encyclopedia of Fishes.* 2d ed. San Diego: Academic Press.

Scott, W. B., and E. J. Crossman. 1973. *Freshwater Fishes of Canada.* Fisheries Research Board of Canada, Bulletin 184. Ottawa.

Walden, H. T., II. 1964. *Familiar Freshwater Fishes of America.* New York: Harper and Row.

Amphibians and Reptiles

Bishop, S. C. 1947. *Handbook of Salamanders.* Ithaca, N.Y.: Comstock.

Carr, A. 1952. *Handbook of Turtles.* Ithaca, N.Y.: Cornell University Press.

Cogger, H. G., and R. G. Zweifel, eds. 1998. *Encyclopedia of Amphibians and Reptiles.* 2d ed. San Diego: Academic Press.

Duellman, W. E., and L. Trueb. 1994. *Biology of the Amphibians.* Baltimore: Johns Hopkins University Press.

Ernst, C. H., and R. W. Barbour. 1989. *Snakes of Eastern North America.* Fairfax, Va.: George Mason University Press.

———. 1989. *Turtles of the World.* Washington, D.C.: Smithsonian Institution Press.

Ernst, C. H., J. E. Lovich, and R. W. Barbour. 2000. *Turtles of the United States and Canada.* Washington, D.C.: Smithsonian Institution Press.

Greene, H. W. 1997. *Snakes: The Evolution of Mystery in Nature.* Berkeley and Los Angeles: University of California Press.

Haliday, T., and K. Adler. 2002. *Firefly Encyclopedia of Reptiles and Amphibians.* Buffalo: Firefly Books.

Holman, J. A. 2001. "Fossil Dunes and Soils Near Saginaw Bay: A Unique Herpetological Habitat." *Michigan Academician* 33:135–53.

Klemens, M. W., ed. 2000. *Turtle Conservation.* Washington, D.C.: Smithsonian Institution Press.

Lannoo, M. J., ed. 1998. *Status and Conservation of Midwestern Amphibians.* Iowa City: University of Iowa Press.

Petranka, J. 1998. *Salamanders of the United States and Canada.* Washington, D.C.: Smithsonian Institution Press.

Pough, F. H., R. M. Andrews, J. E. Cadle, M. R. Crump, A. H. Savitzky, and K. D. Wells. 1998. *Herpetology.* Upper Saddle River, N.J.: Prentice-Hall.

Seigel, R. A., J. T. Collins, and S. S. Novak, eds. 1987. *Snakes: Ecology and Evolutionary Biology.* New York: Macmillan.

Smith, H. M. 1946. *Handbook of Lizards.* Ithaca, N.Y.: Comstock.

Stafford, P. 2000. *Snakes.* Washington, D.C.: Smithsonian Institution Press.

Wright, A. H., and A. A. Wright. 1949. *Handbook of Frogs and Toads.* Ithaca, N.Y.: Comstock.

Zug, G. R., L. J. Vitt, and J. P. Caldwell. 2001. *Herpetology: An Introduction to the Biology of Amphibians and Reptiles.* 2d ed. San Diego: Academic Press.

Birds

Barrows, W. B. 1912. *Michigan Bird Life.* East Lansing: Michigan Agricultural College Special Bulletin.

Bent, A. C. *Life Histories of North American Birds.* A series of volumes from 1919 through 1958. Washington, D.C.: United States National Museum Bulletins.

Collias, N. E., and E. C. Collias. 1984. *Nest Building and Bird Behavior.* Princeton: Princeton University Press.

Forshaw, J., ed. 1998. *Encyclopedia of Birds.* 2d ed. San Diego: Academic Press.

Girard, J. M., and G. R. Bortolotti. 1988. *The Bald Eagle. Haunts and Habitats of A Wilderness Monarch.* Washington, D.C.: Smithsonian Institution Press.

Palmer, R. S., ed. 1962. *Handbook of North American Birds.* Vol. 1. New Haven: Yale University Press.

———, ed. 1976. *Handbook of North American Birds.* Vols. 2 and 3. New Haven: Yale University Press.

Palmer, R. S., ed. 1988. *Handbook of North American Birds.* Vol. 4. New Haven: Yale University Press.

Peters, J. L. 1931–51. *Birds of the World.* 7 vols. Cambridge: Harvard University Press.

Sibley, C. G., and J. E. Ahlquist. 1990. *Phylogeny and Classification of Birds.* New Haven: Yale University Press.

Stattersfield, A., M. Crosby, A. Long, and D. Wege. 1998. *Endemic Bird Areas of the World.* Washington, D.C.: Smithsonian Institution Press.

Terres, J. J. 1980. *The Audubon Society Encyclopedia of North American Birds.* New York: Alfred A. Knopf.

Van Tyne, J., and A. J. Berger. 1959. *Fundamentals of Ornithology.* New York: John Wiley and Sons.

Wallace, G. J. 1963. *An Introduction to Ornithology.* 2d ed. New York: Macmillan.

Welty, J. C. 1962. *The Life of Birds.* Philadelphia: W. B. Saunders.

Mammals

Chapman, J. A., and G. A. Feldhammer. 1982. *Wild Mammals of North America.* Baltimore: Johns Hopkins University Press.

Franzmann, A. W., and C. C. Schwartz. 1998. *Ecology and Management of the North American Moose.* Washington, D.C.: Smithsonian Institution Press.

Gould, E., and G. McKay, eds. 1998. *Encyclopedia of Mammals.* San Diego: Academic Press.

Hall, E. R. 1981. *The Mammals of North America.* 2d ed. New York: John Wiley.

Hamilton, W. J., Jr., and J. O. Whitaker, Jr. 1979. *Mammals of the Eastern United States.* Ithaca, N.Y.: Cornell University Press.

Henry, J. D. 1996. *Red Fox.* Washington, D.C.: Smithsonian Institution Press.

Jones, J. K., Jr., and E. C. Birney. 1988. *Handbook of Mammals of the North-central States.* Minneapolis: University of Minnesota Press.

Jones, J. K., Jr., and R. W. Manning. 1992. *Illustrated Key to the Skulls of Genera of North American Mammals.* Lubbock: Texas Tech Press.

Nowak, R. M. 1991. *Walkers Mammals of the World in 2 Volumes.* Baltimore: Johns Hopkins University Press.

Parker, S. B., ed. 1990. *Grzimek's Encyclopedia of Mammals.* New York: McGraw-Hill.

Wilson, D. D., and S. Ruff. 1999. *The Smithsonian Book of North American Mammals.* Washington, D.C.: Smithsonian Institution Press.

Wilson, D. E., and D. M. Reeder, eds. 1993. *Mammal Species of the World: A Taxonomic and Geographic Reference.* 2d ed. Washington, D.C.: Smithsonian Institution Press.

Archaeology

The best way for you to learn more about archaeology is to seek out people who are knowledgeable about the subject. Although additional reading beyond the sources in the first chapter is certainly not discouraged, there are many opportunities to learn about archaeology first-hand. Professional and avocational archaeologists in this state are members of the Michigan Archaeological Society. This organization is divided into chapters throughout the state that meet regularly to present programs about Michigan archaeology. Many chapters have projects working with artifacts and members who volunteer at excavations. The MAS has a quarterly publication the *Michigan Archaeologist* that comes with membership in the society. Other states, such as Wisconsin, and provinces, such as Ontario, have similar societies that also have programs, publications and projects. Most of these societies have web sites where you can obtain information about them. If you wish to write for information, the address of the Michigan Archaeological Society is P.O. Box 359, Saginaw, MI 48606. The Office of the State Archaeologist is at the Michigan Historical Center at 717 W. Allegan in Lansing. The staff at this office is a source of information about archaeology in the state, including opportunities to volunteer in labs or on excavations. The archaeologists at the state office hold an annual Archaeology Day at the state Historical Museum. This event which takes place in the fall provides an opportunity for people to meet archaeologists, see artifacts, and exhibits. Professional archaeologists at the state's colleges and universities, and museums can provide much of the same information. Many chapters of the Michigan Archaeological Society meet at a university or museum. Finally, we will recommend a book that is useful for identifying the age and distribution of the most common artifacts recognized by people, spear and arrow points: N. D. Justice, *Stone Age Spear and Arrow Points of the Midcontinental and Eastern United States* (Bloomington: Indiana University Press, 1987). This book will help you get started if you have a collection that you have found or inherited. If you do have such a collection, take it to an archaeologist who can tell you more about it. The archaeologist will advise that you keep your collection organized according to the site it came from so that the critical association of materials with the site is retained. Again, it is this association that is so important for learning about the past. The archaeologist can also help you get a state site number if that seems appropriate. Other references for material presented in this book are as follows.

Cleland, C. E. 1966. *The Prehistoric Animal Ecology and Ethnozoology of the Upper Great Lakes Region.* Anthropological Papers, no. 29. Ann Arbor: Museum of Anthropology, University of Michigan.

Douglass, J. F., M. B. Holman, and J. H. Stephenson. 1998. "Paleoindian, Archaic, and Woodland Artifacts from a Site at Green Lake, Grand Traverse County, Michigan." *Michigan Archaeologist* 44:151–92.

Fagan, B. M. 1991. *Ancient North America.* New York: Thames and Hudson.

Fitting, J. E. 1975. *The Archaeology of Michigan: A Guide to the Prehistory of the Great Lakes Region.* Cranbrook Institute of Science Bulletin 56. Bloomfield Hills, Mich.: Cranbrook Institute of Science.

Halsey, J. R., and M. D. Stafford, eds. 1999. *Retrieving Michigan's Buried Past: The Archaeology of the Great Lakes State.* Cranbrook Institute of Science Bulletin 64. Bloomfield Hills, Mich.: Cranbrook Institute of Science.

Hinsdale, W.B. 1931. *Archaeological Atlas of Michigan.* Michigan Handbook Series No. 4. Ann Arbor: University Museums, University of Michigan.

Holman, M. B., J. G. Brashler, and K. E. Parker, eds. 1996. *Investigating the Archaeological Record of the Great Lakes State: Essays in Honor of Elizabeth Baldwin Garland.* Kalamazoo: New Issues Press, Western Michigan University.

Martin, S. R. 1999. *Wonderful Power: The Story of Ancient Copper Working in the Lake Superior Basin.* Detroit: Wayne State University Press.

Paleo-Indian

Buckmaster, M. M., and J. R. Paquette. 1996. "Surface Indications of a Late Pleistocene and Early Holocene Occupation at Silver Lake Basin, Marquette County, Michigan." In *Investigating the Archaeological Record of the Great Lakes State: Essays in Honor of Elizabeth Baldwin Garland,* ed. M. B. Holman, J. G. Brashler, and K. E. Parker, 1–54. Kalamazoo: New Issues Press, Western Michigan University.

Cleland, C. E. 1965. "Barren Ground Caribou (*Rangifer arcticus*) from an Early Man Site in Southeastern Michigan." *American Antiquity* 30:350–51.

Cleland, C. E., M. B. Holman, and J. A. Holman. 1998. "The Mason-Quimby Line Revisited." In *From the Northern Tier: Papers in Honor of Ronald J. Mason,* ed. C. E. Cleland and R.A. Birmingham. Special issue, *Wisconsin Archeologist* 79:8–27.

Dekin, A. H. 1966. "A Fluted Point from Grand Traverse County." *Michigan Archaeologist* 12:35–36.

Mason, R. J. 1958. *Late Pleistocene Geochronology and the Paleo-Indian Penetration into Lower Michigan.* Anthropological Papers, no. 11. Ann Arbor: Museum of Anthropology, University of Michigan.

Quimby, G. I. 1960. *Indian Life in the Upper Great Lakes, 11,000 B.C. to A.D. 1800.* Chicago: University of Chicago Press.

Shott, M. J. 1993. *The Leavitt Site: A Parkhill Phase Paleo-Indian Occupation in Central Michigan.* Michigan Memoir, no. 25. Ann Arbor: Museum of Anthropology, University of Michigan.

Simons, D. B., M. J. Shott, and H. T. Wright. 1984. "The Gainey Site: Variability in a Great Lakes Paleo-Indian Assemblage." *Archaeology of Eastern North America* 12:266–79.

Archaic

Brantsner, M. C., and M. J. Hambacher, eds. 1994. *1991 Great Lakes Gas Transmission Limited Partnership Pipeline Expansion Projects: Phase III Investigations at the Shiawassee River (20SA1033) and Bear Creek Sites (20SA10453), Saginaw County, Michigan.* Report no. 94–01. Williamston, Mich.: Great Lakes Research Associates.

Cleland, C. E., and D. L. Ruggles. 1996. "The Samels Field Site: An Early Archaic Base Camp in Grand Traverse County, Michigan." In *Investigating the Archaeological Record of the Great Lakes State: Essays in Honor of Elizabeth Baldwin Garland,* ed. M. B. Holman, J. G. Brashler, and K. E. Parker, 55–100. Kalamazoo: New Issues Press, Western Michigan University.

Egan, K. C. 1993. "Hunter-Gatherer Subsistence Adaptations in the Saginaw Valley, Michigan." Ph.D. diss., Michigan State University.

Garland, E. B., ed. 1990. *Late Archaic and Early Woodland Adaptations in the Lower St. Joseph River Valley.* Michigan Cultural Resource Investigation Series, vol. 2. Lansing: Michigan Department of State and Michigan Department of Transportation.

Lovis, W. A. 1986. "Environmental Periodicity, Buffering, and the Archaic Adaptations of the Saginaw Valley of Michigan." In *Foraging, Collecting, and Harvesting: Archaic Period Subsistence and Settlement in the Eastern Woodlands,* ed. S. W. Neusius, 99–116. Occasional Paper, no. 6. Carbondale: Center for Archaeological Investigations, Southern Illinois University at Carbondale.

Lovis, W. A., ed. 1989. *Archaeological Investigations at the Weber I (20SA581) and Weber II (20SA582) Sites, Frankenmuth Township, Saginaw County, Michigan.* Michigan Cultural Investigation Series, vol. 1. Lansing: Michigan Department of State and the Michigan Department of Transportation.

Robertson, J. A. 1987. "Inter-Assemblage Variability and Hunter-Gatherer Settlement Systems: A Perspective from the Saginaw Valley of Michigan." Ph.D. diss., Michigan State University.

Shott, M. J. 1999. "The Early Archaic: Life after the Glaciers." In *Retrieving Michigan's Buried Past: The Archaeology of the Great Lakes State,* ed. J. R. Halsey and M. D. Stafford, 71–82. Cranbrook Institute of Science Bulletin 64. Bloomfield Hills, Mich.: Cranbrook Institute of Science.

Smith, B. A., and K. C. Egan. 1990. "Middle and Late Archaic Faunal and Floral Exploitation at the Weber I Site (20SA581), Michigan." *Ontario Archaeology* 50:39–54.

Early Woodland

Garland, E. B. 1986. "Early Woodland Occupations in Michigan: A Lower St. Joseph Valley Perspective." In *Early Woodland Archaeology*, ed. K. B. Farnsworth and K.B. Emerson, 47–77. Kampsville Seminars in Archaeology, vol. 2. Kampsville, Ill.: Center for American Archaeology.

Garland, E. B., and S. G. Beld. 1999. "The Early Woodland: Ceramics, Domesticated Plants and Burial Mounds Foretell the Shape of the Future." In *Retrieving Michigan's Buried Past: The Archaeology of the Great Lakes State*, ed. J. R. Halsey and M. D. Stafford, 125–46. Cranbrook Institute of Science Bulletin 64. Bloomfield Hills, Mich.: Cranbrook Institute of Science.

Ozker, D. B. 1982. *An Early Woodland Community at the Schultz Site 20SA2 in the Saginaw Valley and the Nature of the Early Woodland Adaptation in the Great Lakes Region.* Anthropological Papers, no. 70. Ann Arbor: Museum of Anthropology, University of Michigan.

Middle Woodland

Brashler, J. G., and B. E. Mead. 1996. "Woodland Settlement in the Grand River Basin." In *Investigating the Archaeological Record of the Great Lakes State: Essays in Honor of Elizabeth Baldwin Garland*, ed. M. B. Holman, J. G. Brashler, and K. E. Parker, 181–249. Kalamazoo: New Issues Press, Western Michigan University.

Brose, D. S. 1970. *The Archaeology of Summer Island: Changing Settlement Systems in Northern Lake Michigan.* Anthropological Papers, no. 41. Ann Arbor: Museum of Anthropology, University of Michigan.

Fitting, J. E., ed. 1972. *The Schultz Site at Green Point: A Stratified Occupation Area in the Saginaw Valley of Michigan.* Memoirs, no. 4. Ann Arbor: Museum of Anthropology, University of Michigan.

Garland, E. B. 1990. "New Information on Early Post-Hopewell Ceremonialism from the Sumnerville Mounds Site: The Brainerd Phase in Southwestern Michigan." In *Pilot of the Grand: Papers in Tribute to Richard E. Flanders*, ed. T. J. Martin and C. E. Cleland. Special issue, *Michigan Archaeologist* 36:191–208.

Garland, E. B., and A. DesJardins. 1995. "The Strobel Site (20SJ180): A Havana Encampment on Prairie River in Southwest Michigan." *Michigan Archaeologist* 41:1–40.

Griffin, J. B., R. E. Flanders, and P. F. Titterington. 1970. *The Burial Complexes of the Knight and Norton Mounds in Illinois and Michigan.* Memoirs, no. 2. Ann Arbor: Museum of Anthropology, University of Michigan.

Hill, M. 1995. "The Timid Mink Site: A Middle Woodland Domestic Structure in Michigan's Western Upper Peninsula." *Wisconsin Archeologist* 76:338–64.

Kingsley, R. G. 1981. "Hopewell Middle Woodland Settlement Systems and Cultural Dynamics in Southern Michigan." *Midcontinental Journal of Archaeology* 6:131–78.

Prahl, E. J. 1991. "The Mounds of the Muskegon." *Michigan Archaeologist* 37:59–125.

Late Woodland

Brashler, J. G. 1981. *Boundaries and Interaction in the Early Late Woodland of Southern Lower Michigan.* Anthropological Series, vol. 3, no. 3. East Lansing: Publications of the Museum, Michigan State University.

Brashler, J. G., E. B. Garland, M. B. Holman, W. A. Lovis, and S. R. Martin. "Adaptive Strategies and Socioeconomic Systems in Northern Great Lakes Riverine Environments: The Late Woodland of Michigan." In *Late Woodland Societies: Tradition and Transformation across the Midcontinent,* ed. T. E. Emerson, D. L. McElrath, and A. C. Fortier, 543–82. Lincoln: University of Nebraska Press.

Brunett, F. V. 1966. "An Archaeological Survey of the Manistee River Basin: Sharon, Michigan to Sherman, Michigan." In *Edge Area Archaeology,* ed. J. E. Fitting. Special issue, *Michigan Archaeologist* 12:169–82.

Cleland, C. E. 1982. "The Inland Shore Fishery of the Northern Great Lakes: Its Development and Importance in Prehistory." *American Antiquity* 47:761–84.

Fitting, J. E. 1965. *Late Woodland Cultures of Southeastern Michigan.* Anthropological Papers, no. 24. Ann Arbor: Museum of Anthropology, University of Michigan.

Hambacher, M. J. 1992. "The Skegemog Point Site: Continuing Studies in the Cultural Dynamics of the Carolinian-Canadian Transition Zone." Ph.D. diss., Michigan State University.

Hambacher, M. J., and M. B. Holman. 1995. "Camp, Cache and Carry: The Porter Creek South Site (20MN100) and Cache Pits at 20MN31 in the Manistee National Forest." *Michigan Archaeologist* 41:47–94.

Holman, M. B., and R. G. Kingsley. 1996. "Territoriality and Societal Interaction During the Early Late Woodland Period in Southern Michigan." In *Investigating the Archaeological Record of the Great Lakes State: Essays in Honor of Elizabeth Baldwin Garland,* ed. M. B. Holman, J. G. Brashler, and K. E. Parker, 341–82. Kalamazoo: New Issues Press, Western Michigan University.

Holman, M. B., R. G. Kingsley, and J. A. Robertson. 1988. "Archaeological Investigations at the Caseville Airport Site (20HU164) in Huron County, Michigan." *Michigan Archaeologist* 26:1–90.

Krakker, J. J. 1999. "Late Woodland Settlement Patterns, Population, and Social Organization Viewed from Southeastern Michigan." In *Retrieving Michigan's Buried Past: The Archaeology of the Great Lakes State,* ed. J. R. Halsey, and M. D. Stafford, 228–33. Cranbrook Institute of Science Bulletin 64. Bloomfield Hills, Mich.: Cranbrook Institute of Science.

Lovis, W. A. 1976. "Quarter Sections and Forests: An Example of Probability Sampling in the Northeastern Woodlands." *American Antiquity* 41:364–72.

————. 1985. "Seasonal Settlement Dynamics and the Role of the Fletcher Site in the Woodland Adaptations of the Saginaw Drainage Basin." *Arctic Anthropology* 22:153–70.

Martin, S. 1989. "A Reconsideration of Aboriginal Fishing Strategies in the Northern Great Lakes Region." *American Antiquity* 54:594–604.

Martin, T. J. 1990. "A Reconsideration of Animal Exploitation at the Spring Creek Site." In *Pilot of the Grand: Papers in Tribute to Richard E. Flanders*, ed. T. J. Martin and C. E. Cleland. Special issue, *Michigan Archaeologist* 36:123–40.

McHale Milner, C., and J. M. O'Shea. 1998. "The Socioeconomic Role of Late Woodland Enclosures in Northern Lower Michigan." In *Ancient Earthen Enclosures of the Eastern Woodlands*, ed. R. C. Mainfort and L. P. Sullivan, 181–201. Gainesville: University Press of Florida.

McPherron, A. L. 1967. *The Juntunen Site and the Late Woodland Prehistory of the Upper Great Lakes Area*. Anthropological Papers, no. 30. Ann Arbor: Museum of Anthropology, University of Michigan.

Shott, M. J., ed. 1987. "Archaeology in Ann Arbor." *Michigan Archaeologist* 33:5–117.

Smith, B. A. 1996. "Systems of Subsistence and Networks of Exchange in the Terminal Woodland and Early Historic Periods in the Upper Great Lakes." Ph.D. diss., Michigan State University.

Wobst, H. M. 1968. "The Butterfield Site, 20 BY 29, Bay County, Michigan." In *Contributions to Michigan Archaeology*, ed. J. E. Fitting, J. R. Halsey, and H. M. Wobst, 173–275. Anthropological Papers, no. 32. Ann Arbor: Museum of Anthropology, University of Michigan.

Zurel, R. J. 1999. "Earthwork Enclosure Sites in Michigan." In *Retrieving Michigan's Buried Past: The Archaeology of the Great Lakes State*, ed. J. R. Halsey and M. D. Stafford, 244–48. Cranbrook Institute of Science Bulletin 64. Bloomfield Hills, Mich.: Cranbrook Institute of Science.

Upper Mississippian

Cremin, W. M. 1996. "The Berrien Phase of Southwest Michigan: Proto-Potawatomi?" In *Investigating the Archaeological Record of the Great Lakes State: Essays in Honor of Elizabeth Baldwin Garland*, ed. M. B. Holman, J. G. Brashler, and K. E. Parker, 383–414. Kalamazoo: New Issues Press, Western Michigan University.

Cremin, W. M., and D. G. De Fant. 1987. "The Indian and the Prairie: Prehistoric and Early Historic Utilization of Native Grassland Environments in Kalamazoo County, with Emphasis on Gourd-Neck Prairie in Schoolcraft Township." *Michigan Archaeologist* 33:118–53.

Holman, M. B., and T. J. Martin, eds. 1980. "The Sand Point Site (20BG14)." *Michigan Archaeologist* 26:1–90.

Historic

Branstner, S. 1985. "Excavating a Seventeenth-Century Huron Village." *Archaeology* 38:58–59, 73.

Cleland, C. E. 1999. "Cultural Transformation: The Archaeology of Historic Indian Sites in Michigan, 1670–1940." In *Retrieving Michigan's Buried Past: The Archaeology of the Great Lakes State,* ed. J. R. Halsey and M. D. Stafford, 279–90. Cranbrook Institute of Science Bulletin 64. Bloomfield Hills, Mich.: Cranbrook Institute of Science.

Davis, J. R., C. S. Demeter, J. G. Franzen, G. L. Grosscup, B. Hawkins, K. E. Lewis, P. E. Martin, T. J. Martin, K. R. Pott, R. B. Stamps, and N. E. Wright. 1999. "Forts, Shipwrecks, and Thomas Edison? Late Period Archaeology on Land and Underwater." In *Retrieving Michigan's Buried Past: The Archaeology of the Great Lakes State,* ed. J. R. Halsey and M. D. Stafford, 323–74. Cranbrook Institute of Science Bulletin 64. Bloomfield Hills, Mich.: Cranbrook Institute of Science.

Esarey, M. E. 1991. "Socio-Economic Variation at American Forts in the Upper Great Lakes: An Archaeological Perspective from Fort Gratiot (1814–1879)." Ph.D. diss., Michigan State University.

Heldman, D. P., A. R. Pilling, D. L. Anderson, and M. C. Branstner. 1999. "From Fleur-de-Lis to Stars and Stripes: Euro-American Archaeology in Michigan." In *Retrieving Michigan's Buried Past: The Archaeology of the Great Lakes State,* ed. J. R. Halsey and M. D. Stafford, 291–322. Cranbrook Institute of Science Bulletin 64. Bloomfield Hills, Mich.: Cranbrook Institute of Science.

Lewis, K. E. 2002. *West to Far Michigan: Settling the Lower Peninsula, 1815–1860.* East Lansing: Michigan State University Press.

Martin, P. E. 1985. *The Mill Creek Site and Pattern Recognition in Historical Archaeology.* Archaeological Completion Report Series, no. 10. Mackinac Island: Mackinac Island State Park Commission.

Quimby, G. I. 1966. *Indian Culture and European Trade Goods: The Archaeology of the Historic Period in the Western Great Lakes Region.* Madison: University of Wisconsin Press.

Stone, L. M. 1974. *Fort Michilimackinac, 1715–1781: An Archaeological Perspective on the Revolutionary Frontier.* Anthropological Series, vol. 2. East Lansing: Publications of The Museum, Michigan State University.

Ethnohistory

Blackbird, A. J. 1887. *History of the Ottawa and Chippewa Indians of Michigan: A Grammar of Their Language, and Personal and Family History of the Author.* The Ypsilantian Job Printing House, Ypsilanti. Reprint, Petoskey, Mich.: Little Traverse Regional Historical Society.

Cadillac, A. L. 1947. "The Memoir of Lamothe Cadillac." In *The Western Country in the Seventeenth Century: The Memoirs of Lamothe Cadillac and Pierre Liette,* ed. M. M. Quaife, 3–86. Chicago: Lakeside Press, R. R. Donnelley and Sons.

Cleland, C. E. 1992. *Rites of Conquest*. Ann Arbor: University of Michigan Press.

Clifton, J. A., G. L. Cornell, and J. M. McClurken. *People of the Three Fires: The Ottawa, Potawatomi and Ojibway of Michigan*. Grand Rapids, Mich.: Grand Rapids Intertribal Council.

Dunbar, W. 1980. *Michigan: A History of the Wolverine State*. Rev. ed., ed. G. S. May. Grand Rapids, Mich.: William B. Eerdmans.

Gringhuis, D. 1972. *Moccasin Tracks: A Saga of the Michigan Indian*. Educational Bulletin 1. East Lansing: Publications of The Museum, Michigan State University.

Henry, A. 1969. *Travels and Adventures in Canada and the Indian Territories between the Years 1760 and 1776*, ed. J. Bain. Rutland, Vt.: Charles E. Tuttle Co.

Kinietz, V. W. 1965. *The Indians of the Western Great Lakes*. Ann Arbor: University of Michigan Press.

Thwaites, R. G. 1959. *The Jesuit Relations and Allied Documents: Travel and Explorations of the Jesuit Missionaries in New France 1610–1791*. New York: Pageant Books.

GENERAL INDEX

The General Index covers the "Prologue to Travel" section, pp. 3–125.

Blueberries, 94
Blue-green algae, 18, 37
Blue racer snake, 45, 75
Blue-spotted salamander, 44
Boardman River, 116
Bobcat, 45, 68
Bog: definition of, 58–59; "quaking," 59
Bois Blanc Island, 21, 23, 106, 122
Bones, by the roadside, 73–74
Booming, definition of, 116
Brachiopods, 37
British occupation of Fort Michili-mackinac, 112
Brook trout, 60
Brown snake, 45
Bullfrog, 44
Bulrush, 59
Burial mounds, 98
Burials, law regarding, 124–25
Burt Lake, 32
Butler's garter snake, 45, 75
Buttonbush, 59

Cadillac, Antoine de la Mothe, 111
Cambrian period, discussion of, 19–20
Canada goose, 62, 76
Carboniferous period, 24
Carolinian Biotic Province, preset-tlement forests of, 52–53
Casnovia, 30
Cass River, 91–92, 94, 115
Cattail, 59
Cedarville, 22
Chapel Rock, 20
Charcoal, from lumber fires, 118
Chenopodium, 106
Chippewa Indians: Fort Michili-mackinac captured by, 112; at Fort Pontchartrain, 111; inter-tribal exchange of food, 105
Chippewa stage of ancient Lake Michigan, 89

Chronology: absolute, 13–14; rela-tive, 11–13
Chubs, 60
Climax dominant species, definition of, 59
Climax forest, definition of, 59
Clovis spearpoints, 35
Coho salmon, 60
Coleman, 30
Common gray fox, 45
Common loon, 62
Common map turtle, 45
Common musk turtle, 45, 91
Common porcupine, 45, 64
Common raccoon, 45, 72, 74, 75, 91
Common raven, 72, 77
Converse Mounds, 98
Cooper's hawk, 77
Cope's gray treefrog, 44
Copper: caches of, 101; exchanges of, 101; mining of, in Middle Archaic, 92
Corals, 37
Corn, 105–7, 111, 114
Cottonwood, 59
Covenanted communities, definition of, 114
Coyote, 45, 67
Crow, 72
Culture diffusion, definition of, 88
Cultures, about archaeological, 119–26

Dating, geological, 11–14
Detroit, 111, 113, 116
Devonian period, discussion of, 23
Dinosaurs, lack of fossils of, in Michigan, 25
Disconformities, 11
Domestic animals, at Fort Michili-mackinac, 112
Duck bone, in Pleistocene, 30
Duckweed, 59
Dunbar, Willis, 114, 116
Dunes: blowouts of, 34; discussion

of, 33–35; foredune ridges, 34; habitats in, 56–57; high, 34; inland, 34–35; migration of, 33–34; perched, 34
Dutch elm disease, 51

Earthwork enclosures: definition of, 105; Early Woodland, 98
Eastern American toad, 44, 60
Eastern box turtle, 45, 61, 73, 75
Eastern cottontail, 45, 73
Eastern fox snake, 45
Eastern fox squirrel, 45
Eastern gray squirrel, 45, 66
Eastern garter snake, 44, 61, 75
Eastern hog-nosed snake, 45, 61
Eastern massasauga rattlesnake, 45, 71, 75
Eastern milksnake, 45
Eastern mole, 45
Eastern newt, 44
Eastern smooth green snake, 44, 61
Eastern tiger salamander, 44, 72
Echinoderms, 37
Ecological succession: definition of, 59; in wetlands, 57–59
Eden-Scottsbluff points, 86, 90
Elderberries, 94
Elk, 68, 91
Escanaba, 116
Evening bat, 47

Farmstead sites, Late Woodland, 106
Faunal succession, of fossil assemblages, 13
Fayette State Park, 118
Fen, definition of, 59
Fir, 51
Fires, as a result of lumbering, 117–18
Fishhooks, of copper, 101
Five-lined skink lizard, 44
Flat River, 32
Fledgling birds, as roadkill, 72

Fletcher Lake, 32
Flint River, 92, 115
Flotation, use of, to discover small bones and seeds, 124
Forest associations: distinctive, 56; elm-ash-cottonwood, 56; pine-oak-aspen, 56; spruce-fir, 56
Fort de Repentigny, 112
Fort Dubaude, 110
Fort Gratiot, 114–15
Fort Michilimackinac, 110–12
Fort Pontchartrain, 111–12
Fort St. Joseph: at Port Huron 111; on St. Joseph River, 112
Fossils: definition of, 36; of Precambrian and Paleozoic, in Michigan, 36–37
Four-toed salamander, 44
Fowler's toad, 44
Frankenmuth, 91
French: missionaries, 109–10; traders, 109
Frog safety tunnels, 72
Fur trade, Indians and Europeans, 109

Gainey points, 84
Gainey site, 83–84
Garden beds, definition of, 106
Garden Peninsula, 22
Gas and oil deposits, location of, 22
Gastropods, 37
Geological formations, 14–15
Geologic cycle: deposition, 11; erosion, 11; uplift, 11
Geologic timescale, 11
Gogebic Iron Range, 118
Grand Ledge, 18
Grand Rapids, 99, 116
Grand River, 24, 32, 98–99, 102, 108, 116
Grand Traverse County, 84
Gray squirrel, 45, 66
Gray treefrog, 44
Gray wolf, 45, 67

Great blue heron, 62, 75
Great Lakes, origin and development of, 29–32
Green frog, 44, 60
Green Point, 115
Gypsum, deposits of, 22

Half-life, definition of, in radiocarbon dating, 122
Harper site, 91
Harpoons, of antler, 101
Hartwick Pines State Park, 54
Hell Gap points, 87
Hemlock, 51, 53–55, 90
Hickory, 59
Hickory nuts, 92
Higgins Lake, 32
Hi-Lo points, 88
Historic period, general discussion of, 108–9
Hixton silicified sandstone, 86, 90
Hogs, 114
Holcombe Beach site, 81, 84
Holcombe points, 84
Holland, 114, 118
Holocene, definition of, 42
Honey, 114
Hopewell: grave goods, 98; from Havana of Illinois River Valley, 99; mound burial, 98
Houghton stage of ancient Lake Superior, 89
Huron Indians: at Fort Pontchartrain, 111; intertribal exchange of food, 105; village at St. Ignace, 110–11
Hypsithermal interval: definition of, 43; prairie relicts in, 56

Ice Age: discussion of, 25–36; glacial ages of, 26; interglacial ages of, 26
Ice Age mammals: discussion of, 37–40; extinction of, 40; flat-headed peccary, 39, 45, 81; giant beaver, 39, 45, 81; Scott's

moose, 39, 40, 81; woodland musk ox, 40, 45, 81
Ice Age topography: as formed by glacial ice, 26–29; drumlins, 29; eskers, 29; kames, 29; kettle holes, 29; moraines, 27–29; outwash deposits, 27; till, 27
Indiana bat, 47
Indiana hornstone, 95, 97
Indian Lake, 32
Ionia County, 88
Iron Ore, 118
Ironwood, 87, 90
Iroquois Indians, 111
Isle Royale, 67, 68, 70, 101
Isostatic rebound, definition of, 89

Jack pine, 55
Jacobsville Sandstone, as example of Precambrian formation, 18
Jurassic period, discussion of, 24

Kalamazoo River, 98–99, 108
Kalkaska County, 30, 41
Kestrel, 72, 77
Keweenaw Peninsula, 54, 101
Kirk points, 88
Kirtland's snake, 45
Kirtland's warbler, 55, 63
Kramer points, 96

Lake Erie, 30, 32, 111, 113
Lake Forest Middle Woodland: discussion of, 100–101; Laurel ware of, 100
Lake Huron, 30, 32, 80, 100, 109, 111, 118
Lake Michigan, 30, 32, 80, 100, 109, 118
Lake Ontario, 32
Lake sturgeon, 94, 101
Lake Superior, 30, 32, 100, 116, 118
Lake trout, 60, 103
Landforms, discussion of, 30
Lansing, 18, 24, 91

Lapeer County, 30, 43, 84
Larch, 54
Largemouth bass, 91
Late Woodland: cultural change in, 104; discussion of, 101–7; Juntunen phase of, 106; Juntunen ware of, 104; Mackinac ware of, 103; Spring Creek ware of, 102, 103; Traverse ware of, 104; use of transition zone in, 102
Laughing Whitefish Falls, 20–21
Least shrew, 47
Logging camps, 117
Long lots, 111
Looking Glass River, 32
Lost interval, in Michigan, 11, 25
Lumber and mines, discussion of, 115–19
Ludington, 116
Lycopods, 37

Mackinac Island, 21, 23, 112
Macomb County, 84
Mallard, 91
Mammoths: differences from mastodonts, 39; discussion of, 25, 35; reinvasion of, after Ice Age, 45; relation to Paleo-Indians, 81; relative to salt distribution, 38
Manistee, 116
Manistee River, 102, 116
Manistique Lake, 32
Maple, 51, 59
Maple River, 32
Maple syrup, 114
Marbled salamander, 45
Marquette, 118
Marquette, Father, 110
Marquette Iron Range, 118
Marquette Mission, 110–11
Marquette stadial, 86
Marshall, 14
Marshall Formation, 14, 24
Marshes, 58, 59; definition of, 58
Marsh hawk, 77

Marsh thicket, 59
Mason, R. J., 35
Mason-Quimby Line: discussion of, 35; relative to coyotes and black bears, 67; relative to mammoths and mastodonts, 38; relative to Paleo-Indians, 83–84
Mastodonts: differences from mammoths, 39; discussion of, 25, 35; reinvasion of, after Ice Age, 45; relation to Paleo-Indians, 81; relative to salt distribution, 38
Meadow vole, 45
Meadowood points, 96
Megablocks, 27
Menominee, 116, 118
Menominee Iron Range, 118
Menominee River, 106, 116
Mesozoic era, discussion of, 24
Michigan, as a vegetational transition zone, 51
Michigan Archaeological Society, 119
Michigan Basin, 16–18
Midland, 22
Mill Creek archaeological site, 112
Mill Creek vertebrate paleontological site, 30
Minerals, definition of, 10–11
Miners Castle, 19–20
Miners Falls, 20
Mink, 45
Mink frog, 44
Mississippian period, discussion of, 23–24
Monroe, 113
Moose, 45, 68
Morel mushrooms, 57
Mudpuppy, 44
Mullett Lake, 32
Multicomponent sites, definition of, 121
Munising Falls, 20–21
Munising Formation, 19–20
Munuscong Lake, 21

Muskeg, definition of, 59
Muskegon, 116
Muskegon County, 41–42
Muskegon River, 98–99, 102, 116
Muskrat, 45, 64, 73
Muskrat house, 64

Napoleon, 24
Narrow gauge railroads, use in lumbering, 116–17
Nautiloids, 37
Negaunee, 118
Netsinkers, of stone, 101
Nipissing stage in ancient Great Lakes, 89–91, 94
Northern copperbelly snake, 45
Northern leopard frog, 44, 60, 72
Northern red-bellied snake, 44
Northern ribbon snake, 45, 76
Northern ring-necked snake, 44
Northern river otter, 45
Northern short-tailed shrew, 45
Northern spring peeper, 44
Northern water snake, 44
North Manitou Island, 42
Northwest Ordinance of 1785, 112–13
Norton Mounds, 99
Norwood chert, 85

Oak, 59, 87, 90
Oak-hickory climax, 59
Onondaga chert, 95–96
Ontonagon River, 116
Ordovician period, discussion of, 20–21
Ossuary burial, definition of, 105
Ottawa Indians: intertribal exchange of food, 105; village at St. Ignace, 110

Painted turtle, 44, 60, 71, 73, 74, 91
Paleo-Indian period, 35, 80–87
Paleo-Indians: common artifacts of, 81–82; multicomponent sites of,

82; relative to spruce-parkland environment, 83
Paleozoic era, discussion of, 18–19
Paleozoic fishes: acanthodians, 37; cartilaginous forms, 37; placoderms, 37
Pelecypods, 37
Pennsylvanian period, discussion of, 24
Pere Marquette River, 116
"Petoskey Stone," 37
Pickerel frog, 44
Pictured Rocks, 19–20
Pine, 51
Pipe Creek chert, 96
Plant associations: modern, 47–57; reestablishment of, after Ice Age, 41–43
Pond weed, 59
Portage Lake, 32
Port Huron, 89, 111, 114–15
Potawatomi Indians: 106; relative to capture of Fort St. Joseph, 112
Pottery: earliest use of, 95; Early Woodland, 96; grit-tempered, 107; Juntunen ware, 104; Laurel ware, 100; Mackinac ware, 103; Middle Woodland, 99; shell-tempered, 107; Spring Creek ware, 102–3; Traverse ware, 104
Prairie, 56
Prairie vole, 47
Precambrian era, discussion of, 18
Preforms, definition of, 85
Presque Isle, 18

Queen snake, 45
Quimby, G. I., 35

Railroad grades, as evidence of lumbering, 117
Reciprocal exchange, definition of, 95
Red-backed salamander, 44
Red Cedar River, 32

TRAVEL INDEX

The Travel Index covers the "Seven Michigan Highway Trips" section, pp. 127–295, and deals only with place names.

Printed and bound by CPI Group (UK) Ltd, Croydon, CR0 4YY

09/06/2025

14685675-0004